Elder Neglect and Abuse

Elder Neglect and Abuse

An Annotated Bibliography

Compiled by
TANYA F. JOHNSON,
JAMES G. O'BRIEN, *and*
MARGARET F. HUDSON

Bibliographies and Indexes in Gerontology, Number 1

Greenwood Press
Westport, Connecticut • London, England

Library of Congress Cataloging in Publication Data

Johnson, Tanya F.
Elder neglect and abuse.

(Bibliographies and indexes in gerontology,
ISSN 0743-7560 ; no. 1)
Includes index.
1. Aged—United States—Abuse of—Bibliography.
2. Aged—Services for—United States—Directories.
I. O'Brien, James G. II. Hudson, Margaret F.
III. Title. IV. Series.
Z7164.04J56 1985 [HV1461] 016.3626 84-27982
ISBN 0-313-24589-4 (lib. bdg.)

Library of Congress Catalog Card Number: 84-27982
ISBN: 0-313-24589-4
ISSN: 0743-7560

First published in 1985

Greenwood Press
A division of Congressional Information Service, Inc.
88 Post Road West, Westport, Connecticut 06881

Printed in the United States of America

10 9 8 7 6 5 4 3 2 1

CONTENTS

PREFACE

RATIONALE

The subject of elder neglect and abuse touches the lives of many. Besides affecting laypersons in a variety of ways, elder mistreatment involves human service professionals as diverse as journalists to judges and dietitians to demographers. As awareness of the conditions and consequences of elder neglect and abuse increases, so does the need to know what researchers and practitioners are discovering in the areas of identification, treatment, and public policy. This annotated bibliography has been compiled in order to keep pace with the spread of knowledge on the subject. The more that is known about elder mistreatment, the better prepared society will be to help protect elders and their families from this problem and to hasten the prospects for prevention.

AUDIENCE

Due to the multidisciplinary nature of elder mistreatment, the recentness of systematic studies on the subject, and the limited literature published thus far, this problem has been difficult to grasp. This reference brings together into one volume material from a number of disciplines and sources. Collecting the literature in this fashion will enable assessment of the nature and scope of the problem and contribute to an understanding of the progress made in intervention. In addition to providing a benchmark for the field of elder neglect and abuse, the annotated bibliography is a guide for the professional and the private sectors who seek to preserve the quality of life for both the elder and the family. This book is written for human service professionals who have confronted or anticipated involvement with the issues raised by the problem of elder mistreatment.

INTRODUCTION

SIGNIFICANCE OF THE PROBLEM

Most older persons live with or close by their families and are physically, psychologically, and financially independent. Among those who are disabled, the majority are cared for by their families. Indeed, researchers report that most family members treat old persons with love and respect. Therefore, it is hard to believe that the greatest number of elder abusers are family members. Although there is no reliable documentation on the prevalence of elder abuse at the present time, researchers' estimates range from 4 percent to 10 percent, or from one million to two and a half million older persons. There is also evidence that the number of neglected and abused elders will increase in the future. Current indicators include (1) the growing number of older members in the community, (2) long-term aging with the greater likelihood of sustained dependence, and (3) fewer social and material resources to manage the process of long-term aging. However, the important issue on which researchers and practitioners need to focus is not how many of our elders are neglected and abused but that the condition exists at all. Our American society should be able to guarantee a better quality of life for potential victims.

DEFINITIONS

Definitions of neglect and abuse vary. It is difficult to conceptualize and approach elder mistreatment as a social problem when there is no clear-cut definition. The authors of this volume have chosen to define neglect and abuse in the following manner: neglect refers to the omission of an act of essential care that results in some type of psychological, sociological, biological, or legal harm to the older person; abuse is the commission of an act that results in psychological, sociological, biological, or legal harm to the older person.

COVERAGE

The bibliograpy includes literature on elder mistreatment written since 1975. Although cases of elder neglect and abuse have been cited in the past, researchers and practitioners in gerontology and geriatrics began to focus on this subject as a social problem first in England in 1975 with the work reported by A. A. Baker and G. R. Burston, then in the United States in 1978 through the research of Suzanne K. Steinmetz. Professional consciousness was quickly transferred to the applied setting. Between 1979 and 1983, seventeen empirical studies were conducted on the nature and scope of elder neglect and abuse. In addition, the literature contains reviews, reports, training guides, detection instruments, and a variety of theoretical, policy, and discussion papers. All of the elder mistreatment literature found dating from 1975 to the time of the compilation of the annotated bibliography has been reviewed. However, only those materials providing considerable substantive information on the subject of elder mistreatment have been included.

SCOPE

Because the subject of elder neglect and abuse has been reported so recently, it was necessary to look for material in places other than traditional sources. Letters of inquiry were sent to state aging services and state-level adult protective service departments requesting available printed material on elder mistreatment. Requests for copies of their presentations were sent to authors who had presented papers on the subject at professional meetings. Finally, an informal communications network was established with researchers and practitioners in the field to request names of persons they knew who had prepared unpublished manuscripts on elder neglect and abuse. Some of these contracts produced written manuscripts which appear in the annotation section. This search for unpublished documents has demonstrated that there is significant work generated on the subject of elder mistreatment but that it is relatively inaccessible to the public. The authors are pleased to have conducted this original search for literature so that readers may have as current and comprehensive a collection of resources as is presently possible. However, if any contributions to the subject have been overlooked, our apologies go to those whose works have been unintentionally omitted.

Although elder neglect and abuse is found in a number of settings, the annotations in the bibliography focus on elder abuse in family settings. The unannotated section contains a selected listing of elder mistreatment in both family and non family settings.

FORMAT

A classification index follows the introduction and precedes the bibliography. It presents in table form a quick reference to material contained in the annotations. Two tables appear along with a glossary of key terms and other descriptive material clarifying the classification index. Table I indicates the professional orientation of the first listed author and then the type of exposition used in the reference. Table II includes the professional orientation once again and then the key substantive issues discussed in the reference. Numbers representing citations in the annotation section appear within the appropriate categories in the tables. By referring to the numbers, readers can identify the type of entry they find of interest.

The book contains two major sections. The first of which is the bibliography. The first subsection contains the annotated portion of the bibliography. Each citation is preceded by orientation information and includes the threefold categories used in the classification index: the professional orientation of the first listed author; the type of exposition; and the substantive issues cited in the entry. These classifications are followed by the citation information and the annotation, which includes the topic, objective(s), method(s), findings, and conclusions. Inclusion of some or all of these section headings depended on the nature of the material reviewed. Descriptions of these annotation categories are as follows: _topic_ refers to a sentence or statement indicating the focus of the book, article, or presentation; _objective(s)_ are statements of the goal(s) the author or authors wish to achieve in the exploration of the topic; _method(s)_ include a brief review of the techniques used in the study of the topic; _findings_ involve the presentation of results of an empirical study; and _conclusions_ refer to an assessment of findings of an empirical study; the presentation of information on a particular subject through library research or clinical observation, or a recommendation for some kind of action. The next subsection contains an unannotated bibliography on elder neglect and abuse. It includes a selected professional bibliography, articles on elder mistreatment found in newspapers, and state and federal publications on elder neglect and abuse. Section two consists of a directory of agencies and organizations serving older persons that might be helpful in preventing or protecting older persons and their families against elder mistreatment. It includes state adult protective service departments, state aging services, state Medicaid offices, state mental health organizations, and national organizations whose programs may serve the needs of older persons and their families in some way. The appendix includes the Model Adult Protective Services Act. This is followed by an author index. The index identifies all the authors in the annotated bibliography and the selected professional bibliography by the number of the entry in which the author's work appears.

ENTRIES

The annotated bibliography contains a variety of references. These include books, chapters from books, journal articles, articles from the popular press, reports from investigative committees, hearings, conference proceedings, prepared statements, testimonies, research reports, monographs, pamphlets, plays, papers presented at professonal meetings, and unpublished manuscripts.

ACKNOWLEDGEMENTS

This reference volume has been supported in part by the National Institute of Mental Health Adult Development grant number 5-T32 MH14660 administered through the Center for the Study of Aging and Human Development at Duke University Medical Center and in part by the Biomedical Research Support Grant number 71-0941 from Michigan State University.

Portions of others' published works also appear in the bibliography. The authors wish to express their gratitude to these authors and organizations for the opportunity to add their material to the bibliography. These include Maine's Bureau of the Elderly; the U.S. Congress, House Select Committee on Aging Report, Elder Abuse: (An Examination of the Hidden Problem); the same committee's publication number 97-362 A Directory of State Area Agencies on Aging; and Ruth Kane and Gladys Krueger's publication by the National Institute of Mental Health, A Resource Guide for Mental Health and Support Services, for the elderly.

Because of the limited published literature which prompted the original national search for other literature, the preparation of this annotated bibliography has been a heady task. However, the undertaking was accomplished with relative ease because of the assistance of a number of individuals. In alphabetical order they are Lucy Bearon, Deborah Coley, Beth Cuddy, Janet Francis, Deborah Long, and Cindee Moore. Thanks to their dedication, patience, and humor the authors were able to complete the project.

CLASSIFICATION INDEX

The 144 annotated references were cross-classified according to the professional orientation of the first author, the type of exposition on the subject, and the key substantive issues addressed in the citation. The professional orientation refers to nine disciplines: _Journalism_; _Law_; _Medicine_; _Nursing_; _Psychiatry_; _Psychology_; _Public Health_; _Social Work_; and _Sociology_. In addition, there is an _Other_ category that includes miscellaneous disciplines other than the nine mentioned above. The category of _Unidentified_ was used when the author's name was not mentioned or the discipline was unknown.

The type of exposition represents the author's approach to the subject. Nine major types of expositions were also identified in this category: _Theoretical_; _Discussion or Position Papers_; _A Review of Symposium_; _Survey Research_; _Case Studies_; _Clinical Observations_; _Advocacy or Advice-Giving_; _Training Guides_; _Congressional Briefings or Hearings_; _Research Methods_; and _Reports_. The category of _Other_ is used here for the types of expositions that do not fall in the nine categories mentioned above.

A number of substantive issues on elder neglect and abuse have also been addressed in the literature. These key issues have been synthesized into twenty-one topics. The following Glossary of Terms clarifies the meaning of these substantive issues.

GLOSSARY OF TERMS*

1. Definitions of neglect and abuse: Basic definitions of neglect and/or abuse are presented which identify the problem, the victim, and the perpetrator.

2. Information on aging: Discussions are included on some aspect of the aging process such as loss of certain senses or other dimensions of normative aging.

3. Scope: Incidence or prevalence of neglect and/or abuse: Statistics reporting the number of neglected and/or abuse older persons indicate incidence. Prevalence refers to the number of new cases of neglect and/or abuse.

4. Types of neglect and/or abuse: A classification system used to distinguish among the various forms of neglect and abuse.

5. Varieties of family violence: Refers to discussions that compare other types of family violence with elder neglect and abuse. These include child abuse, spouse abuse, and parent abuse.

6. Identification: Discussions on the methods of professional identification of neglect and abuse.

7. Treatment: This refers to strategies that may be used to ameliorate neglect or abuse situations.

8. Causal Factors: Conditions, events, or individual characteristics that attempt to explain the reasons for neglect and/or abuse.

9. Theory: A systematic scientific set of deductive propositions that offer predictive explanations of neglect and/or abuse.

10. Characteristics of the abused and abusers: Refers to discussions focusing on demographic information on the victims and perpetrators of abuse.

11. Family Dynamics: Relational processes taking place in the daily living of a family that affect the older member in some way.

12. Cultural Patterns: Refers to discussions of values, beliefs, symbols, and norms in the society or in subgroups in the society which have some bearing on aging.

13. Social Structure: Systems of organization in the family or other social institutions that influence the lifestyle of the older person. Others include religion, education, politics, economic, and health.

---

*The underlined portion of the phrase is contained in the annotation.

14. Laws: Legislation related to reporting, treatment, protection, or prevention of elder neglect and abuse.

15. Reporting: Refers to all aspects of the process of notifying authorities of the presence of elder neglect or abuse.

16. Barriers to resolution of neglect and abuse: Discussions of blocks to detection, reporting, and treatment.

17. Professional Responsibility: Clarification of the professional's role in the management of elder neglect and abuse.

18. Community Responsibility: Refers to clarification of the community's role in the management of elder neglect and abuse.

19. Attitudes toward aging: Discussions that focus on the stereotyping of older persons in American society.

20. Policy: Refers to discussions on the evaluation of current practices in elder abuse and neglect or proposals to implement specific practices.

21. General: When six or more substantive issues are listed, the material was judged to deal with elder neglect and abuse in general.

TABLE I
PROFESSIONAL ORIENTATION AND TYPE OF EXPOSITION

	Theor./Dis./ Position	Review Sym.	Survey Research	Case Studies	Clin. Obser.	Adv/Adv- Giving	Train. Guide	C. Brief/ Hearing	Res. Meth.	Report	Other
Journalism	028*	036,048,089									
Law	053,076 109,110	022,040 087,098				086,108	136	014,046 057			
Medicine	111,138	077	030,031,114			024,096	124			032,064	
Nursing	013	005,006 012,074	011,112	034,084 102			052,054 055,072 075	051		004	
Psychiatry	061				008,009	090					
Psychology	016,017,042 092	130	018,131 144					019	073		
Public Health		043	044,066,067				045				
Social Work	007,047,056 071,088,123 125,140,142	035,059 065,080 115,116,143	029,060 083	082 104	106,113 137	020,070 105	062,107 134,135	117		026,139	069,079
Sociology	025	027,093 094,099	095,118 119,121 126,127,129			100		128	120		
Other	068		002,037,141		133			091,101			122
Uniden-tified	015	010,023,033 038,039,078 081,097,132	001,003,050 058,063,085 103			049		021		041	

* Numbers refer to the number of the entry in the annotated bibliography section.

TABLE II (page 1 of 3)
PROFESSIONAL ORIENTATION AND SUBSTANTIVE ISSUES

	Definitions	Info.	Scope/ Inc./ Prev.	Types	Varieties	Identification	Treatment	Causal Factors	Theory
Journalism			048*					048	
Law		022	076		053,076	098	014,022 086,110	076	
Medicine	077,096	064		030,031,064 077,114		064,096 111	030,031,032 096,111,114 124	138	
Nursing	006,052	006		005,012,034	074	004,052 054,055 072,075,102	004,005,034 052,054,072 075,112	005,006 012,013 052,054	
Psychiatry	090	061		008,009			008,009	061	
Psychology			019	019,131		073,144	144	016,019 092,130	130,144
Public Health	066	045	066	066		045	066	066	
Social Work	020,137 142		082	060,104		069,071 134	007,020,026 069,070,071 079,080,082 105,106,107 113,125,134 137,139,140	029,079 080,105 140	082
Sociology	099		118	120,127	119,120 128	118,120 121	094,110,119 121,126	129	099
Other				122,133		002	068	141	
Unidentified	078		050	021,050	049	041	103	078	

* Numbers refer to the number of the entry in the annotated bibliography section.

TABLE II (page 2 of 3)
PROFESSIONAL ORIENTATION AND SUBSTANTIVE ISSUES

	Charac-teristics	Family Dynamics	Cult. Patterns	Soc. Structure	Laws	Reporting
Journalism					028,048	
Law					022,040,053,057 076,086,087,098 108,109,110	087,098
Medicine	077	111		138		
Nursing	052,084	012,013 054				055
Psychiatry		061				
Psychology	019,130 131,144	130				
Public Health						045
Social Work	029,082 104,137	020,029 060,079 080,105 106	020	069 105	047,071,115,116 117,123,125,139	
Sociology	027,099 121	027,100 119,120 121,126 127,128 129	027 126	027 119 126		
Other	002,068 141	122			091	
Unidenti-fied	015,021 050,078	015		015	003,049	

TABLE II (page 3 or 3)

PROFFESSIONAL ORIENTATION AND SUBSTANTIVE ISSUES

	Barriers	Professional Respon.	Community Respon.	Attitudes	Policy	General
Journalism	028	048			036	089
Law	108	098,108 110	108	022		046,136
Medicine		024,030 031,032 114		077,124		
Nursing	084	004,005 006,034 072,102	005		084	011,051
Psychiatry		008,090				
Psychology		092,130		092	016,017	018,042
Public Health		045				043,044 067
Social Work	020 047	070,080 125	069 070 080		047,082 088,105 117,125 137	035,056,059 062,065,083 135,143
Sociology	094,118	121			025,027,094 099	093,095
Other		068,133			002,091	037,101
Unidentified	021	103		039	003,049	001,010,023 033,038,058 063,081,085 097,132

LIST OF JOURNAL ABBREVIATIONS

Abbreviation	Title
Age and Ageing	Age and Ageing
Age Concern England	Age Concern England
Aging	Aging
Am J Nurs	American Journal of Nursing
Am J Psychiatry	American Journal of Psychiatry
Am J Public Health	American Journal of Public Health
Ann Intern Med	Annals of Internal Medicine
Br Med J	British Medical Journal
Concern	Concern
Conn Med Assoc J	Connecticut Medical Association Journal
Crim Just Eld Newsl	Criminal Justice and the Elderly Newsletter
Dynam Yrs	Dynamic Years
Encore	Encore
Fam Advo	Family Advocate
Fam Comm Health, Aspen Sys	Family and Community Health, Aspen Systems
Fam Law Q	Family Law Quarterly
Fam Pract Annu	Family Practice Annual
Fam Relat	Family Relations
Fifty Plus	Fifty Plus
Ger Consult	Geriatric Consultant
Ger Nurs	Geriatric Nursing
Gerontopics	Gerontopics
Geriatrics	Geriatrics
Gray Pan Net	Gray Panther Network
Hum Behav	Human Behavior
Hum Dev News	Human Development News - Department of Health, Education and Welfare
Hum Serv	Human Services Monograph Series
Iss Ment Health Nurs	Issues in Mental Health Nursing

J Fam Law	Journal of Family Law
J Geront Nurs	Journal of Gerontological Nursing
J of Geront Soc Work	Journal of Gerontological Social Work
J Geront	Journal of Gerontology
JAGS	Journal of the American Geriatrics Society
JAMA	Journal of the American Medical Association
J Leg Med	Journal of Legal Medicine
J NY State Nurs Assoc	Journal of the New York State Nurse's Association
Lancet	Lancet
Maine Health Care Assoc News	Maine Health Care Association Newsletter
Mass Nurs	Massachusetts Nurse
Ms Mag	Ms. Magazine
Mod Ger	Modern Geriatrics
Nurs Forum	Nursing Forum
Nurs Mirror	Nursing Mirror
Nurs Pract	Nurse Practitioner
Nurs Puls New Eng	Nursing Pulse of New England
Nurs Times	Nursing Times
Old Amer Rep	Older American Reports
Phys Occ Ther Ger	Physical and Occupational Therapy in Geriatrics
Response	Response
Soc Casework	Social Casework
Soc Prob	Social Problems
Soc Work	Social Work
Society	Society
Coord	The Coordinator
Fam Coord	The Family Coordinator
Gerontologist	The Gerontologist
Urb Soc Change Rev	Urban and Social Change Review
US News World Rep	U.S. News and World Report
William Mary Law Rev	William and Mary Law Review

SAMPLE ENTRIES

SAMPLE BOOK ENTRY

Professional Orientation:
- Sociology

Type of Exposition:
- Survey Research

Substantive Issues:
- Causal Factors
- Family Dynamics

129 Steinmetz, Suzanne K., and Amsden, Deborah J. "Dependent elders, family stress, and abuse." In: Brubaker, Timothy H., ed. _Family Relationships in Later Life_. Beverly Hills, California: Sage Publications, Inc., 1983. 173-92. (38 References).

TOPIC: The authors examine the nature of caregiver and care-receiver relationships when elders become dependent in order to determine the level of stress, the assessment of caregiver burden, and the likelihood of abuse.

OBJECTIVES: There are three objectives in this chapter. "The goal of this study is to ascertain the relationship between dependency measured by the frequency with which tasks or services need to be provided for the elder, stress as perceived by the caregivers, and the abusive techniques utilized to gain or maintain control."

METHODS: A "snowball technique" was used to secure a nonrandom sample of 119 adult respondents. Print media was used to ask for volunteers who were middle-aged "child" caregivers living with and caring for an elderly parent. Out of the total, 104 were interviewed by means of structured and semistructured questions.

FINDINGS: Families are faced with a new form of intergenerational relationships -- generationally inverse relationships. Adult and older caregivers are caring for elderly and very old relatives who are dependent upon the family in some way. The care of dependent older family members can be stressful. Issues such as personal time, privacy, medical care of the elderly and financial strain illustrate the kinds of stressors families experience. However, there is another variable which must be included before abuse can be considered a possibility. Burden is defined as the subjective perception of the situation and can be an ameliorator of caregiver stress. How the individual perceives the dependency may be a more important predictor of abuse than stress itself. Finally, abuse in family settings can be in both directions -- caregiver abuse and carereceiver abuse.

The study of dependency, stress, and abuse represented a sample in which 91% of dependent elders were 70 years or older, 94% were cared for by women, and about 66% of the caregivers were above age 50. With regard to dependency, the elderly were dependent on family for (1) household management (99% of elderly), (2) grooming (70%), (3) mobility (61%), (4) financial management (90%), (5) social-emotional needs (98%), and (6) mental health needs (94%). Fifteen stressors were presented to adult caregivers. The least stressful condition was the older person's trying to maintain an authority role in the family and the most stressful was the elder's loneliness. Respondents were also asked whether they felt burdened or not. The results show that neither the tasks performed for the dependent elder nor the stress produced by the task were necessarily correlated with burdensomeness. "In fact, many more families report being stressed by some aspect of caregiving than they are burdened."

Conflict resolution techniques differed between caregivers and carereceivers. While adult children used talking as their major strategy (83%), older relatives pouted or withdrew (60%). Nineteen other strategies fall somewhere in between.

Drawing the four variables of dependency, stress, burden, and abuse together, social-emotional and mental health dependency were the most stressful and burdensome and were "strongly (and significantly) correlated" with abuse.

CONCLUSION: Dependency can lead to stress, burden and abuse. Families need to understand the aging process in order to make the adult/elder communication process more effective. Caring for the dependent elderly is not an easy task. "There is a point when even the most dedicated, loving child is ill-equipped to deal with personal grooming, physical, social-emotional, and mental health needs of an elderly parent." Support services in the community can help relieve stress and burden, and create better communication between the caregiver and carereceiver.

1. Item number
2. Author(s)
3. Title of book
4. Place of publication
5. Publisher
6. Date of publication
7. Number of pages
8. Presence of bibliography
9. Annotation

SAMPLE JOURNAL ENTRY

Professional Orientation:
- Psychologist

Type of Exposition:
- Survey Research

Substantive Issues:
- Characteristics
- Types

131 Steuer, Joanne, and Austin, Elizabeth. "Family abuse of the elderly." JAGS 28(8):372-6, August, 1980. (8 References).

TOPIC: The authors describe the abuse of the disabled elderly by family members.

OBJECTIVE: The goal is to bring the problem of elder abuse by family members to the attention of health professionals and to offer possible methods of intervention and prevention.

METHOD: Findings were reported from a study of 12 cases of abuse of elderly victims identified as victims when they were hospitalized for an acute medical problem or who were visited by a social worker at the request of a home-care nursing service.

FINDINGS: The majority of the abused victims were women, ages 76 to 86, who had some form of physical or mental disability. Abuse tended to be either physical or verbal/psychological. Neglect was the most common form of abuse. In four of the cases, financial problems and established family conflicts or long-term strained family relationships appeared to contribute to the abuse.

CONCLUSIONS: Additional research is needed on elder abuse in the community and at the agency level. A major goal of that research should be to set standards of care for the elderly which are acceptable to private families, service agencies and local communities. Another focus for future study should be to establish guidelines for prevention which include public dissemination of resources available to the elderly. In addition, more facilities are needed for temporary relief for home caretakers.

1. Item number
2. Author(s)
3. Title of article
4. Name of journal (abbreviation)
5. Volume and issue number
6. Inclusive pagination
7. Month and year of publicaton
8. Number of bibliographical references
9. Annotation

Elder Neglect and Abuse

I. BIBLIOGRAPHY

A. ANNOTATED BIBLIOGRAPHY

Professional Orientation:
- Unidentified

Type of Exposition:
- Survey Research

Substantive Issue:
- General

001 ______. A survey of abuse of the elderly in Texas. Austin, Texas: Gray Panthers of Austin, February, 1983. 9p. (0 References).

TOPIC: This paper presents the results of a survey of professionals' experience with elder abuse in the state of Texas in 1982.

OBJECTIVE: The survey on elder abuse in Texas seeks to assess the nature and scope of elder abuse and determine some basic factors associated with elder abuse.

METHODS: A mailed questionnaire was sent to 1,508 individuals and agencies "whose practice brings them into contact with elderly persons or their families, or who might possibly get reports of elder abuse." Key respondents included: home health service professionals, legal service and social service professionals, physicians, nurses, law enforcement officers, and others. The questionnaire was based on one used by Mary Ann Beachler of the Visiting Nurse Association of Brazoria county in Texas in 1979. The response rate to the statewide survey was 33.6% or 507 responses.

The results of the survey show that responses came from all over the state of Texas and from urban, rural and urban-rural areas. Approximately 62% of the respondents report having encountered elder abuse, with each of the seven groups having some involvement. In addition, respondents indicate that they have seen all types of abuse that are often multiple. The factor most frequently reported as the cause of abuse is long-term environmental conditions which include crowded living quarters, extreme poverty, and marital conflict. This factor comprised 59% of the total of the six factors included in the causal factors list.

CONCLUSIONS: A note of caution is given regarding the high incidence of self-neglect. Some 82% of the respondents encountered this type of abuse. On the one hand, it may be a consequence of long-term environmental conditions, or it may be the easiest form of abuse to report since no one else is blamed for the abuse. The survey has generated a number of recommendations: (1) a centralized system should be developed for finding and reporting cases, (2) services should be available to help both the elderly and caretaker, (3) the public and the professional need to have more knowledge about "the nature and causes of elder abuse," and (4) families who are potential elder caretakers need to have counseling regarding the aging process and what they may expect in their elder care role.

Due to the secrecy which accompanies other forms of family violence, we may assume that the same condition holds true in elder abuse. This means that many cases probably go unreported. There is also the probability that the more contact the professional has with the victim of abuse "the more likely he/she is to recognize and report the abuse."

Professional Orientation:
- Other

Type of Exposition:
- Survey Research

Substantive Issues:
- Identification
- Characteristics
- Policy

002 Ames, Margery E., and Popper, Robert L. Prepared statement in <u>Domestic Abuse of the Elderly</u>. April 28, 1980, Union, New Jersey. Committee Publication Number 96-259. Washington, D.C.: U.S. Government Printing Office, 1980. 37-39. (0 References).

TOPIC: The authors report on an informal elder abuse survey of community agencies providing services to the elderly.

OBJECTIVE: The goal is to look at non-institutional elder abuse in order to explore its scope and severity.

METHODS: Staff members from some of the Federation of Protestant

Welfare agencies serving the older population were asked to report on the nature and scope of elder abuse. This informal survey led the authors to several policy recommendations for the protection and prevention of abuse.

FINDINGS: Staff members reported that elders were highly unlikely to report abuse. Five percent of the physically and mentally impaired older persons who were served by agencies specializing in these disabilities were believed to be abused. However, its discovery was always indirect. Although prevalence is slight, it has been important enough to be recognized by all levels of government. In agencies where abuse came to the staff's attention, fifty percent of the victims lived with relatives. While the perpetrators of the abuse tended to be relatives, others were identified as friends and neighbors. In severe cases, agencies referred victims to other professionals. However, older persons tended to reject the referral because victims often felt the situation was inevitable. Refusal of treatment was frustrating to the professional who wished to help the victim.

CONCLUSIONS: A number of recommendations emerged from this informal survey. First, there should be mandatory reporting laws for the elderly, just as there are for children. Second, there should be more federal funding for adult protection service programs. Third, elder abuse must be more inclusive than just family abuse. The focus should be on elder abuse wherever it occurs rather than the particular context. Fourth, there is a need to conduct national surveys on elder abuse to have a better picture of the nature of the abuse. And, fifth, programs which provide older persons with a number of options, such as living, working, and medical alternatives should be developed in order to help the elder live independently in the community.

Professional Orientation:
- Unidentified

Type of Exposition:
- Survey Research

Substantive Issues:
- Law
- Policy

003 _____. _An analysis of state mandatory reporting laws on elderly abuse._ Syracuse, New York: Alliance/Elder Abuse Project. 28p. (0 References).

TOPIC: This paper reports the findings from a survey of the 17 states with mandatory reporting laws.

OBJECTIVE: The major objective of the survey was to assess the effectiveness of existing mandatory reporting laws. The primary public policy issue examined was the required reporting of any suspected abuse or neglect case.

METHODS: The Metropolitan Commission on Aging, an agency serving Syracuse and Onondago counties in New York, was awarded an Administration on Aging demonstration grant to design a model response system for elder abuse. Data were collected in the fall of 1980 by a survey mailed to the state Departments of Social Services on Aging in the 17 states that had mandatory reporting laws. In the spring of 1983, a follow-up survey was conducted by the Elder Abuse Project of 13 states that had enacted mandatory reporting laws since the first survey was conducted.

FINDINGS: The response rate to the survey was 100 percent. No one model for a mandatory reporting system was identified. The one common provision found in the reporting laws of most states was immunity for the reporter.

In general, the 17 reporting laws studied either included adults 18 years old and older or adults 60 years old or older.

Of the 11 states with a central registry, eight viewed the registry as vital to the success of the mandatory reporting system.

Provisions in the laws for mandatory reporting varied widely in entry and investigation rights, expungement of unfounded records, penalty for failure to report, penalty for the abuser, and emergency and involuntary removal.

While 10 of the states that have enacted mandatory reporting laws have seen an increase in the number of abuse incident reports, the specific provisions of a state's law seemed to have no effect on increased abuse reporting.

The majority of the states indicated that their protective services departments had the capacity to respond to all reported elder abuse cases.

A number of states questioned the overall effectiveness of mandatory reporting laws in increasing reports of elder abuse. The states believed that community education had the most significant impact on increasing reports of elder abuse. The follow-up survey uncovered 13 more states that had passed elder abuse laws since 1981. The questionnaires sent to these states regarding their effectiveness also show that community education was important in the reporting of elder abuse. While there were some technical differences between the two sets of laws -- the original 17 and the 13 which were enacted later -- immunity for those reporting was a consistent feature of all 30 mandatory reporting laws.

CONCLUSION: Adequate funding to departments of protective services and a clear legal mandate for these protective service workers to intervene also determine the effectiveness of mandatory reporting laws.

In addition to the question of the effectiveness of mandatory reporting laws in identification and intervention, there is the question of elder rights. Since the laws vary in scope, the civil rights of the older person would have to be viewed in the context of a specific law. There is also the question of how society defines the older person. Do mandatory laws tend to infantilize the elder by treating him/her like a child rather than an adult?

Professional Orientation:
- Nursing

Type of Exposition:
- Report

Substantive Issues:
- Identification
- Treatment
- Professional Responsibility

004 Anastasio, Charlotte J. "Elder abuse: Identification and acute care intervention." In: First National Conference on Abuse of Older Persons, Cambridge, Massachusetts, March, 1981, Conference Proceedings. Boston, Massachusetts: Legal Research and Services for the Elderly, 1981. 25p. (1 Reference).

TOPIC: The author focuses upon the detection of abuse and neglect among hospitalized older persons.

OBJECTIVES: A multidisciplinary assessment tool is presented along with a report of how the Elder Abuse Committee at Brigham and Women's Hospital in Boston, Massachusetts manages cases of elder abuse.

METHODS: A description is given of the multidimensional assessment tool for detecting elder abuse designed by the Elder Abuse Committee. Characteristics of victims and their abusers are also described very briefly along with treatment options and recommendations for improved protective services.

CONCLUSIONS: The Elder abuse assessment protocol includes a diagnosis of functional impairment, physiological changes, mental status changes, family or caregiver coping changes, and changed in the elder's home management skills. This tool serves a twofold purpose -- detecting abuse and, at the same time, identifying the specific problem areas related to abuse. The tool is multidimensional in two senses. First, it covers the several facets of the quality of life of the older person, and second, the assessment involves a variety of health care professionals. This latter multidimensional approach insures a more accurate assessment of the patient's situation.

The results of a fourteen month study of victims and abusers at Brigham and Women's Hospital show that victims tend to be female, very old, functionally and economically dependent on their caregivers, and who have some type of memory problems. On the other hand, caregivers reported that there was some type of stress in their caregiving role with the older person.

A variety of care plans are used with victims of elder abuse. Family interviews, monitoring living situations, and other kinds of follow-up procedures are used. However, all of these procedures are tempered by the patient's cooperation with the intervention protocol and the kinds of facilities present in the community. One response to limited facilities was the implementation of a coffee hour by the Elder Abuse Committee. These gatherings were designed to bring community agencies together for the purpose of developing and improving the resource network of managing elder abuse cases.

Several problem areas still remain in adult protective services. These include problems of housing alternative for victims, financial and legal constraints in intervention and the overutilization of acute-care hospitals. Preventive steps should be taken in both the hospital and community settings. A number of recommendations are proposed in order to provide these preventive interventions.

Professional Orientation:
- Nursing

Type of Exposition:
- Review

Substantive Issues:
- Types
- Causal Factors
- Professional Responsibility
- Community Responsibility
- Treatment

005 Anderson, Cheryl L. "Abuse and neglect among the elderly." J Geront Nurs 7(2):77-85, February, 1981. (55 References).

TOPIC: The article presents a discussion and illustrations of physical and emotional neglect and abuse of older persons.

OBJECTIVE: Although no goals are stated, the implied goal is to characterize types of abuse in order to make health care professionals more aware of the complex nature of abuse and neglect.

METHOD: The presentation of information includes reporting on and reviewing other work which addresses the meaning of types of abuse and neglect and the use of "case histories" to illustrate the various forms.

CONCLUSIONS: The elderly are vulnerable to physical and psychological abuse and neglect. Because of this fact, health care providers should work toward improving the health care of older persons and developing plans to provide alternative facilities for the care of older persons other than traditional institutional or home care.

Professional Orientation:
- Nursing

Type of Exposition:
- Review

Substantive Issues:
- Definitions
- Causal Factors
- Information
- Professional Responsibility

006 Bahr, Sister Rose Therese. "The battered elderly: Physical and psychological abuse." Fam and Comm Health 4(2):61-69, August, 1981. (11 References).

TOPIC: The author reviews noninstitutional and institutional abuse of the elderly.

OBJECTIVE: To describe the characteristics of physical and psychological abuse of the elderly.

METHODS: Newspaper articles, review of other research, and a case history present the reality of elder abuse as part of this article's discussion on physical and psychological abuse of the elderly in family and institutional settings. Legal definitions of abuse are also discussed.

FINDINGS: Physical and psychological abuse are the central foci of the article. Physical abuse exists in a variety of forms and settings. It is sometimes camouflaged by symptoms which accompany the normal aging process. Sometimes, it is the result of ignorance regarding the appropriate care of the elderly. Psychological abuse also takes on many forms and is found at home and in health care institutions.

CONCLUSIONS: Educating the general public about the aging process, identifying potential abusive families, and reporting evidence of abuse are ways in which nurses can help combat elder abuse.

Professional Orientation:
- Social Work

Type of Exposition:
- Position Paper

Substantive Issue:
- Treatment

007 Baily, Thelma. "Some practical issues in delivering protective services to the elderly." In: First National Conference on Abuse of Older Persons, Cambridge, Massachusetts, March, 1981. Conference Proceedings. Boston, Massachusetts: Legal Research and Services for the Elderly, 1981. 5p. (0 References).

TOPIC: This presentation addresses several of the problems which arise when adult protective service workers attempt to intervene in abuse and neglect cases.

OBJECTIVE: The presenter seeks to identify the adult protective service worker as a family support person rather than an unwelcomed intruder.

METHODS: Key features of the adult protective services role are highlighted in order to show how these social workers can serve as vital support persons to families with older members who are victims of abuse.

CONCLUSIONS: Professionals must be well-prepared to deal with the inevitable resistance families exercise when these helping agents involve themselves in the lives of neglecting and abusing families. Both the victim and the abuser see the adult protective worker as an adversary rather than a support person. The worker enters the home involuntarily which constitutes an invasion of privacy. Elder and family members may deny the violence because of embarrassment, the inability to articulate the problem or search for solutions. In particular, the older person may fear that exposing the violence may lead to even worse consequences.

Service workers must show clients that their role in cases of neglect and abuse is supportive rather than punitive. In fact, the social worker can offer support to the whole family by sharing information about community programs which reduce caregiver stress. In addition, social worker professionals should develop inter-agency communication in order to insure the delivery of appropriate services to families. Other tasks include watching out for mandatory reporting laws as they develop in one's state in order to utilize the authority of the legal system to work with families, and being "solidly prepared" for the decision of when to intrude into the privacy of the household and when not to. In sum, even though federal cutback will hamper the services social workers can provide families, these families need to know that they can rely on service workers for support in helping them care for their older members.

Professional Orientation:
- Psychiatry

Type of Exposition:
- Clinical Observations

Substantive Issues:
- Types
- Treatment
- Professional Responsibility

008 Baker, A.A. "Granny battering." Nurs Mirror 144(8):65-66, February 24, 1977. (2 References).

TOPIC: This article focuses on nursing practices for the elderly.

OBJECTIVE: The author's goal is to examine common nursing practices which contribute to the devastation suffered by a hospitalized elderly person.

METHODS: Brief citations from case histories and observations by the author as a Consultant Psychiatrist in a British hospital reveal commonplace nursing practices which actually cause the elderly patient's health to deteriorate.

CONCLUSIONS: Once removed from familiar home surroundings, the elderly patient becomes disoriented and may adopt a completely different personality. In addition, nursing practices may cause the elderly patient to become more dependent on hospital care. Prolonging life for the dying elderly through good nursing practices may be a serious detriment to the elder's quality of life. These life-extending measures can mean stress and misery for the elderly patient. Therefore, the nursing staff need to re-evaluate the importance of life for the older person when it means unnecessary pain and a loss of dignity.

The problems of geriatric nursing can best be solved by changing negative attitudes toward older patients and by establishing and coordinating hospital policy for their care.

Professional Orientation:
- Psychiatry

Type of Exposition:
- Clinical Observations

Substantive Issues:
- Types
- Treatment

009 Baker, A.A. "Slow euthanasia -- or "she will be better off in hospital." Br Med J 2(6035):571-72, September 4, 1976. (1 Reference).

TOPIC: The author raises the question of whether the self-neglecting elderly in the community are better or worse off than if they are placed in the hospital for medical treatment.

METHODS: Observations are made of the changes in self-neglecting patients after hospital admission and after having lived on a long-stay ward. An illustrative case history is also used to collect data to show what happens to the socio-emotional and physical well-being of older self-neglecting patients who are moved from their home to the hospital setting by health care professionals.

CONCLUSIONS: While hospitalization of the frail and neglected elderly may prolong the patient's life, it may not offer the patient a quality of life of the same magnitude which s/he experienced in the familiar home environment. A case can be made for hospitalization being a cruel action if it removes the privacy and sense of dignity which the frail elderly often do retain when they remain in their own home.

Professional Orientation:
- Unidentified

Type of Exposition:
- Review

Substantive Issue:
- General

010 ______. "Battered elderly: A hidden family problem." Human Dev News, Dept. of H.E.W., July, 1980. (0 References).

TOPIC: The review summarizes two Administration on Aging funded research studies on elder abuse.

METHODS: The two Administration on Aging projects discussed in this article are the Douglass, Hickey and Noel research study conducted at the University of Michigan Institute of Gerontology and the Block and Sinnott project at the University of Maryland, Center on Aging. Information was based on interviews with social, spiritual, mental, and physical health care professionals, police officers, and older persons.

CONCLUSIONS: Both studies found that psychological abuse was more frequent than physical abuse, although a variety of forms of abuse and neglect were identified. In addition, they agreed that victims of abuse were likely to be dependent elders, while the abusers were family members suffering some kind of personal stress. However, Douglass and his colleagues found that abuse was not the consequence of a lack of love for the victim, but, rather, the absence of personal resources to manage elder care successfully. The survey results of the two studies differed on the socio-economic status of the abused and abusers. Douglass et al. identified lower-class as the typical profile. Block et al. data showed that the abused and abusers tended to come from the middle-class. Both studies indicated that victims and families were reluctant to report abuse because the consequences of the acknowledgement might be worse than the abuse. Institutionalization of the elder or the vulnerability of the family to possible community stigma are reasons why elders and families were reticent to report the abuse. The two reports also revealed that little attention is paid to the problem of elder abuse. When there was reporting, Block et al. point out that little help was given, thus discouraging further attempts to seek help. A key policy recommendation both groups advocate is a mandatory reporting law. Further recommendations include emphasizing family support rather than blame in elder abuse cases, and greater professional awareness of the problem.

Professional Orientation:
- Nursing

Type of Exposition:
- Survey Research

Substantive Issue:
- General

011 Beachler, Mary Ann. "Mistreatment of elderly persons in the domestic setting." <u>Unpub Man</u> 9p. (0 References).

TOPIC: The author examines the phenomenon of elder mistreatment in Brazoria County, Texas.

OBJECTIVES: The author outlines several objectives. They include the scope and nature of mistreatment of older persons, causal factors, identification, and treatment.

METHODS: A questionnaire was mailed to 208 "agencies and individuals whose practice brings them into contact with elderly persons or their families, or who might feasibly get reports of mistreatment of the elderly." Six individuals or agencies were involved: physicians, social workers and counselors, home health agencies, attorneys, police departments, and funeral homes. Sixty-two questionnaires were returned which constituted a response rate of 29.8 percent.

FINDINGS: Some 26 (41.9%) of the individuals or agencies who responded to the questionnaire had encountered some kind of elder mistreatment. The only group who did not see elder mistreatment were those working in funeral homes. Among those encountering mistreatment all identified passive neglect, verbal/emotional neglect, active neglect, and physical abuse. These were ranked in terms of frequency in the same manner they are listed above. Passive neglect was the most frequently reported type, while both active neglect and physical abuse were reported as the least frequently encountered. Four causative factors mentioned in the literature were used as categories for causal factors in the questionnaire -- vulnerability/dependency of the victim, development disorders of the abuser, situational crises in the environment of the perpetrator or victim and long term environmental conditions. When respondents were asked to rank these factors, long-term environment was the most frequently mentioned factor, while situational crisis was the least frequently mentioned. Ninety-two percent of the respondents learned of the mistreatment through self-reporting by the victim or someone close to them. The remaining 8% said that they detected signs. However, all observed that detection took more than one visit with the victim. Actions taken by these five groups were varied, ranging from mental health services to nursing home placement.

CONCLUSIONS: Elder mistreatment appears to be a problem which is neither normally discussed nor referred to law enforcement agencies for resolution. When cases are identified and referred, they "seem to be made to established agencies, providing social, mental, and physical health services." These services tend to correspond to the needs implied in causative factors to which respondents replied in the questionnaire.

Professional Orientation:
- Nursing

Type of Exposition:
- Review

Substantive Issues:
- Types
- Causal Factors
- Family Dynamics

012 Beck, Cornelia M., and Ferguson, Doris. "Aged abuse." J Geront Nurs 7(6):333-36, June, 1981. (14 References).

TOPIC: The meaning of four types of elder abuse are discussed.

CONCLUSIONS: The literature on elder abuse includes four types -- violation of rights, material abuse, physical abuse, and psychological abuse. The violation of elder rights can occur without adequate community support services which preserve the older person's independence. Older persons are also vulnerable to material abuse if they are no longer able to handle financial matters. Physical abuse includes a spectrum from benign neglect, to oversedation, to bruises. In like manner, psychological abuse involves a wide range of behaviors. Some of these circumstances include provoking fear, threatening the elder, a failure to grasp the social needs of the older person, and treating the latter like a child.

Two causes for elder abuse may be explained by means of role theory and family systems theory. Shifts in role definitions for both the elder and the family provide sources of frustration. In the case of family systems theory, the need for stability may create a scheme of denial and distortions which may, in turn, serve to sustain abuse.

Professional Orientation:
- Nursing
Type of Exposition:
- Discussion
Substantive Issues:
- Causal Factors
- Family Dynamics

013 Beck, Cornelia M., and Phillips, Linda R. "Abuse of the elderly." J Geront Nurs 9(2):97-101. February, 1983. (21 References).

TOPIC: Family dynamics of those families caring for a "confused, frail elderly person."

OBJECTIVE: The goal is to examine the effect that a frail elderly person has on family structure and to examine the behavioral characteristics of a frail elderly person and his caretaker.

METHODS: This article represent a summary of the findings in the literature on elder abuse.

CONCLUSIONS: The high stress levels in the family system, the "spoiled identity" of the elder family member, and the caretaker's viewpoint that the elder family member's confused behavior merits some form of punishment all contribute to elder abuse. In addition, the distinct cognitive and social behavior of a dependent elderly family member along with typical responses from the caretaker serve to contribute further to elder abuse.

Professional Orientation:
- Law
Type of Exposition:
- Congressional Briefing
Substantive Issue:
-Treatment

014 Bergman, James A. "Testimony." In: First National Conference on Abuse of Older Persons, Cambridge, Massachusetts, March, 1981. Conference Proceedings. Boston, Massachusetts: Legal Research and Services for the Elderly, 1981. 14p. (0 References).

TOPIC: This presentation offers an overview of developments in both research and clinical practice in the area of elder abuse.

OBJECTIVES: The author wishes to synthesize the results of research and treatment over the course of the three years (1979-81) that active study of elder abuse has taken place.

METHODS: The presentation includes a report on case management at Legal Research and Services for the Elderly, and the assessment portion of Margaret O'Rourke's presentation at the National Conference on Elder Abuse entitled "Elder abuse: The state of the art."

FINDINGS: Legal Research and Services for the Elderly is a multifaceted program. Among its services are managing elder abuse cases, training staff to handle cases, conducting research on the subject, and lobbying for legislation which would serve abused elderly. The case of a 70 year old woman who refuses assistance despite her verbal and physical abuse by an adult child is typical of those who refuse help.

The presentation concludes with portions taken from the presentation of Margaret O'Rourke. See entry for Margaret O'Rourke No. 097. Four types of elder abuse cases are identified: (1) the competent/consenting person, (2) the competent/non-consenting person, (3) the incompetent person, and (4) the emergency case. Victims tend not to report abuse, services may not be available even when they do, and abusers need counseling.

Professional Orientation:
- Unidentified

Type of Exposition:
- Discussion

Substantive Issues:
- Characteristics
- Family Dynamics
- Social Structure

015 Birkley, Michael M. Protecting Wisconsin's elderly. Madison, Wisconsin: Office on Aging, Bureau of Human Resources, Division of Community Services, Department of Health and Social Services, May, 1983. 34p. (5 References).

TOPIC: The author shares his knowledge and perspective on elder abuse with members of the human services professions whose role is to protect the older population in the state of Wisconsin.

OBJECTIVE: The goal of this discussion paper is to examine strategies for intervention in elder abuse.

METHODS: The information presented here was gathered through material provided by and discussions with personnel in the Office of Aging, a special committee from the legislative council studying elder abuse, and those persons who work in the field of aging in the state of Wisconsin.

CONCLUSIONS: Elder abuse may occur in two to four percent of the older population. It occurs for a variety of reasons and is complicated to resolve. There are four kinds of abuse - physical, psychological, financial, and abuse of basic rights. In each instance, there is the belief that the abuse was intentional. The abused are older women who are dependent on others in some way and are most likely to live with other members of the family. They refuse to testify against those who abuse them for a number of reasons. Abusers tend to be caregivers who are related to the victim. Primary abusers are those who suffer some kind of personal stress and "accept violence as a normative aspect of family life." Secondary abusers are those who permit the abuse to occur and may even be victims themselves. The major cause of abuse is stress. Some of the environmental stressors come from the family, the social setting of the elder member. When we examine the victims of abuse, the abuser and the environment, a profile emerges which depicts elders at risk.

There are three major objectives which should be met in order to protect older persons from abuse. The first involves keeping the older person from social isolation. Community-based informal support networks are more beneficial in this regard than formal programs. A second goal involves the development of a caregiver support system. The government should support community programs which help at-risk families to resolve conflicts rather than removing some of the parties to the conflict from the home. Finally, there are some legal barriers involved which complicate identification, reporting, and treatment. Intervention policy should encourage voluntary community programs which help at-risk families to resolve conflicts rather than removing some of the parties to the conflict from the home. Finally, there are some legal barriers involved which complicate identification, reporting, and treatment. Intervention policy should encourage voluntary reporting of abuse rather than impose punishments for those who do not report cases. While Wisconsin's state law of adult protective services provides for these goals, implementation is uneven because each county has its own service priorities and resource limitations.

Protecting the elderly in the community does not require new programs. Rather, there is a need to re-direct, reconstruct, and expand programs already in existence. There should be one agency in the community whose task it is to provide information on services to the elderly. Advocacy and support of the needs of older persons is also an important priority in elder care protection. Finally, service delivery systems can take a more active role in identifying elders at risk and providing for preventive measures before abuse takes place. Elder protection involves both the availability of services and their active implementation.

Professional Orientation:
- Psychology

Type of Exposition:
- Position Paper

Substantive Issues:
- Causal Factors
- Policy

016 Block, Marilyn R. "Elder abuse research issues for the future." In: First National Conference on Abuse of Older Persons, Cambridge, Massachusetts, March, 1981. Conference Proceedings. Boston, Massachusetts: Legal Research and Services for the Elderly, 1981. 2p. (0 References).

TOPIC: This is a statement before the House Select Committee on Aging on future research needs on the subject of elder abuse.

CONCLUSIONS: Violence between adult members of the household and their older relatives is different from other forms of family violence. New directions in research should include determinations of scope, causes, and how changing lifestyles will influence the family structure. Future research must review methods of identification and reporting, legislation, how helping resources are delivered, and the training needs of those in the service delivery system. The most important need in research is "the development of a data base that will allow long-range study of the epidemiology of abuse." This data base needs to be organized at the federal level. In sum, more information on elder abuse is needed before sound public policy can be developed.

Professional Orientation:
- Psychology

Type of Exposition:
- Position Paper

Substantive Issue:
- Policy

017 Block, Marilyn R.; Davidson, Janice L.; Sinnott, Jan D. "Elder abuse and public policy." In: Block, Marilyn R. and Sinnott, Jan D. eds. The battered elder syndrome: An exploratory study. College Park, Maryland: University of Maryland Center on Aging, November, 1979. 85-95. (6 References).

TOPIC: A comprehensive public policy system is proposed for solving the problem of elder abuse.

OBJECTIVE: The goal in this chapter is to present options which could be utilized in a public policy system dealing with elder abuse.

METHODS: Using the scheme of three levels of policy -- nominal, procedural, and material in which the first level assumes adequacy of resources and the last inadequacy -- the author proposes that we enact the third level. The plan for the third level of material policy is comprehensively reviewed.

CONCLUSIONS: An Elder Abuse Prevention and Treatment Act should provide for the establishment of a National Center on Elder

Abuse and Neglect. This center should promote research, provide information on elder neglect and abuse, and offer a variety of services in the area of intervention. Finally, this Act should contain the requirement for all states to have MRL's (mandatory reporting laws).

Elder abuse public policy must also be involved in intervention. This can be either social, such as institutionalization, or legal which takes on a variety of alternatives. Civil sanctions are preferred to criminal in cases of elder abuse. Criminal charges against an abuser, especially one who is a relative, make rehabilitation of the abuser difficult to achieve, require the burden of proof to be on the elder, and provide for less immediate protection than in civil sanctions.

Prevention strategies should include family caregivers as well as the older person. Support services such as home-care services, transportation, educational, and financial assistance could supplement some of the family's elder caregiving functions. Increasing the fund of resources for older persons should also make the older person less dependent. Societal changes which focus on the positive aspects of aging must also be implemented.

Professional Orientation:
- Psychology

Type of Exposition:
- Survey Research

Substantive Issue:
- General

018 Block, Marilyn R., and Sinnott, Jan D. "Methodology and results." In: Block, Marilyn R. and Sinnott, Jan D. eds. The battered elder syndrome: An exploratory study. College Park, Maryland: Center on Aging, University of Maryland. November, 1979. 67-84. (0 References).

TOPIC: The results of three research designs on elder abuse are examined.

OBJECTIVE: The authors wished to determine the best methods of data gathering on elder abuse, and through the process of data collection wanted to examine the nature, scope, and dynamics of abuse.

METHODS: Data for this exploratory study were collected by means of three research plans. Plan A called for contacting agencies that assisted elders in the Washington, D.C. and Baltimore areas in order to obtain access to confidential records on elders who were abuse victims. This would permit retrospective case analysis. Plan B involved mailing a survey to nurses, doctors, social workers, and professionals in Maryland who were likely to be in contact with abused elders. Plan C collected data directly from community-dwelling elders in the D.C. and Maryland area. Analysis of the data was based on four research questions: (1) What is the extent of elder abuse in a representative population of urban/suburban elderly?, (2) Can profiles of the abused elder or of the abuser be determined?, (3) Are the dynamics in the elder abuse situation comparable to the dynamics in other dependent abuse situations?, and (4) Which method of obtaining data on elder abuse yields the highest quality data and is the most feasible?

FINDINGS: Plan B had the highest response rate of the three plans. Slightly more than four percent of the community-based elder respondents in Plan C reported elder abuse, suggesting that approximately one million cases of elder abuse occur across the nation. The abused elders were found to be very old (75+) and physically impaired in the majority of abuse citings in the three research plans. Also, these victims were found in both the middle and lower classes. Frequently, these abused elders lived with their children who abused them repeatedly. Many of these victims sought help only to find none was available.

CONCLUSIONS: The findings of the three research plans confirm and dispute findings of earlier studies. Contrary to a report by Lau and Kosberg (1978), more psychological abuse than physical abuse occurred. The three research plans also found that most respondents (88%) were aware of elder abuse even though they had experienced no cases of abuse. Another contradiction of this study was that abuse was found in middle-class families rather than largely lower-class families as previously supposed. Victims in this study were vulnerable because of failing health, and abusers were often stressed by economic and psychological factors. Similar results were found in other studies.

Professional Orientation:
- Psychology

Type of Exposition:
- Congressional Briefing

Substantive Issues:
- Scope
- Types
- Characteristics
- Causal Factors

019 Block, Marilyn R., and Sinnott, Jan D. Prepared statement for the Select Committee on Aging, U.S. House of Representatives, Ninety-Sixth Congress, First Session. June 23, 1979. Boston, Massachusetts. Elder abuse: The hidden problem, Washington, D.C.: U.S. Government Printing Office. 1980. 10-12. (0 References).

TOPIC: The presenters discuss abuse of the elderly by their caretaking children.

OBJECTIVE: Their goal is to report on the scope of elder abuse, its nature, the characteristics of the abused elder, and the causes of abuse.

METHODS: Journal articles, state statutes, research studies and police department reports support this statement's discussion.

CONCLUSIONS: Since data have not been collected in an orderly manner, no statistics exist that document the number of incidences of abuse. Findings from the few studies conducted reveal that the elderly victim suffers from several kinds of abuse -- severe beatings, shakings, slapping, overdoses of medication, sleeping pills or tranquilizers, theft, forced relocation to a nursing home, and forms of psychological abuse. Many of these victims are physically or mentally impaired and tend to deny abuse because of fear or because of embarrassment.

Although many factors contribute to elder abuse, a hasty decision to care for an aging parent in one's home, the increasing disability of that parent and the attempt to perform those tasks that s/he can no longer perform, and family power struggles all increase the likelihood for abuse to occur.

Professional Orientation:
- Social Work

Type of Exposition:
- Advice-Giving

Substantive Issues:
- Family Dynamics
- Cultural Patterns
- Treatment
- Definitions
- Barriers

020 Bookin, Deborah, and Dunkle, Ruth E. "Elder abuse: Issues for the practitioner." Cleveland, Ohio: School of Applied Social Sciences, Case Western Reserve University. 23p. (28 References).

TOPIC: This paper examines some of the problems practitioners face in dealing with elder abuse cases.

OBJECTIVES: The goal of this paper is to clarify the problems the social worker must address when intervening in cases of elder abuse and to propose strategies for dealing with these problems.

METHODS: Barriers to effective treatment of elder abuse victims by caseworkers are reviewed. These include the personal limitations of the social worker, limitations within the social work profession itself, and limitations of the families with whom they work.

CONCLUSIONS: Human service professionals find the task of identifying cases of elder abuse very difficult. There is not a uniform definition; and due to workers "limited exposure to cases," they tend to have little experience in this area of abuse and neglect. There is also a problem with differential access to abuse by various helping agents. For example, mental health workers may see families at a different phase of abuse than medical practitioners. These assessments lead to differential perceptions and profiles.

Another difficulty faced by the practitioner is the variation in cultural biases between the family and the caseworker. For example, in households where violent behavior is a matter of course, the worker may find resistance to interventions designed to stop the violence. Perceptions about family stress also may be viewed differently by the practitioner and the family. When the caseworker observes caregiver stress, and the caregiver does not agree, treatment to resolve the stress is unproductive. Or, sometimes, perceptions about force vary between casework staff members, creating problems for agreement on treatment strategies. Since elder abuse generally occurs within the family, the social worker also needs to be aware of the interpersonal dynamics of the members. Determining the nature of family relationships and conflict areas is an additional difficulty the caseworker must face, since each family system is different.

Both the worker and the victim of elder abuse feel powerless in a situation in which family cooperation is needed. Elders often deny the abuse because of the fear that exposure may bring shame and further conflict. On the other hand, the worker may find it difficult to establish trust with either the client or the family. One of the reasons for a lack of acceptance of help from the worker is the recognition that social workers have yet to gain knowledge and skill in working with the older client.

Caseworkers are confronted with ageism and attitudes toward dependency which create problems in elder care intervention. These attitudes can be counteracted through community education, better detection of elder abuse, and more dialogue among professionals in the human services. Elder abuse must be clearly defined in terms of "its effect upon the elder." While workers should rely on their own personal interpretation, they must also (1) know themselves, (2) understand aging, (3) understand the nature of abuse in families, (4) be aware of cultural and and societal biases, and (5) know appropriate methods of intervention. Finally, workers must be able to identify variables pertinent to identification and treatment and utilize age appropriate helping techniques in cases of elder abuse.

Professional Orientation:
- Unidentified

Type of Exposition:
- Congressional Briefing

Substantive Issues:
- Types
- Characteristics
- Barriers

021 Boydston, Linda S., and McNairn, James A. "Elderly abuse by adult caretakers: An exploratory study." Physical and Financial Abuse of the Elderly, Appendix 2. Hearing of the Select Committee on Aging, House of Representatives, April 3, 1981. San Francisco, California: U.S. Government Printing Office, 1981. 135-36. (0 References).

TOPIC: This statement reports the findings of a survey on elder abuse in San Diego, California.

OBJECTIVE: The purpose of this study was to determine preliminary estimates of the prevalence of elder abuse in San Diego, California. In particular, the goals of the survey were to determine whether elder abuse is a significant problem in American society, to determine which professionals were most likely to encounter cases of elder abuse and neglect, to establish "characteristics of the maltreatment", and to determine current intervention strategies in elder neglect and abuse cases.

METHODS: Data were collected by mailed questionnaires from a survey of medical, legal, social service, and law enforcement professionals likely to encounter elder abuse. Some 431 questionnaires were distributed. One hundred and one were returned with 67 of these questionnaires citing an elder abuse case. The returns represented a response rate of 24%.

FINDINGS: Social services workers and visiting nurses reported most of the abuse citings. The victims were most often women (73%) between 70 and 84 years of age. In 76% of the citings some type of physical abuse occurred, whereas 85% of the citings indicated that some type of psychological abuse occurred. Mental or physical impairments were found in 76% of the citings. Incidents of abuse seemed to recur twice or more in 70% of the citings.

Family members were the most frequent abusers and most were male relatives. Seventy percent of the respondents viewed the elderly person as a source of stress to the abuser. Most of the abuse case referrals were made by observations of the respondents or by the report of the victim.

Although a variety of interventions were used, there was some barrier to intervention in 76% percent of the cases. In 43% of the citings, it was the victim who was the barrier, while 42% of the abusers failed to co-operate in incidences of intervention.

CONCLUSIONS: The results of this study are similar to those studies on elder abuse found elsewhere in the country. The problem of elder abuse has been demonstrated by this study. What is needed is social, legal and medical support for both the abused and the abuser. The abused "need not be embarrassed to admit the problem" and the abuser must recognize that helping agencies are ready to help relieve the stress which inevitably accompanies caring for an older person.

Professional Orientation:
- Law

Type of Exposition:
- Review

Substantive Issues:
- Treatment
- Information
- Laws
- Attitudes

022 Bragg, David F.; Kimsey, Larry R.; Tarbox, Arthur R. "Abuse of the elderly: The hidden agenda. II. Future Research and Remediation." <u>JAGS</u> 29(11):503-7, November, 1981. (16 References).

TOPIC: Present and future solutions are proposed in order to treat neglect and abuse.

OBJECTIVES: The authors propose treatment goals in three sectors: (1) the community-at-large, (2) the medical community, and (3) the legal community which may lead to a reduction of abuse and neglect of older persons.

METHOD: Recommendations for protecting older persons are based on a review of work done by others as well as the professional experiences of the writers of the article.

CONCLUSIONS: The community-at-large needs to learn more about the aging process in constructive ways; members of the community ought to involve themselves in nursing home settings through volunteer programs and offer day care so that older persons may get away from institution and/or family from time to time. The medical community must offer more geriatric medical training, develop better methods of detection and follow-up on medical records, and must be educated to know the importance of reported suspected cases of abuse and neglect. Finally, the legal community needs to create legislation in order to protect older persons in nursing home settings, then make neglect and abuse unlawful, provide for "a minimum recovery for damages" and penalties for neglect and abuse or perhaps rewards for giving the elderly good nursing care. In summary, the various sectors need to combine efforts in order to bring the problem of elder neglect and abuse to the attention of others and to develop intervention strategies for the resolution of the problem.

Professional Orientation:
- Unidentified
Type of Exposition:
- Review
Substantive Issue:
- General

023 Briley, Michael. "Battered parents." Dynam Yrs 14(2):24-27, January/February, 1979. (0 References).

TOPIC: The author presents a review of the work of several persons prominent in the study of elder abuse.

CONCLUSIONS: The article focuses on prevalence and characteristics of elder abuse, some causes and intervention strategies. Two researchers, Suzanne K. Steinmetz and Eloise Rathbone-McCuan, report that it is difficult to know just how many elderly are victims of abuse, but they both predict an increase in elder abuse in the future.

The causes for abuse are still not clear. In some families violence has been a way of life. Elder abuse is simply one manifestation. Closely aligned with this pattern is the fact that the elder may actually provoke the abuse in some instances. Then, there are families who are not prepared for elder care, especially dependent elders. In these cases, elder abuse is the result of too much stress on the caregiving family.

Some of the useful strategies to help solve the problem of elder abuse include an increasing professional and community awareness of the problem, more in-depth research studies to help professionals know how to be better prepared to treat cases of elder abuse, helping families adjust to elder care and understand the aging process, and informing families about community resources which can assist them in elder care. In some cases, when professionals know that the families are unsuited for elder care, they urge families to locate a good nursing home for the elder member.

Finally, Alice Dempsey, Director of the Boston Visiting Nurses Association, observes that psychological abuse can be just as damaging as physical abuse of the elderly. It is her hope that calling our attention to physical abuse will bring us closer to the recognition that psychological abuse of the elderly is present in our society and "can be more significant to the elderly than physical battering..."

Professional Orientation:
- Medicine
Type of Exposition:
- Advocacy
Substantive Issue:
- Professional Responsibility

024 Burston, G.R. "Granny-battering." BMJ 3(5983):592, September, 1975. (1 Reference).

TOPIC: This letter to the editor calls professionals attention to the phenomenon of elder abuse in order to raise their consciousness about the problem.

METHOD: The author relates personal knowledge with the subject of elder abuse.

CONCLUSION: The problem of elder abuse appears to be a natural outcome when professionals fail to support caregivers of older persons. The situation known as "granny-battering" should be recognized in the same way that "baby-battering" has been.

Professional Orientation:
- Sociology

Type of Exposition:
- Position Paper

Substantive Issue:
- Policy

025 Callahan, James J. "Elder abuse programming -- will it help the elderly?" Urb Soc Change Rev 15(2):15-19, Summer, 1982. (11 References).

TOPIC: This presentation urges caution in the development of public policy on the subject of elder abuse.

OBJECTIVE: The goal is stated in the form of a question. "To what extent will the well-being of older persons be protected and enhanced by conceptualizing the above-described behavior as "elder abuse" for which special programming is required?"

METHOD: The author begins his discussion by answering the question posed in the objective in the negative. This is followed by an explanation of the author's response. The explanation for why the author believes that older persons may not be well-served by focusing on elder abuse includes five categories: "Issues of Definitions and Expectations; Problems with Data and Research; The Role of the Media; Supply Side Economics; and the Potential Effectiveness of Proposed Solutions to the Problem."

CONCLUSIONS: Definitions of elder abuse vary from research study to research study and from practitioner to practitioner. "Abuse like beauty, is in the eye of the beholder." This poses problems in assessment and treatment. In addition, attempts to define elder abuse can undoubtedly misinterpret relationships and family needs which, in turn, may lead to inappropriate intervention.

Research, per se, has suffered from design flaws many of which have their roots in sampling techniques. Therefore, generalizing to larger populations is impossible. Another problem with the research studies is their focus on abuser/abused characteristics rather than information which would be useful in problem-solving.

The media is of little value in promoting the well-being of older persons because it tends to distort the nature of abuse by sensationalizing instances, and repeating the same reports and cases. In the process, it colors the way we look at abuse.

With regard to the issue of supply side economics, there are some social programs in which demand followed supply. When there is a supply of professionals, we tend to generate services whether needed or not. This may be the case with elder abuse. Law schools and schools of gerontology may have overproduced professionals.

Finally, solutions may be examined in three spheres - political, legal and service. In the political area, policy should be more encompassing than elder abuse since politics impacts on institutions rather than particular groups of individuals. Law and the use of force do not change behavior. Resources would be better placed in nurturing institutions. Service programs need to be evaluated to determine effectiveness, and procedures need to be designed to make sure that intervention addresses the cause/s of the problem as well as the symptom/s. Elder abuse as a problem area should not be abandoned, but it should be treated as a side issue of a family centered approach. A particular focus may be on the support systems which individuals need.

Further recommendations include (1) more funds being made available as the age structure and the elderly's consumption needs change, (2) the formation of a single public agency to treat all forms of family violence, (3) the preservation of aging services networks and the co-ordination of these with other programs, and (4) financial resources which will provide decent housing, health maintenance and insure independence.

Professional Orientation:
- Social Work

Type of Exposition:
- Report

Substantive Issue:
- Treatment

026 Cash, Tim. "Abuse and neglect of the elderly." In: First National Conference on Abuse of Older Persons, Cambridge, Massachusetts, March, 1981. Conference Proceedings. Boston, Massachusetts: Legal Research and Services for the Elderly, 1981. 3p. (0 References).

TOPIC: This presentation involves a summary of the development of South Carolina's Adult Protective Services Program and recommendations for an effective program to protect the elderly.

OBJECTIVE: The author offers an illustration of the scope and depth of elder abuse in South Carolina and suggests effective care at the state level.

METHODS: A review of the program procedures for the Adult Protective Services in South Carolina from 1974 to 1981 are reviewed.

CONCLUSIONS: South Carolina identifies three groups of mistreated elderly: abused, neglected, and exploited. In the six years that the Adult Protective Services Program has been in operation, 7,000 cases have been reported. The number of new reports increase by about 25% each year. The Adult Protective Services Program employs 4 staff attorneys, 46 supervisors, and 150 caseworkers. The overall cost of this program is less than $1,000,000.

The essential components of a successful program involve two important ingredients. The first is a state law which requires both mandatory reporting and mandatory treatment and also provides for criminal action when necessary. In addition, the law should provide for immunity of the reporter and protection of the rights of the victim. The second ingredient for a successful program includes administration on the state level which requires training of caseworkers and lawyers in the special area of elder abuse, and which develops a centralized reporting procedure at the state level, supportive community services, and emergency shelters.

Funding should increase at the federal level to provide for emergency shelters, better services for in-home care, and specialized training in adult protective services for caseworkers and lawyers who work with these cases.

Professional Orientation:
- Sociology

Type of Exposition:
- Review

Substantive Issues:
- Characteristics
- Family Dynamics
- Cultural Patterns
- Social Structure
- Policy

027 Cazenave, Noel A. "Elder abuse and black Americans: Incidence, correlates, treatment and prevention." In: Kosberg, Jordon I., ed. Abuse and maltreatment of the elderly: Causes and interventions. Littleton, Massachusetts: John Wright, PSG Inc., 1983. 187-203. (43 References).

TOPIC: The author cautions viewing elder abuse as an individual phenomenon. Instead, he proposes to look at elder abuse as it relates to diverse subgroups in American society. The author focuses on features and experiences in the black subculture which bear on the occurrence and deterrence of elder abuse.

OBJECTIVE: The author correlates conditions which promote elder abuse with patterns found in the black community. In addition, factors in the black community which may be insulators against elder abuse are also reviewed, and proposals are offered for the reduction of elder abuse in the black subculture.

METHOD: Empirical data from studies on family violence are correlated with factors peculiar to the black subculture. Using a systems model for identifying the dynamics in abuse, the author analyses four levels of variables (1) societal, (2) family, (3) individual, and (4) precipitating factors.

CONCLUSIONS: Societal factors which correlate with family violence include poverty, a high proportion of elderly who are women and neighborhoods with high crime rates. Since Blacks tend to experience all three of these conditions, they should be considered at risk for elder abuse.

Family variables are much less predictive. The factors of multigenerational households, the presence of non-nuclear members in the household, social isolation, and shared values in the family may operate differently in the black subculture because of differences in both the cultural patterns of Blacks and the social structure in the black family; therefore, research needs to be conducted in these areas before we will know whether these family variables are buffers or causes for black elder abuse. Individual characteristics for the abused elder and the abuser tend to be congruent with the demographic and health conditions in the black community. For example, Blacks are reported to experience more physical and mental health problems than whites, making them more vulnerable to abuse. Substance abuse and other problems of health factors which correlate with elder abuse are also high in low income, black communities.

Finally, other research has shown that stress is a precipitating cause for elder abuse. Since Blacks tend to live under stressful conditions in a stressful environment, they are vulnerable for elder abuse. Indeed, comparing all four levels of variables, Blacks appear to be at risk for elder abuse.

Treatment programs should be sensitive to the conditions in the black community, and practioners should be non-prejudicial in their treatment. In addition, families need assistance in the custodial care in order to reduce caregiver stress in the black community. Helping agents must also be aware of the nature of friendship networks in the black community and "realize that these existing natural helping networks can often be incorporated into the intervention strategy." Finally, intervention must deal with the root causes of abuse in the black community rather than the symptoms of abuse. This will mean "changes" in the social predicaments in which many black families and many black aged find themselves."

Professional Orientation:
- Journalism

Type of Exposition:
- Discussion

Substantive Issues:
- Barriers
- Laws

028 Champlin, Leslie, "The battered elderly." Geriatrics 37(1):115-21, July, 1982. (0 References).

TOPIC: The author presents an overview of several of the barriers to the prevention of elder neglect and abuse.

OBJECTIVE: Social, medical and legal issues leading to limitations in intervention in cases of elder neglect and abuse are examined.

METHOD: Information from a variety of sources is presented in order to clarify and illustrate the barriers in the prevention of elder neglect and abuse. Several experts in this area are quoted.

CONCLUSIONS: Investigations of neglect and abuse by social workers are made difficult by laws which protect the privacy of the family. Even when confronted, families often deny the abuse because of fear of retaliation by the abuser or adverse publicity in the community. The fact that federal legislation has yet to be passed establishing mandatory reporting also makes detection lag behind where it should be. Although some states have now passed such laws, since there is no financial support to enter into a treatment program, mandatory reporting is a moot point. Increased financial support does not seem likely under the Reagan Administration and such a policy of cutbacks as is now seen could mean that a "greater number of elderly" are at risk of abuse. In light of retrenchment, we must make good use of the resources we have.

Professional Orientation:
- Social Work

Type of Exposition:
- Survey Research

Substantive Issues:
- Family Dynamics
- Characteristics
- Causal Factors

029 Chen, Pei N.; Bell, Sharon L.; Dolinsky, Debra L.; et al. "Elderly abuse in domestic settings: A pilot study." J Geront Soc Work 4(1):3-17. Fall, 1981. (32 References).

TOPIC: Conditions which contribute to persons becoming abused elderly victims or abusers of the elderly, and the effects of abuse on the abused and the abuser are the focus of this article.

OBJECTIVE: The goal of the study was to gain insight on the problem of elder abuse in the home from those practitioners who have had contact with elder abuse cases.

METHODS: A pilot study was conducted in Boston, Massachusetts. There were three phases of the study: (1) a survey of experts on elder abuse who were professors and administrators, (2) a preliminary survey to identify those practitioners who had had contact with elder abuse in domestic settings, and (3) a cross-sectional survey of the 90 practitioners identified in the second phase.

FINDINGS: Of the 30 respondents in phase three, 90% were aware of the elder abuse problem. Victims of abuse were mainly white women between the ages of 60 and 80 who were single or widowed and had low incomes, education, and socio-economic status. Abusers, on the other hand, were white males between 40 and 60 who were often a close relative of the victim, single or married and of a similar socio-economic, educational and income level as the abused.

These 30 respondents identified a number of causes for abuse including situational, societal, and family problems. Abusers and their victims also varied in terms of provocation peculiar to their circumstances. The effects of the abuse were also determined by the particular situation. Respondents saw the public at large as being unaware of and unconcerned about elder abuse. Methods of intervention and community resources to aid the victim and the abuser were considered inadequate. The majority of the respondents recommended that further research and public awareness programs be initiated as types of intervention for the problem of elder abuse.

Professional Orientation:
- Medicine

Type of Exposition:
- Survey Research

Substantive Issues:
- Types
- Treatment
- Professional Responsibility

030 Clark, A.N.G. "The Diogenes syndrome." Nurs Times 71(21):800-2, May 22, 1975. (1 Reference).

TOPIC: The focus of the article is on self-neglect by the elderly.

OBJECTIVE: The authors wish to identify the shared characteristics of elders who are neglectful of their health and living conditions.

METHODS: Hospital personnel studied 30 severe cases of self-neglect by the elderly in the community of Brighton, England. The physical appearances of these elderly victims of self-neglect, their health status, and their living environment were compared for common characteristics.

FINDINGS: Self-neglect affected elderly persons of either sex. Most self-neglectors lived alone. While depression and psychoses were not present, patients did exhibit common features of detachment, aggressiveness, and a tendency to distort reality. Those elderly who were hospitalized suffered from severe malnutrition, and many were seriously ill. Half the group examined were educated professionals with high intelligence, who chose to live a spartan existence, or who were hoarders surrounded by useless items and filth. Although all were known to both medical and social security officers before hospitilization, one-third refused help. Others showed reticence and resentment if health care professionals sought to alter their personal habits and living conditions.

CONCLUSIONS: Caution should be exercised when considering moving the self-neglecting elderly from their homes. If a move is necessary or if home care services are sought, it is best to involve only one contact person in persuading the victim of self-neglect to comply. Welfare homes or hospital admission for these elderly persons should be used only as a last resort. This will insure that the victims of self-neglect will have as much freedom as possible to determine their own life style.

Professional Orientation:
- Medicine

Type of Exposition:
- Survey Research

Substantive Issues:
- Types
- Treatment
- Professional Responsibility

031 Clark, A.N.G.; Mankikar, G.D.; Gray, Ian. "Diogenes Syndrome: A clinical study of gross neglect in old age." Lancet 1(7903): 366-68, February 15, 1975. (21 References).

TOPIC: The authors discuss self-neglect by the elderly.

OBJECTIVE: The goal of the article is to determine the characteristics of a syndrome in which elderly persons exhibit gross self-neglect.

METHODS: A study of 14 male and 16 female victims (ages 66 to 92) of self-neglect, who were admitted to the geriatric unit of a British hospital, was conducted using medical and intelligence examinations. In addition, close attention was given to the social and physical environment of each patient.

FINDINGS: All patients lived in squalor and were filthy in appearance. Their diet consisted mostly of breads and cakes stored in tins. Although some patients were admitted because of a critical illness, 17 patients suffered from a fall or collapse. Twenty-eight of the patients lived alone, and all were known by community authorities prior to hospital admission. None of the patients suffered from poverty despite the appearance of their home, and most had enjoyed professionally satisfying and rewarding careers. A surprising finding was the high I.Q. range (97 to 134) of the patients which placed them in the top quarter of their contemporaries. No abnormal personality traits were identified in the 15 patients tested; however, the patients did appear somewhat detached from reality.

CONCLUSIONS: Two possible explanations for the behavior of these patients are (1) a lifetime tendency towards giving personal and home care a low priority and (2) a reaction to the stresses that accompany old age that may be peculiar to certain personality types. However, in the last analysis, "care by consent" should guide community agencies in helping victims of self-neglect. It is the latter's choice to live in squalor and isolation.

Professional Orietation:
- Medicine

Type of Exposition:
- Report

Substantive Issues:
- Professional Responsibility
- Treatment

032 Clark, Curtis B. "Formation and utilization of an interdisciplinary geriatric abuse team." Department of Family Medicine. Jackson, Tennessee. Unpub Man 12p. (2 References).

TOPIC: The formation and function of a hospital-based geriatric abuse intervention team is described.

OBJECTIVES: The author proposes to assess the successes and dilemmas of a geriatric abuse intervention team, and to demonstrate how it functions in elder abuse cases.

CONCLUSIONS: A review of the literature shows that members of the society and the medical professional are prejudiced against older persons. At the same time, the elder population is growing. This means that expanded efforts to reduce this negative attitude toward aging need to take place.

The Geriatric Abuse Intervention Team or GAIT was formed to manage elder abuse cases more effectively and to have its professional members serve as role models for medical residents in family medicine. The team is composed of a family physician, nurse clinicians, clinical psychologist, two residents, pharmacist, and a medical educator. Some of the problems GAIT has experienced are (1) the difficulties in identifying cases, (2) the time and role assignments required for a multidisciplinary effort to be undertaken, and (3) the power struggles which sometimes take place among the members of the team. Nevertheless, this interdisciplinary process can be the best way to serve the needs of older abused persons.

Five cases are used to illustrate how the GAIT identifies and follows up on treatment and aftercare. Actions taken beyond medical treatment included a court order to obtain custody of the older person, removal of the elderly from the home, and encouragement for the older person to be placed in a nursing home in the patient's best interest. In one case, however, the abuse was discovered too late and the victim died while being medically treated.

Professional Orientation:
- Unidentified

Type of Exposition:
- Review

Substantive Issue:
- General

033 Cloke, Christopher. Old age abuse in the domestic setting: A review. Surrey, England: Age Concern England, August, 1983. 32p. (28 References).

TOPIC: The author presents an overview of elder abuse in domestic settings in both the United Kingdom and the United States.

METHODS: Developments since the mid-seventies in research and practice in the field of elder abuse are traced by highlighting the key areas of interest. These include: the definition, scope, causes, characteristics of abused/abusers, family dynamics, treatment and policy in elder abuse. Research in these areas is summarized and the work of four practitioners in the United Kingdom, A.A. Baker, G.R. Burston, Elizabeth Hocking, and Mervyn Eastman, is reviewed. The first three are physicians and the last is a social work professional.

CONCLUSIONS: Elder abuse has, indeed, come to be recognized as a problem. However, professionals find that its resolution is hindered by the lack of a common definition; inadequate research efforts in examining the nature, scope, and causes for abuse; attempts to compare elder abuse with child abuse; and problems in establishing effective treatment. While there is a need to develop policy, research thus far is insufficient to use for this purpose. The United Kingdom has responded by leaving "the respective professions to develop their own approaches." At the same time, all professionals should be responsible for identifying cases of elder abuse and for providing appropriate services to the family.

The article by A.A. Baker stresses the need for the physician to go beyond the medical model to look at older persons in the social and personal aspects of their lives as well. This could be achieved by working with a multidisciplinary team, more home visits, and by better training of the physician. G.R. Burston focuses on some catalysts for abuse -- fragility of the elder, living with younger family members, caregiver frustration, crowding, and the continuous presence of the elder in the household. Elizabeth Hocking finds three situations in which abuse might occur (1) when families have used violence over the years, then adult children may simply return it to their older parents, (2) relatives may resent the care they give to the older person manifesting it in abuse, and (3) after considerable dependent elder care, the caregivers may succumb to violence through fatigue. Finally, Mervyn Eastman considers several "signals" which point to elders at risk -- physical/ mental dependency, poor communication, lifestyle of the caregiver, role-reversal, repeated falls, bruising, crowding, other family dependents, caregiver medical visits for "nerves", and caregiver alcoholism. Overall, elder abuse is a family problem and treatment should focus on the family as a whole. It is ongoing rather than a single incident, and the medical and social work professions need to be better prepared to identify and treat the problem.

Some of the current issues of concern in elder abuse in the United Kingdom are caregiver burden, the complexities of family dynamics in elder care, and the role of the government. Several researchers have shown that caregivers are under considerable stress when they care for older members. The causes for stress may be a key to the possible causes for elder abuse. The literature on family dynamics points out that abuse can be two-way, from the caregiver to the elder and from the elder to the caregiver. Therefore, family intervention should involve the development of positive communication among family members. Finally, during the last parliament, the Secretary of State for Social Services was asked to provide guidelines to practitioners for intervention in elder abuse. His response indicated that the government preferred to leave such questions in the hands of the individual practitioner.

American research has emphasized the caregiver role, the frequency and nature of abuse, characteristics of the abused and abuser, potential causes of abuse, and agency responses. Caregivers indicate that their role is appropriate, but at the same time stressful. With regard to frequency and the nature of abuse, there is still no definitive research. The literature on characteristics of the abused and abuser and causes are also variable and, in some cases, contradictory. Agencies do not have a clear protocol for treatment. This is the result of failure to recognize the problem, fear of mis-diagnosis, narrowly defined agency-specific services, or concern about becoming unpopular if the worker labels too many people in this way.

Professional Orientation:
- Nursing

Type of Exposition:
- Case Studies

Substantive Issues:
- Types
- Treatment
- Professional Responsibility

034 Cornwall, Julia V. "Filth, squalour and lice." Nurs Mirror 153(10):48-99, September 2, 1981. (0 References).

TOPIC: The author focuses on self-neglect of the elderly.

OBJECTIVE: The goal of this article is to raise the question of whether hospitalization of self-neglecting elderly is the most beneficial approach for the older person.

METHODS: The hospital care provided for a 74-year-old victim of self-neglect is chronicled from the time of his admission to his death 19 hours later.

FINDINGS: Self-neglectors appear to be above average in intelligence. Their lifestyle and personal habits reveal poor hygiene, a filthy environment, refusal to be helped, and a desire for social isolation. These self-neglecting elderly are especially vulnerable to trauma when there is a need to be hospitalized for medical attention. In fact, about half of these self-neglecting elderly die while under hospital care.

Harry, the self-neglect victim, is used as an illustration of what might happen to such a person when hospitalized against one's will. Neighbors became involved when his physical health deteriorated. Subsequently, he was hospitalized and subjected to a number of changes in his personal habits and level of privacy. Although the hospital staff were kind and well-meaning, their disruption of his day-to-day existence may have contributed to an earlier death than he would have experienced had he stayed at home.

CONCLUSIONS: Even though he may have died at home soon after the time he did die in the hospital, the question remains of how much authority the victim of self-neglect should have over his or her life. Perhaps the older person should be free to decide what is best with regard to remaining at home or being hospitalized.

Professional Orientation:
- Social Work

Type of Exposition:
- Review

Substantive Issue:
- General

035 Coslo, Judith, and Thomas, Sandra. "The history of elder abuse and society's response." In: Schultz, Leroy G. ed. Elder abuse in West Virginia: A policy analysis of system response. Morgantown, West Virginia: West Virginia University, 1983. 20p. (30 References).

TOPIC: The authors review literature on elder abuse to explain why it is not adequately understood and/or responded to. Political "clout" exercised by the elderly is one possible answer to the problem.

METHODS: A considerable number of writings on domestic abuse are cited to reveal why society in general and West Virginia in particular have not dealt with elder abuse in any significant way. The development of the elderly as a political force is considered. Existing and pending national and state legislation are also discussed.

CONCLUSIONS: Socialization processes, stress and society's tolerance for violence are seen as causes for all sorts of domestic abuse including elder abuse. However, the research supporting such analysis is faulty and, therefore, can't be depended upon. Much of what is supposed about elder abuse is drawn from an analogy with spouse and child abuse, an analogy which has its strengths but also its limitations. There are problems in reporting such abuse and no clear-cut ways seen to remedy these problems. The elderly are rapidly increasing their percentage of the population and, hence, they might constitute a "voting bloc" dedicated to achieving their own interests, like the Townsend Movement of the 30's. However, despite a number of organizations which serve these interests wholly (such as AARP) or in part (such as the West Virginia Council of Churches), elders are not reckoned with as having political "clout" at the present time. This is due to a diversity of interests within their population, and to a frequent unwillingness of elders to identify themselves as such. It is hoped that as elder abuse becomes more visible, older persons might use this problem as a rallying point around which to unite. There are two pieces of national legislation affecting the abused elderly: the Older American's Act of 1965 and the still pending HR 769. And, there are two such West Virginia statutes: SB 121 and HB 743. The issue of protective services has been left to the individual states where it has been addressed inconsistently. More legislation must be passed to assure adequate funding for protective services; more research must be carried out that will lead to better informed service providers; the elderly should be helped toward political cohesiveness and personal independence; and the state should be less paternalistic in its attitude toward elders and more sensitive to their rights.

Professional Orientation:
- Journalism

Type of Exposition:
- Review

Substantive Issue:
- Policy

036 Crist, Karen, and Lerman, Lisa. "Responding to elder abuse: Using spouse abuse models." In: First National Conference on Abuse of Older Persons, Cambridge Massachusetts, March, 1981. Conference Proceedings. Boston, Massachusetts: Legal Research and Services for the Elderly, 1981. 23p. (11 References).

TOPIC: This presentation points out the differences between spouse abuse and elder abuse but, nevertheless, finds some common features.

OBJECTIVES: The presenters review the course of programs and legislation regarding spouse abuse in order to assess the degree to which older persons may benefit from the same interventions and policies.

METHOD: Three key areas are discussed: shelters, state laws regarding spouse abuse, and the merits of treating abusers as criminals.

CONCLUSIONS: The history and nature of shelters for battered women are reviewed. In many ways, shelters are ill-equipped to meet the health care and social-psychological needs of older persons. Since these shelters are sex-specific, older men cannot use these facilities. Even with changes in sex-related accommodations, shelters for battered women are not prepared to meet the special needs of the older population at the present time.

Alternatives to staying in the violent home are limited for the older person. The nursing home might be psychologically traumatic and/or the cost of elder care in the nursing home might be too draining on the family's resources. The safe-home network used in cases with battered women might be expanded to include elders who must leave their homes in order to protect themselves against violence.

Law enforcement is also important in family violence cases. Inadequate enforcement may be seen from police to prosecutors. The latter group must make family violence a priority and must be cognizant of the victim's needs. In both spouse and elder abuse, the victims do not necessarily wish to sever the relationship with the abuser. They just want to stop the abuse. With regard to treating the abuser, there are three main reasons for doing so: (1) the failure of the criminal justice system in law enforcement against abusers seems to perpetuate abuse in families, (2) if family violence is viewed as a crime, then the police would be more likely to make arrests, and (3) criminal prosecution can offer the victim protection and can oblige the abuser to seek rehabilitative treatment. Abuser counseling programs of various kinds seem to be effective in stopping abuse, especially if the abuser is ordered by the court to participate in the program. The diversion program used in a Miami, Florida, intervention project illustrates one type of counseling. The more independent the older person, the fewer the problems in finding alternatives to living with the abuser. Nevertheless, domestic violence legislation should provide older persons with a number of legal options to prevent recurrence of abuse. In addition, more resources need to be available to families who care for older persons.

Professional Orientation:
- Home Economics

Type of Exposition:
- Survey Research

Substantive Issue:
- General

037 Crouse, Joyce S.; Cobb, Deborah C.; Harris, Britta B.; *et al*. *Abuse and neglect of the elderly in Illinois: Incidence and characteristics, legislation, and policy recommendations*. Springfield, Illinois: Sangamon State University and Illinois Department on Aging. June 30, 1981. 128p. (76 References).

TOPIC: This study focuses on the phenomenon of abuse and neglect in domestic settings in the state of Illinois.

OBJECTIVES: The intent of this study was the development of a strategy to estimate the nature and scope of elder neglect and abuse. The study has focused on legal research in order to identify basic legal issues in intervention and legal provisions within Illinois and other states. Finally, the authors wished to examine policy options for treatment of elder abuse and neglect.

METHODS: Community research on the objectives involved a number of stages. Illinois was first divided according to five demographic criteria. Then, seven communities were studied at random. At that point, research was divided further into three stages. First, interviews were conducted with people in the community who were involved in services for the elderly. For the second stage, questionnaires were sent to 1,890 service providers to learn more about their attitudes and experiences with elder abuse. Some 1,260 people responded to the questionnaire which resulted in a response rate of 67%. Finally, respondents from the first phase who had identified cases of abuse and neglect were sent a questionnaire in order to provide information on individual cases.

State statutes and social service programs were also studied for the purpose of evaluating legislation and policy recommendations in elder abuse cases.

FINDINGS: This study showed that each of the six types of elderly neglect and abuse identified by the researchers did occur in each of the communities involved. Abuse related to crime was more prevalent in urban communities. In the survey of service providers, 11,739 cases of elder abuse and neglect were reported. Urban and rural areas had the highest incidence of abuse with passive neglect or verbal abuse being the most common form. Projecting to the entire states, it is estimated that there are 18,716 to 20,065 cases of neglect and abuse with 80% of the cases assumed to be neglect.

Although home care professionals were believed to be more likely to encounter abuse cases, hospital emergency room personnel, police, and clergy actually reported more cases of elder abuse. Respondents identified personal contact as the most frequent method of identifying abuse cases.

In the second survey of service providers, data on 148 abuse cases were collected. One-third of the cases represented severe neglect or abuse. Dependency seemed to be more a factor in neglect than in abuse cases.

Examination of states' laws showed many states leaning toward adult protective service laws and mandatory reporting statutes. Seventeen states have both types of laws at present. In relation to Illinois, the state's Guardianship and Advocacy Act is central to maintaining the balance between state intervention rights and an individual's rights to liberty. It is important to keep in mind the motives for intervention and who is being served.

An analysis of state social services systems revealed no coherent statewide system of services. Community networks usually coordinated services to the elderly. Of the three model service systems examined, the advocacy model was considered superior to the child abuse or domestic violence models. With this model, the older person has an advocate to look after his or her rights. This advocate operates independently of the social services system.

Professional Orientation:
- Unidentified

Type of Exposition:
- Review

Substantive Issue:
- General

038 Davidson, Janice L. "Elder abuse." In: Block, Marilyn R. and Sinnott, Jan D. eds. The battered elder syndrome: An exploratory study. College Park, Maryland: Center on Aging, University of Maryland. November, 1979. 49-55. (10 References).

TOPIC: The subject of this chapter is abuse of the elderly by their caretaking children.

OBJECTIVE: The author's goal is to report the findings of family violence literature on topics related to elder abuse by caretaking children.

METHODS: Approximately 12 sources from family violence literature are cited. Topics discussed include frequency and nature of elder abuse, the characteristics of the abused elder and the abuser, and the potential causes of elder abuse. The latter topic concludes the paper with a somewhat detailed discussion.

FINDINGS: Those adult children who care for their elderly parents largely because of a sense of responsibility represent the negative aspects of their caretaking role. Those who have found this role the most difficult are those who still have children at home and those whose elderly parents suddenly become dependent. One study reported over three-fourths of its cases involved physical abuse and over half related to psychological abuse. There seems to be a correlation between impairment (mental and physical) and abuse. In addition, older persons tend to deny abuse or refuse to report incidences. With respect to cause, the literature suggests that violence is learned. Those who were abused as children may very well retaliate in later life in the form of elder abuse. Causal factors contributing to the potential for abuse have been identified in the following trends: a growing elderly population, diminishing economic resources, changes in the older person's or adult child's life that conflict with previous expectations, strained family relationships, and the relocation of the elderly parent to the adult child's home.

Professional Orientation:
- Unidentified

Type of Exposition:
- Review

Substantive Issue:
- Attitudes

039 Davidson, Janice L.; Hennessey, Susan; Sedge, Suzanne. "Additional factors related to elder abuse." In: Block, Marilyn R. and Sinnott, Jan D. eds. The battered elder syndrome: An exploratory study. College Park, Maryland: Center on Aging, University of Maryland. November, 1979. 57-66. (32 References).

TOPIC: The authors review attitudinal factors present in society that contribute to elder abuse within the family.

OBJECTIVE: The authors wish to provide background information for the possible association of ageism, attitudes towards the disabled, disability perceptions of the elderly, and learned helplessness with elder abuse by family members.

METHODS: The paper's causal theories are supported by the studies of approximately 30 anthropologists and social psychologists.

CONCLUSIONS: Studies in anthropology reveal that a culture's behavvior is learned rather than innate. Many societies teach negative attitudes toward the elderly through their treatment of the elderly. In the United States, old people are viewed as isolated, deteriorated, and cognitively deficient. Other studies reveal that rejection of the disabled because of their physical differences relates to a rejection of the elderly because of their differences. A negative portrayal of those who are physically different predicts a negative opinion towards the elderly. Further studies show that those elderly who share society's negative attitudes and who view themselves as "old" have less control over their lives and may be subject to abuse. Furthermore, once individuals feel no control over a situation, studies show that they develop a psychological state of helplessness. That is, they learn to become helpless. This learned helplessness may be explained by the social exchange theory and the theory of learned helplessness itself. The problem of ageism needs to be carefully considered in programs of public awareness, education and treatment for elder abuse.

Professional Orientation:
- Law
Type of Exposition:
- Review
Substantive Issue:
- Laws

040 de la Hunt, William. "Legal remedies for elderly victims of abuse." In: First National Conference on Abuse of Older Persons, Cambridge, Massachusetts, March,1981. Conference Proceedings. Boston, Massachusetts: Legal Research and Services for the Elderly, 1981. 6p. (0 References).

TOPIC: The author presents a simple overview of all the possible legal actions the abused elderly in Massachusetts may take.

OBJECTIVE: The author wishes to demonstrate that victims of elder abuse have some recourse under the law.

METHODS: Massachusetts' statutes and civil suits which may be employed in the defense of the abused elderly are reviewed.

CONCLUSIONS: The civil order 209A protects the elder from physical abuse by home caregivers when s/he takes the initiative in reporting the mistreatment. Elders may also file a criminal complaint which imposes greater sanctions on the abuser. A third legal approach is a civil suit by the older person. This may involve payment for damages in the case of injury, or damages for the violation of the elder's civil rights. Finally, the M.G.L.C. 258A compensates victims for losses as a result of violent crime.

There are clear drawbacks to utilizing either criminal or civil law, but these options are available to abused older persons if they are aggressive enough to protect their rights. For those who do not assert themselves, mandatory reporting and treatment is the next step.

Professional Orientation:
- Unidentified

Type of Exposition:
- Report

Substantive Issue:
- Identification

041 Delp, Gladys. "Hospital elderly abuse committee develops criteria for identifying abuse." Nurs Pulse of New Eng. 1(40):1,3, November 29, 1981. (0 References).

TOPIC: The article summarizes a detection protocol for elder abuse which may be used in a medical setting.

OBJECTIVE: The goal of the report is to offer a method for nurses to use to assess whether elder abuse has occurred.

METHODS: The article reports on the work of the multidisciplinary committee formed by Charlotte Anastasio in order to identify elder abuse at Brigham and Women's Hospital in Boston, Massachusetts.

CONCLUSIONS: The multidisciplinary committee developed a two-step protocol. If patients presented with one or more risk factors for elder abuse, then the next step was to determine the level of functioning of the older person as well as the ability of the caregiving person to cope with elder care. If patients or caregivers were reticent to move to the second step of reporting on functioning and caregiving, then the nurse employed questions which achieved the same ends. Patients also give clues that they may be victims of elder abuse by withdrawing from physical touch or eating voraciously after it has been reported that they have eaten normally during the day. Nurses must show empathy toward caregivers in order to reassure the caregiver that nurses understand the stress the caregivers are under.

If the patient appears to be at risk for abuse, the assessment tool is used. This tool includes demographics, nursing assessment, social service assessment, medical assessment, nutritional assessment and a plan for intervention. The goal is to work within the family system. Families may react differently to the diagnosis of elder abuse. The important thing is to gain their cooperation in the resolution of the problem. If families are uncooperative by denying the abuse or resisting care, then it is hard for the nursing staff to stand by and watch the abuse of the older person continue. "But, on the other hand, that's what they know as family, that's what they know as love."

Professional Orientation:
- Psychology

Type of Exposition:
- Position Paper

Substantive Issue:
- General

042 DeRidder, Lawrence, and Dietz, Siegfried. "Counseling and counseling services for the abused older person." In: Tennessee Conference: Abuse of Older Persons. Knoxville, Tennessee, December, 1980. Conference proceedings. Knoxville, Tennessee: School of Social Work, Office of Continuing Social Work Education, 1981. 89-102. (9 References).

TOPIC: The elderly is a group which deserves much more counseling specific to their needs than they have been getting. Such counseling might be an important factor in preventing elder abuse.

METHODS: The article looks at reported statistical data and other articles on the elderly to try to separate fact from fiction with regard to elder abuse and the elderly in general. Elder abuse and some of its causes are discussed along with the implication of the demographic data for counseling services to the elderly abused. Specific factors counselors need to be aware of are mentioned.

CONCLUSIONS: The demographic data about aging in the United States establish some perhaps unexpected facts and dispel some myths. Some of the former, with important implications for counseling, are the facts that (1) at age 65, the life expectancy is fifteen more years and at age 75, it is ten more, (2) there is probably a wider range of differences among the elderly than between the elderly as a group and any other age group, and (3) learning ability does not decline with age. A typical myth is that aggression/abuse is more prevalent in the lower socio-economic classes and among Blacks. Given the data about the nature and causes of elder abuse, there are a number of things that are important to know as a counselor of the abused including the following: One should use local rather than national demographic data; One should expect that there will be more women than men counselees; And one should adapt to the fact that a higher percentage than normal of one's counselees will be homebound. There is a great potential for the positive use of counseling among the abused elderly in order to increase their sense of freedom, hope and flexibility. Black Americans have special needs in this regard, and these needs require a specific response.

Professional Orientation:
- Public Health

Type of Exposition:
- Review

Substantive Issue:
- General

043 Douglass, Richard L. "Domestic neglect and abuse of the elderly: Implications for research and services." Fam Relat 32(3):395-402, July, 1983. (15 References).

TOPIC: The author reviews six research studies on elder neglect and abuse and concludes by raising issues for practitioners and researchers to address.

OBJECTIVE: The goal of the article is to summarize the findings of the six studies on abuse of the elderly by family members in order to provide professionals from urban planners to social workers with information useful in prevention and intervention of elder neglect and abuse.

METHODS: Five studies are reviewed very briefly and the sixth (Douglass et al., survey, 1980) is reviewed in depth. Recommendations for practitioners and researchers reflect some observations about the changing demographics in the family.

CONCLUSIONS: Population dynamics suggest that older persons will be living longer and increasing in numbers, but opportunities for their adequate care will be decreasing. This sets the stage for neglect and abuse. Some contributions from other research studies on elder neglect and abuse include some in-depth case reports; documentation that informal caregivers do abuse and neglect elders; stress as a cause for abuse; the resistance of victims to report incidences; and the observation that there is a variety of forms of abuse and neglect.

The summary of the Michigan research addressed the questions of whether neglect and abuse really existed, what the mistreatment characteristics were, and why professionals think it occurs. In the case of the latter objective, four causal hypotheses were explored: (1) elder dependency, (2) exposure to abuse in childhood, (3) life crises, and (4) environmental factors. The result was that all four were considered valid with no one causal factor outstanding.

Observing the hard fiscal times facing us, one way to insure help for older persons and their families is through action at the local level and assistance from volunteer agencies. Also, lawmakers must use care in modeling elder abuse reporting and intervention after child abuse laws. In order to protect the rights of older persons, they must be treated as adults, not children. Finally, researchers must use care in comparing elder abuse with other forms of family violence because the older population has its own place in the family structure. Researchers must first test the models derived from these other forms to determine similarities and differences and be open to the information available from the several disciplines, tracing the new family structure resulting from long-term aging.

Professional Orientation:
- Public Health

Type of Exposition:
- Survey Research

Substantive Issue:
- General

044 Douglass, Richard L.; Hickey, Tom; Noel, Catherine. A study of maltreatment of the elderly and other vulnerable adults. Ann Arbor, Michigan: Institute of Gerontology, The University of Michigan, February, 1980. 197p. (60 References).

TOPIC: This research report presents findings on the nature, scope, and causes for abuse to older persons and other vulnerable adults.

OBJECTIVES: Four objectives guided the research. The first goal of the research study was to examine the scope of research in the area of elder mistreatment. The rationale for this objective was to determine whether elder maltreatment was significant enough to warrant the utilization of professional, scientific, and governmental resources in order to deal with the problem. The second objective focused on characteristics of abuse. The third objective addressed the issue of case finding procedures. The fourth explored possible causes for elder maltreatment.

METHODS: Researchers at the Institute of Gerontology and the School of Public Health at the University of Michigan received funds from the Administration on Aging to conduct an exploratory study on elder neglect and abuse. The research project was conducted from October 1, 1978 through June 30, 1979. Three research designs were implemented. The first design involved the study of vulnerable persons in the community. These included older persons, the mentally retarded, the emotionally impaired, and the physically handicapped. The second design included a study of basic or skilled care nursing homes. Finally, the third component included secondary data analysis based on Detroit City Police Department records and records from the Michigan Department of Social Services.

In the domestic setting, interviews were conducted with practitioners at five sites in Michigan (city of Detroit, Oakland County, Lake County, Kent County, and Marquette County). Selection of practitioners was based on their level of involvement with vulnerable adults. These vulnerable adults include the elderly, the mentally retarded, the emotionally impaired and the physically handicapped. A semi-structured interview schedule was administered to 288 respondents. Each interview was approximately one hour in length. There were ten respondent categories. These included police, physicians, nurses/aides, caseworkers, adult service workers, mental health counselors, lawyers, services to the aging personnel, clergy, morticians and coroners.

In addition, nursing home personnel were interviewed. These included administrators and nursing home staff from a non-random selection of 12 nursing homes in Oakland County and the city of Detroit. Nursing home administrators were asked to be interviewed themselves along with a nursing staff member and a nurse's aide. Therefore, a total of 36 persons were interviewed among the twelve institutions.

Secondary data analysis was conducted on the city of Detroit Police Department's Preliminary Case Report data for 1978. The researchers used this data set to determine the victim's familiarity with the perpetrator. A second data set was secured from the Michigan Department of Social Services nursing home data. The objective in using these data was to assess the vulnerability to neglect and abuse of newly admitted public patients or nursing home residents.

FINDINGS: Maltreatment in the domestic setting survey was classified as passive neglect, active neglect, verbal abuse, emotional abuse, and physical abuse. Most of the 228 respondents were in mid-career, between the ages of 30 and 39, were about equally divided between males and females and tended to be better educated than the average citizen. The respondents did not report any major differences in the neglect and abuse conditions according to the type of vulnerable adult. It was also found that the least severe forms of neglect and abuse occurred more frequently, and the most severe were reported to be less frequent. This meant that passive neglect appeared more frequently than active neglect. The occurrence of active neglect was reported more frequently than emotional abuse. Emotional abuse was reported more frequently than verbal abuse. And, physical abuse reported to be the least frequent form of mistreatment.

Cause of neglect and abuse were identified by means of three questions. The first was an open-ended question about what the respondent considered the causes to be, and the other two were pre-coded questions. The second of the pre-coded questions asked the respondent to rank four identified cause -- dependency causing neglect and abuse, child abuse victims reversing the abuse when they become elder caregivers, some kind of life crises for the victim of abuse or the perpetrator, or the living environment as a cause of neglect and abuse. Responses to these four causal hypotheses varied according to occupation of respondent and size of population in the five sites used.

Respondents were also asked about policies for handling cases. Only about a third of the respondents said they did have a policy. But of that group which numbered 63, only 26 respondents indicated that the policy was based on written procedures.

In the nursing home study most of the respondents had had experience with passive neglect. Most nursing home administrators believed that the causes of neglect and abuse were basically the same. Finally, overall, the 36 nursing home respondents did not believe that neglect and abuse were a problem in the nursing home and reported that the nursing home staff offered better care than the older person's family.

The third research component was the secondary data analysis. According to city of Detroit Police Department records for 1978, perpetrators of assaultive and non-assaultive crime were least likely to be relatives or acquaintances. However, police department respondents noted that the crime reports appeared to understate incidences caused by relatives and acquaintances.

Data on nursing home admissions were taken from Oakland County in which there were data on 236 individual assessments. The findings indicate that these nursing home residents were highly dependent on nursing care. They were identified as frail or ill. Therefore, they were considered to be at risk for elder mistreatment.

CONCLUSIONS: Neglect and abuse of vulnerable adults is probably not new. This research study has attempted to call attention to the fact that vulnerable adults who are very dependent on others may not be adequately cared for, and, therefore, may be victims of maltreatment. Nevertheless, there may be no villians. Instead, families and others may be victims of circumstances. Therefore, intervention should be based on assistance rather than punishment. A number of recommendations to provide this assistance are proposed. These fall within the context of practice and research. With regard to the former, several suggestions are made for the legal and helping professions which focus on protection and prevention. Research recommendations stress the need for better research designs and a more comprehensive analysis of the mistreatment of vulnerable adults.

Professional Orientation:
- Public Health

Type of Exposition:
- Training Guide

Substantive Issues:
- Information
- Identification
- Reporting
- Professional Responsibility

045 Douglass, Richard L., and Ruby-Douglass, Patricia. "Domestic abuse and neglect of the elderly." In Braen, G., ed. Management of the physically and emotionally abused. San Diego, California: MacMillan, 1981. 141-50. (10 References).

TOPIC: The authors discuss elder neglect and abuse caused by family caregivers.

OBJECTIVES: There are five objectives presented. These include preparing medical and emergency personnel to learn about family violence, to become aware of elder abuse and neglect, to propose appropriate roles for these health care providers in cases of elder abuse, to suggest standardized identification procedures for elder abuse and neglect, and to challenge others to learn more about the problem.

METHODS: Several methods are used to meet the objectives. These include a review of the literature on elder neglect and abuse, case studies of victims seen at a medical emergency facility, and procedures medical emergency personnel should utilize in order to identify and manage cases of elder abuse.

CONCLUSIONS: Several studies on elder abuse and neglect have been conducted since 1977. Although the results are not conclusive, they do point to some common patterns in abuse characteristics, causes, and possible intervention strategies. These studies report a variety of forms of abuse from psychological and physical to financial abuse and various forms of neglect. Victims of abuse are usually frail older females suffering from some type of mental or physical impairment. "Racial, socioeconomic, or other social criteria that define segments of the population at higher risk of being neglected or abused have not been found."

Causes for abuse are also multiple. However, the most common include caregiver stress, personal problems of the caregiver, long-term family conflict, and failure to take advantage of community support for family caregiving. When cases do surface, identification is hampered by a lack of co-operation on the part of the victim, a lack of training procedures in medical and social service settings, poor communication among helping services and legal problems with the reporting of cases. Five case studies are presented to highlight the complications in assessing and treating elder abuse and neglect cases. Each individual had received medical emergency care as a consequence of the abuse.

Geriatric patients differ from younger patients in a variety of ways. The aging process may contribute to misleading signs such as confusion and disorientation. However, confusion may be the result of abuse or neglect. Older persons differ from children in that they may refuse help. This complicates identification and treatment. The response of the emergency medical team to elder abuse should involve greater suspicion about the possible abuse, the use of an inventory of signs of neglect and abuse and alerting support staff to some common signs. Once the case has been identified, documentation should proceed through "the medical history, physical examination, photographs, and any remarks by the patient." After documentation, referral is based on the nature of the case. However, even when cases are taken over by community agencies, emergency staff should continue to monitor the intervention and provide assistance when appropriate. Since the elder population is increasing, there is the increased probability that elder abuse will increase as well. Further, these victims will probably be seen with greater frequency in emergency departments. Therefore, emergency medical teams need to be prepared to identify and manage cases of severely neglected and abused older persons.

Professional Orientation:
- Law

Type of Exposition:
- Congressional Hearing

Substantive Issue:
- General

046 Dudovitz, Neal S., and Chiplin, Alfred, Jr. Prepared statement in Physical and Financial Abuse of the Elderly. Hearing of the Select Committee on Aging, House of Representatives. April 3, 1981. San Francisco, California: U.S. Government Printing Office, 1981. 32-36. (0 References).

TOPIC: This presentation focuses on the physical and economic abuse of the elderly.

OBJECTIVE: The presenters propose two objectives. First, they would like to call attention to the fact that there are civil rights issues involved in elder abuse, and we must remind ourselves that older persons are citizens of the United States with the same rights as every other citizen. For example, "They have the same right to be free of unwanted government intrusion as do any other citizens." The second objective is to call attention to the economic abuse of the elderly by the federal government.

CONCLUSIONS: The case work of attorneys at the National Senior Citizens Law Center and discussions by the authors with other attorneys, state officials, aging organizations, and legislators support the testimony.

Many legal services available to the elderly do not consider the older person's position as an adult citizen with rights and liberties. Services should not "be provided on an involuntary basis unless the elder has been determined incompetent under appropriate guardianship or conservatorship" laws that follow due process rights of the elderly individual. Involuntary services to elder abuse victims (except in guardianship cases) and public guardianship cases are not in the best interest of the older person.

Another issue which needs to be resolved is "the Social Security Administration's failure to control and police the representative payee system." The federal government, in fact, sends millions of dollars to representative payees without monitoring who actually receives the money. This payee system actually encourages fraud and abuse. Therefore, the House

Select Committee on Aging is urged to "investigate the representative payee system of the Social Security Administration." This investigation should include (1) a demonstration of prevalence of cases of fraud and (2) a proposal which "will make the Social Security Administration accountable for its errors" and guarantee old persons the benefits which are rightfully theirs.

Professional Orientation:
- Social Work

Type of Exposition:
- Discusssion

Substantive Issues:
- Policy
- Laws
- Barriers

047 Dunn, Mary Alice. "West Virginia Department of Welfare: Role, policy and practical issues." In: Schultz, Leroy G. ed. Elder abuse in West Virginia: A policy analysis of system response. Morgantown, West Virginia: West Virginia University, 1983. 19p. (17 References).

TOPIC: The author discusses the strengths and weaknessess of existing West Virginia legislation that bears on elder abuse.

METHODS: The author analyzes Chapter 29,000 of the West Virginia Department of Welfare Social Service Manual as the most relevant document for determining Department of Welfare procedure with regard to elder abuse. She determines its strengths and weaknessess with respect to such things as time and quality of response, division of responsibilities and cooperation among service agencies. Finally, she discusses current problems in funding, training of personnel, and reporting of suspected cases.

CONCLUSIONS: Most victims of elder abuse have a physical or mental disability which makes them a source of stress to the abuser. West Virginia Senate Bill #121, which emphasizes services to "incapacitated adults" is, therefore, very relevant though not limited specifically to elder abuse.

The Department of Welfare is the agency best suited to implement this bill. Therefore, it is useful to see what their current policy is in this area. Chapter 29,000 of the Social Security Manual is most relevant in this attempt. The requirements for governmental response are defined in such a way that they can be adapted to the characteristics of each county. The manual shows an attempt to capitalize on what has been learned from twenty years of experience with Child Protective Services. But if it is to be effective, it needs to establish clear protocols for dealing with such issues as the client's rights to privacy as well as protection, the social worker's legal liability and safety, and the cooperative role to be assumed by the police and courts and other agencies.

Current guidelines require a home visit and certain other procedures within forty-eight hours of notification of a suspected case of elder abuse. But, within this requirement, there is still much to be spelled out, such as whether this is forty-eight "work-time hours," the effect on the response of the reported severity of the case, follow-up visits, and other details. The possibility also exists of dropping the case before a resolution is achieved. Comprehensive and effective services including follow-through should be mandated by law as should reporting by all persons or agencies likely to be involved with a case of elder abuse.

To achieve effective and comprehensive programs, the Department of Welfare should be given overall responsibility for elder abuse treatment. The cooperation of other relevant agencies with the Department of Welfare should be mandated by West Virginia law.

Additional laws should be enacted which would create and maintain family support networks, community-based programs which would be alternatives to institutionalization and programs which would identify and address the conditions which contribute to abuse. Special emphasis should be given to the abuser's situation.

Major problems also exist with respect to (1) the lack of consistent funding -- a lack which severely jeopardizes the project, (2) the development of a thorough and continuing training program, (3) the insurance of adequate funding for a quality program before passage of a mandatory reporting law, and (4) the passage of a mandatory reporting law which details how abuse is to be reported, relieved, prosecuted, and which establishes what safeguards are to exist both for the reporters and the abused.

In line with this, the Department of Welfare should expand the services of the Child Abuse Hotline to also take calls about adult abuse on a twenty-four hour, seven day per week basis.

Professional Orientation:
- Journalism

Type of Exposition:
- Review

Substantive Issues:
- Scope
- Causes
- Professional Responsibility
- Laws

048 Eastman, Peggy. "National spotlight on elder abuse." Ger Consult 1(6):10, June, 1983. (0 References).

TOPIC: The author reviews the findings of a year-long study on elder abuse by the House Select Committee on Aging as well as proposed legislation at the federal level.

CONCLUSIONS: Elder abuse can be found in approximately 4% of the older population; it is recurring and it is expected to increase according to the Select Committee report. This congressional committee also determined that caregiver stress was a major causative factor for elder mistreatment. In addition, elderly victims tended not to report abuse for a variety of reasons which range from shame to a lack of opportunity to lodge a complaint. Physicians can play an important role in identification; however, because of their expected contact with the family and the older person, there is a need for routine medical visits by the latter.

Congresswoman Mary Oaker has unsuccessfully proposed legislation which would establish a National Center on Adult Abuse for the purpose of funding programs on prevention, identification, and treatment of elder abuse. In lieu of federal regulations, states are responsible for elder abuse legislation. The Select Committee's investigation found 26 states with elder abuse laws, 16 of those mandatory, and 20 states failing to sponsor such laws. Most of the officials from the states surveyed reported that they thought state laws for the protection of the elderly were ineffective and preferred federal mandatory legislation. Nevertheless, elder abuse will involve health professionals more and more whether federal legislation is forthcoming or not.

Professional Orientation:
- Unidentified

Type of Exposition:
- Advice-Giving

Substantive Issues:
- Varieties
- Laws
- Policy

049 Edwards, Victor L. "Child abuse laws and services: What can be learned from them to counter elder abuse?" In: Crouse, Joyce S.; Cobb, Deborah C.; Harris, Britta, B.; et al. Abuse and neglect of the elderly in Illinois: Incidence and characteristics, legislation, and policy recommendations, Appendix C. Springfield, Illinois: Sangamon State University and Illinois Department on Aging. June 30, 1981. 20p. (1 Reference).

TOPIC: The author considers the implications of child abuse legislation in Illinois for the subject of elder abuse.

OBJECTIVE: It is the goal of the paper to assist policy planners in elder abuse programs by utilizing the lessons learned in the child welfare system in Illinois.

METHODS: The history of child protective services up through the passage of P.A. 81-1077 and The Abused and Neglected Child Reporting Act in 1980 are reviewed. Then, using child protective services as a frame of reference, the author goes on to draw appropriate parallels with the needs in elder abuse programs.

CONCLUSIONS: While child abuse has always been with us, it was not named and professionally addressed until the 1960's. Now elder abuse seems to be following the same course in the 1980's. Planners are warned about some of the failures coming out of the establishment of a Department of Child and Family Service. Instead of reducing abuse, however, the more active Child Protective Services the more cases seemed to emerge. Therefore, those involved in Adult Protective Services need to be alerted to the prospects of seemingly limitless cases. At the same time, funding for treatment programs is shrinking. Therefore, those individuals engaged in elder abuse services need to set realistic goals for treatment. In addition, they should not fall into the trap of separating the public and private sector as child abuse programs have done. Elder abuse legislation should contain a clear purpose and precise definition of terms. Child abuse legislation has suffered from a lack in both areas. In addition, it is important that lawmakers be guided by the purpose of the law as well as the letter of the law. Issues such as age of reportable cases, when to report, to whom one reports, the requirements for reporting, penalties and immunity must all correspond to the underlying purpose of the elder abuse law. The issue of providing for a central registry to keep track of the nature and scope of cases is controversial. When the information is used to improve services to families it is effective. However, when used as a political tool the utility of a central registry is defused.

Professional Orientation:
- Unidentified

Type of Exposition:
- Survey Research

Substantive Issues:
- Scope
- Types
- Characteristics

050 ______. Elder abuse in Pennsylvania. Harrisburg, Pennsylvania: Pennsylvania Department of Aging, Bureau of Advocacy, January, 1982. 12p. (0 References).

TOPIC: This report contains the findings of a survey on elder abuse in Pennsylvania.

OBJECTIVE: The principal objective of this report was to determine if elder abuse occurred in Pennsylvania; and, if so, what were the characteristics of the abuse incident, the victim, and the abuser.

METHODS: The Pennsylvania Department of Aging mailed a survey to approximately 1,928 professionals and non-professionals representing fourteen occupational categories who were in some way providing services to the elderly population in that state. Data on this non-random sample were collected between July 1980 and June 1981 from 1,138 completed surveys, which represents a return rate of 59%.

FINDINGS: Forty-one percent of those respondents who completed the survey reported knowing of at least one case of elder abuse in the previous 12 months. The total number of respondents was 467, but some of those respondents knew of more than one case. The mean number of abuse cases known to each respondent was five. However, there is no way of knowing whether cases are duplicated. Although all occupations surveyed indicated exposure to at least one abuse case; protective services workers, homemakers, home health aides, and social workers reported more abuse citings than other professions.

The reported cases had actually occurred more than twice in 85% of the respondents' citings. Physical abuse was the most prevalent (44% of citings). Psychological abuse was next (38% of citings). Material abuse was found in 18% of the citings, and 4% involved violation of rights. The highest proportion of abused were in the 70-79 year old group, and 76% were female. In a majority of the citings (81%), the victim was physically disabled with 71% of the citings reporting mental disability. In 69% of the reported citings, the victim lived with the abuser; and in 75% of the reported citings, the abuser was a relative. Most abusers were males (52%). In 67% of the citings, the abuser was a victim of drug or alcohol abuse or had medical and financial problems, all of which contributed to the stress of caring for an elderly dependent. The elders, themselves, were reported as a source of stress in 61% of the citings. Agency responses to these reported cases varied.

CONCLUSION: Two things are clear as a result of this study. Elder abuse in Pennsylvania is appearing at a "significant rate" and service workers who are expected to maintain the quality of life of older persons "must take steps to reduce the impact of that abuse." As a consequence of these conclusions, the following recommendations are made: (1) there is a need for more research, (2) there should be special training for protective service workers who deal with elderly, (3) intervention in elder abuse cases should attempt to be the least disruptive for the victim, (4) support services should be made available to the families who care for dependent elderly, (5) there should be increased visability of programs to protect the elderly, (6) causes for abuse must be eradicated, and (7) housing alternatives should be developed when the elder is removed from the home.

Professional Orientation:
- Nursing
Type of Exposition:
- Hearing
Substantive Issue:
- General

051 ______ "Elder abuse in the home found widespread by Congressional Inquiry." Ger Nurs 1(5):153-54, September/October, 1980. (0 References).

TOPIC: This report reviews the nature of elder abuse and some barriers to treatment.

OBJECTIVE: The goal is to report the findings of a House-Senate Committee probe on abuse of the elderly.

METHODS: Three case summaries of elder abuse victims, reports from various studies across the United States, and comments from affiliates with the New York City Chapter of the National Association of Social Workers, Victim Services of New York, Visting Nurse Service of New York, and a law school dean support the articles' discussion of a House-Senate Committee's probe on elder abuse.

FINDINGS: An estimated two and one-half million elderly people are abused by family members each year, making this form of family violence as widespread as child abuse. The typical victim of abuse is a disabled, middle-class woman who is 75 years of age or older. Most victims live in families that have established patterns of family violence. Societal pressures, especially economic ones, make it hard for family caregivers not to view elder care as a burden. Many victims fear retaliation or shame if they report the abuse, and the lack of adult reporting laws in the majority of states or the presence of weak laws make it difficult for lay or professional persons to intervene. The "Adult Abuse and Protection Act" proposed by Rep. Mary Oaker would provide states with some uniform standards through which to offer treatment and prevention programs.

Professional Orientation:
- Nursing
Type of Exposition:
- Training Guide

Substantive Issues:
- Identification
- Treatment
- Definitions
- Characteristics
- Causal Factors

052 Falcioni, Denise. "Assessing the abused elderly." J Geront Nurs 8(4):208-12, April, 1982. (13 References).

TOPIC: The author presents a health history assessment instrument for the detection of elder abuse.

OBJECTIVE: The author develops an instrument which takes into account both family dynamics and the social structure of relationships between the elderly and caregivers.

METHOD: The literature on elder abuse is reviewed with an emphasis on definitions, causes for abuse and characteristics of the abused and the abuser. This is followed by the proposal and an illustration of an assessment tool which may be used by nurses to detect elder abuse.

CONCLUSIONS: Drawing on the definition by Lau and Kosberg, the types of abuse include physical, psychological, material abuse and violations of rights. Causes for abuse may be the result of developmental dysfunctional, elderly dependence on the caregiver, and situational conditions such as substance abuse or material abuse. Abused/abuser characteristics vary from one individual to another.

The role of the nurse is important in the identification of abused elders. However, an assessment must follow "a complete health history, physical and psycho-social assessment." The particulars of the assessment involve some standard demographic characteristics of the older person: complaints, present and past medical history, personal habits, mental status testing, and the family's history. This is followed by some signs which may point to abuse. An illustration of the detection procedure follows.

Some recommendations for intervention include the need for the nurse to be as supportive of the victim as possible, therapeutic interviewing of both the abused and abuser, an assessment of family needs in order to reduce stress, and awareness of community resources including state laws regarding elder abuse.

Professional Orientation:
- Law

Type of Exposition:
- Position Paper

Substantive Issues:
- Varieties
- Laws

053 Faulkner, Lawrence R. "Mandating the reporting of suspected cases of elder abuse: An inappropriate, ineffective, and ageist response to the abuse of older adults." Fam Law Quart 16(1):69-91, Spring, 1982. (approx 32 References).

TOPIC: The author discusses the implications of the adoption of a mandatory reporting system for suspected elder abuse cases.

OBJECTIVE: The goal of the article is to assist policymakers as they consider mandatory reporting legislation for suspected cases of elder abuse.

METHODS: The author addresses the problems raised by mandatory reporting of suspected elder abuse cases after examining elder and child abuse studies and after comparing enacted state statutes for mandatory reporting of child and spouse abuse. Proposals for mandatory reporting of elder abuse are made.

CONCLUSIONS: Mandatory reporting of elder abuse is only a case-finding tool, and while it will not solve the problem of elder abuse, it is also likely that it will not increase the number of reported cases of elderly abuse. Problems with this system may include ageism, infantilization, and dependency. The negative effects of these laws will be felt especially when reporters of older abuse cases find that few, if any, services are available to help solve the problem.

Before policymakers propose legislation for mandatory reporting laws for elder abuse, agreement on the definition of elder abuse is essential. The most applicable mandatory reporting law model to be used in formulating laws for the reporting of elder abuse is spouse abuse laws. Child abuse laws may have relevance only in the unique setting of child abuse. A parallel model for the elderly should not be implemented.

Professional Orientation:
- Nursing

Type of Exposition:
- Training Guide

Substantive Issues:
- Identification
- Causal Factors
- Treatment
- Family Dynamics

054 Ferguson, Doris, and Beck, Cornelia M. H.A.L.F. -- A tool to assess elder abuse within the family. Ger Nurs 4(5):301-4, September/October, 1983. (7 References).

TOPIC: The authors present an identification measure for detecting abuse or predicting elders who are at risk for abuse in family settings.

METHODS: Four factors identified as potential contributors to abuse are used as the categorical areas to be assessed. These include: "health status of the aged, family and aged adult's attitude toward aging, living arrangements, and finances." H.A.L.F. is an acronym for these factors. A data collection instrument containing 37 items distributed among these four categories is presented; and likert-type scale using the codes of <u>almost, always</u>, <u>some of the time</u> and <u>never</u> is used to determine actual abuse, elders at risk and unabused elders correspondingly.

CONCLUSIONS: This elder abuse identification tool is designed to be filled out by a health care provider. Each of the four sections of the assessment scale calls for the satisfactions and needs of both the elderly and their adult caregivers. H.A.L.F. has been used with some 50 individuals or families and "has proved useful in identifying aged persons who are at risk for abuse or actually being abused." Copyrighted in 1980, plans are being developed to field test the instrument for validity and reliability.

Intervention in families can take place at three levels. Primary prevention calls for (1) the teaching of non-violent coping behavior early in the life course, (2) instructing families about the aging process, and (3) strengthening the family's social support network. Secondary prevention requires prompt treatment because the family is considered to be at risk for abuse. These strategies include: (1) determining role conflicts, (2) assessing which parties in the family need to change roles, (3) clarifying expectations, and (4) support for an appropriate role for the older person. Finally, tertiary prevention comes into play ex post facto. Once abuse has already taken place, there are still some strategies which can be used to prevent further abuse. For example, respite care and placement in another residential setting are commonly used. Two cases are presented in order to show how H.A.L.F. can be implemented. In both instances abuse was detected in all four areas, and in both cases the elder was removed from the caregiver setting.

Families should be continually assessed in order to maintain primary, secondary and tertiary intervention. The H.A.L.F. instrument also has value as a research tool in the area of improving elder care.

Professional Orientation:
- Nursing

Type of Exposition:
- Training Guide

Substantive Issues:
- Identification
- Reporting

055 Fulmer, Teresa T. "Elder abuse detection and reporting." Mass Nur 51:10-12. May 1982. (0 References).

TOPIC: This article summarizes the current demographics, research findings, and reporting issues on elder abuse, in addition to discussing the work of the Department of Nursing at Beth Israel Hospital in Boston concerning a protocol for assessment of elder abuse.

OBJECTIVE: Although the article's overall objective is to summarize the current state of knowledge on elder abuse, the central discussion's goal is to define a protocol for assessing elder abuse.

METHODS: In the fall of 1980, a task force was formed from the nursing staff at Beth Israel Hospital in Boston for the purpose of formulating a protocol for the assessment of elder abuse. This committee was formed in response to a 1980 Massachusetts mandatory reporting statute for abuse of patients in long-term care facilities. The major work of the committee involved a pilot study in the summer of 1981 which was designed to formulate an "Elder Assessment Tool." Douglas Johnson's screening protocol for suspected cases of elder abuse and Block and Sinnott's study "Battered Elder Syndrome" served as models for the assessment tool. For one month, elder assessment forms were attached to emergency room records for patients over 70 years of age. At the end of the month, data were collected from 37% of the 161 assessment sheets that were logged into the hospital's computer system.

FINDINGS: The Beth Israel study was the first research based on a description of patient's history and physical exam. Data from the study indicate that 18% of the elderly seen needed help with hygiene, 18% with feeding, 16% with continence, and 29% with ambulation. While 78% of the patients lived in homes, 12% of the patients were unhappy with their living arrangements. These findings indicate that many elders are "high-risk" for abuse when the impairment theory is viewed as a probable cause for abuse.

CONCLUSIONS: Feedback from the emergency room nurses who participated in the study suggests designing a briefer protocol for determining abuse cases than was used in the study. The revision most often suggested was a check-list format for the assessment form.

Professional Orientation:
- Social Work

Type of Exposition:
- Position Paper

Substantive Issue:
- General

056 Gentry, Charles E., and Nelson, Barbara D. "Developmental patterns of abuse programs: Applications to the aging." In: Tennessee Conference: Abuse of Older Persons, Knoxville, Tennessee, December, 1980. Conference proceedings. Knoxville, Tennessee: School of Social Work, Office of Continuing Social Work Education, 1981. 73-88. (33 References).

TOPIC: The prevalence of abuse and neglect must be uncovered and the problem must be attacked at its source -- within the dysfunctional family.

METHODS: A review of the literature reveals a lack of awareness of the extent of elder abuse and also certain family and characterological traits which must be confronted if the cycle of abuse is to be stopped.

CONCLUSIONS: Abuse which includes both neglect and abuse is defined as misuse in the form of "deprivation, pushing another person, hitting and beating, to homicide." This definition is followed by a number of illustrations. There continues to be little public awareness of elder abuse. Both the family and society tend to deny that the problem exists. Treatment of elder abuse must remove the secrecy surrounding abuse. What is revealed is a variety of conditions and characteristics of families.

There may be environmental stresses such as poverty, substance abuse, or marital problems which may precede abuse. There appear to be parallels between child-abusing parents and parent-abusing children. These include unrealistic expectations, little empathy for the child (elder), the assumption that hitting is legitimate, and unrealistic demands. Interventions which are effective involve the whole family and use multiple community resources. Self-help and rehabilitation approaches are to be preferred over removal either of the abused or the abuser. More protective legislation and adequate funding are required to train those involved with intervention, and contribute to preventing abuse, protecting the abused and rehabilitating the abuser.

Professional Orientation:
- Law

Type of Exposition:
- Congressional Hearing

Substantive Issue:
- Laws

057 Gilfix, Michael. Prepared statement in Physical and Financial Abuse of the Elderly. Hearing of the Select Committee on Aging, House of Representatives. April 3, 1981. San Francisco, California: U.S. Government Printing Office, 1981. 39-42. (0 References).

TOPIC: The presentation focuses on the inappropriateness of mandatory reporting laws for the legal profession.

OBJECTIVE: The goal of this presentation is to examine the ethics of requiring attorneys to report elder abuse or suspected cases of elder abuse.

METHODS: Three cases of financially abused elderly persons which have come to the attention of the Senior Adults Legal Assistance Program in Palo Alto, California, and H.R. 769 (The Prevention, Identification, and Treatment of Elder Abuse Act, introduced by Representatives Mary Oakar and Claude Pepper, serve as the background for this testimony).

CONCLUSION: Because the Code of Professional Responsibility for Attorneys requires that attorneys keep the confidence of their clients, attorneys may be financially exploited through fines for not reporting abuse cases. Yet, attorneys are often the key to identifying cases of elder abuse. Therefore, certain revisions are required before the Elder Abuse Act is passed. These are contained in proposed Rule 1.7 on the Code of Ethics developed by the ABA Kutak Commission which defines professional responsibility for lawyers. First, "a lawyer shall disclose information about a client to the extent it appears necessary to prevent the client from committing an act that would result in death or serious bodily harm to another person....," and secondly, "a lawyer may disclose information about a client to the extent it appears necessary to prevent or rectify the consequences of a deliberately wrongful act by the client, except when the lawyer has been employed after the commission of such an act to represent the client concerning the act or its consequences." Specific recommendations include (1) researching the conflicting implications of reporting laws proposed by the H.R. 769 vis-a'-vis state laws, (2) requesting The House Select Committee to adopt the Code of Ethics advocated by the ABA Kutak Commission, and (3) encouraging state legislators to adopt proposed Rule 1.7 into state laws.

Professional Orientation:
- Unidentified

Type of Exposition:
- Survey Research

Substantive Issue:
- General

058 Gioglio, Gerald R., and Blakemore, Penelope. "Elder abuse in New Jersey: The knowledge and experience of abuse among older New Jerseyans." Trenton, New Jersey: New Jersey Department of Human Resources, New Jersey Division of Youth and Family Services, Bureau of Research and New Jersey Department of Community Affairs, New Jersey Division of Aging. 99p. (47 References).

TOPIC: This study focuses on the nature and scope of elder abuse according to New Jersey's older residents, ages sixty-five and older.

OBJECTIVES: The goal of this research is to identify a representative sample of older New Jerseyans who live in non-institutional settings and to develop a questionnaire which would provide reliable information on the nature and scope of elder abuse in New Jersey.

METHODS: Data were gathered through interviews and mailed questionnaires from a multi-stage stratified random sample of 342 New Jerseyans, aged 65 or older. Sampling was derived from 1980 census data on both households and populations. Only community-dwelling older persons were used. However, this population was drawn in order to be representative of New Jersey's community-dwelling older population, aged 65 and older. The questionnaire consisted of vignette analysis, closed and open questions about this population's knowledge, and experience with elder abuse. When respondents discussed case histories of elder abuse they had observed, they were asked to identify the victim by the initials of the latter's name. It was hoped that this method would reduce the duplication of cases. Finally, a scale was designed by the staff and included in a questionnaire, which was used to measure the attitudes of this older population toward the care and treatment of the elderly.

The questionnaire included five areas: (1) vignettes on elder abuse, (2) questions of actual cases of elder abuse, (3) the respondent's personal involvement with elder abuse, (4) the attitude scale on the care and treatment of older persons, and (5) the interviewer evaluation of the respondent's reaction to the interview.

Fifty interviewers were identified and trained by project staff through the office of the New Jersey Division on Aging.

FINDINGS: Nine hypotheses were tested. These focus on the incidence of abuse and the characteristics of both the abused and the abuser. There were 23 reported cases cited by 16 respondents, five of whom identified themselves as the victim. Based on this sample, it is estimated that about 8,000 New Jerseyans are victims of some type of abuse.

The types of abuse were classified under four categories: financial, neglect, psychological and physical. Respondents reported that financial abuse was the most common form, while physical abuse was the least common. When respondents were asked how close they were to the case of abuse, 74% reported firsthand knowledge.

The data on age of the victim concur with other studies. Most of the abused were age 75 or older. None of the victims were non-white. This may be due to the fact that the sample was not weighted for racial representativeness. Religious identification may also not be representative because of the small abused elder population cited. The data on the abused elder's health status was consistent among most of the victims. About 87% were reported to have "fair to poor" health. Finally, 75% of the victims did not report the abuse to some authority. Reasons given for their failure to do so range from inability to report to feeling that the problem of abuse could be worked out.

Abusers tended not to live with their victims. This may have been due to the fact that financial abuse was predominant. Some 70% of abusers who were identified in the financial abuse category did not live with the victim. Most abusers were male, between ages 16 and 69, and 61% of them were members of the immediate family.

The results of the attitude scale indicate that, indeed, the younger members of the family should care for the old and be willing to share their households with the older member. Improvements in home health care should be important in the prevention of abuse, but elders who once abused their children should expect to experience the abuse in reverse in their later years.

CONCLUSIONS: The results of this survey and those of other similar studies point to several recommendations: future research should focus on causes for abuse rather than incidence; more effective legal provisions should be instituted; the best aspects of traditional, domestic violence, and advocacy models should be incorporated into protective service legislation; there should be more paraprofessional and professional involvement in teaching families how to care for older members; there should be more experiments in intergenerational living, and more governmental and community support for families who care for older members.

Professional Orientation:
- Social Work

Type of Exposition:
- Review

Substantive Issue:
- General

059 Giordano, Nan Hervig, and Giordano, Jeffrey A. "Elder abuse: A review of the literature." Paper presented at the Southern

Gerontological Society Third Annual Meeting. Orlando, Florida: June, 1982. 18p. (Bibliography).

OBJECTIVE: In the authors' words, "The purpose of this paper is to examine the literature on elderly abuse in order to provide a comprehensive view of the nature and extent of the problem, current theoretical viewpoints and the strategies for intervention."

CONCLUSIONS: The literature on elder abuse is flawed by differing definitions of the problem, weaknesses in research methods and sampling, and underreporting of cases. Therefore, we must be cautious about predicting the extent and nature of abuse. Several explanations of abuse have been offered - internal family dynamics, impairment dependency, abuser pathologies, filial crisis, internal family caregiver stress, external family stress, and attitudes toward the elderly. These factors are likely to overlap and fail to isolate the actual causes for abuse.

Services to the elderly are offered to those living alone or those in nursing homes. Help for families is given only when elder care conditions have "deteriorated." "Aging service planners and advocates need to advance the case for a national policy which recognizes that the family and government are _partners_ in the provision of care to the elderly." In addition to improving laws for protecting older persons, service delivery systems should focus on interdisciplinary responses for managing cases of elder abuse. In view of the cost of such an effort, workers need to use resources at hand and begin to coordinate programs through nationwide data collection and dissemination systems.

Current trends suggest that as the number of older members in this society increases, so will the need for caregiving by families. This fact needs to be recognized with a reallocation of resources and services to support families caring for dependent elderly.

Professional Orientation:
- Social Work

Type of Exposition:
- Survey Research

Substantive Issues:
- Family Dynamics
- Types

060 Giordano, Nan Hervig and Giordano, Jeffrey A. "Individual and family correlates of elder abuse." _Unpub Man_ 17p. (9 References).

TOPIC: The authors review data on several cases of elder abuse in order to see if there is a typical family profile.

OBJECTIVE: Two major objectives were cited by the authors. First, the individual and family circumstances of cases of physical abuse, neglect, financial exploitation, psychological abuse, and multiple abuse were explored. Second, the authors wished to develop abused elder profiles for the various forms of abuse and neglect.

METHODS: Case records for the period of January 1976 to January 1982 were secured from Aging and Adult Services Units in seven counties in Florida. The experimental group consisted of 600 abused elders. The control group of non-abused elders numbered 150. Data collection involved (1) identifying the type of neglect or abuse for each case, (2) discerning individual's characteristics, and (3) examining family circumstances. Several statistical procedures were used to identify critical factors in individual and family circumstances which were correlated with various types of abuse.

FINDINGS: The data show that profiles varied according to the types of abuse. Most of the victims were white females between the ages of 66 and 83 whose income was $7,000.00 or less and who lived with the abuser. There were some other family circumstances which were distinguished among the five types. Spouses were frequent perpetrators of physical abuse and, when the victim was not married, sons tended to be the abusers. With regard to neglect, females were more likely than males to be neglectful, especially daughters. Psychological abusers commonly were spouses. And, when the victims were married, the abusers were more likely to be males, especially sons. Males were more likely to be exploited than females, males more often were the abusers and 32% were not related to the abused person. Finally, spouses were often multiple abusers. But, when the victim was unmarried, females, especially daughters, were the perpetrators.

Using a multiple regression analysis, each type of abuse was found to have five to seven variables related to family circumstances which accounted for 15 to 25% of the variance in predicting elder abuse. No two sets were exactly the same, once again demonstrating differences according to type of abuse. Discriminant analysis also predicted some differences among types of abuse. Finally, when abused elders and non-abused elders were compared on 10 variables, those which were better descriptors of the abused were intellectual impairment, living situations, and marital problems.

CONCLUSIONS: Some improvements over others research may be seen by the fact that actual case histories of abused elders are used, and the sample size and scope is much greater than other reported research. In addition, separating the types of abuse reduces the likelihood of overgeneralizations on elder abuse *per se*. More work needs to be done in distinguishing types, in "standardizing case records, and standardizing the reporting of abuse so that more accurate information is readily available."

Professional Orientation:
- Psychiatry

Type of Exposition:
- Discussion

Substantive Issues:
- Information
- Causal Factors
- Family Dynamics

061 Goldstein, Stanley E, and Blank, Arthur. "The elderly: Abused or abusers?" CMAJ 127(6):455-56, September, 1982. (4 References).

TOPIC: This editoral considers the problem of elder neglect and abuse from both the elder's and the caretaker's perspectives.

OBJECTIVE: The authors want to look more carefully at some characteristics and life circumstances of both the older person and the caretaker in order to fully comprehend how neglect and abuse might happen.

METHOD: The authors provide a brief review of the literature on the aging process and the difficulties of both informal and formal caretakers in providing assistance for older persons.

CONCLUSIONS: "The elderly and their caretakers or families are caught together in emotional turmoils that they often cannot comprehend and for which solutions are elusive." There are conditions in the lives of older persons which make the caregiver role difficult to maintain. Older persons tend to become roleless, suffer losses which cannot be recouped, ask for more help than is available to them; and, if confused or incompetent, are especially troublesome. Caring for older persons is difficult both for the family and institutional caregivers. In the case of the latter, sometimes older persons must be confined and restrained for their own safety; but this may be construed by family members as abuse. Because older persons are so vulnerable physically, emotionally and financially, it is easy to take advantage of them. Even though abuse and neglect do occur, most people who care for older persons, nevertheless, are very concerned about their well-being. Certainly abuse and neglect do take place, but we need to sort out the needs of all parties in the relationship (both the caregiver and the older person) before we know how to help.

Professional Orientation:
- Social Work

Type of Exposition:
- Training Guide

Substantive Issue:
- General

062 Greene, Roberta, and Soniat, Barbara. "Clinical interventions with older adults in need of protection." Paper presented at the thirty-sixth annual meeting of the Gerontological Society of America. San Francisco, California: November, 1983. 12p. (19 References).

TOPIC: This paper describes the role of the social worker in cases of dependent elders in need of protective services.

OBJECTIVE: "The purpose of the paper is to sensitize social workers to the issues related to working with the aged and their families in protective service situations involving abuse and neglect."

METHODS: The nature and scope of elder abuse are summarized from the literature. Then, the meaning and uses of the functional family system in detecting and preventing abuse are described.

CONCLUSIONS: Domestic violence is estimated to be found in 10 to 20% of families in the United States. Child abuse was the first form to be exposed about a century ago. Elder abuse is the most recent form; thus, there is less social awareness of it. Its incidence is difficult to document because of the denial by victims and abusers, and professionals' inability to clearly identify this phenomenon. These authors define older adults in need of protection as persons age 60 or older who are physically or mentally incapacitated and cannot manage the affairs of daily living. Abuse includes "physical punishment, psychological harassment, material deprivation and medical neglect." Some literature indicates that psychological abuse is the most frequent form, but abuse may include various forms and is often repetitive. Victims tend to be "white, protestant, female over 75 years of age and from the lower or middle class" and dependent. Abusers are usually adult relatives who are caregivers experiencing emotional stress. Sometimes, the abuser is also a substance abuser.

Social workers need to understand the functional family system (persons who interact with the older person and perform the affective and instrumental roles of the family for the older persons whether relatives or not) in order to "increase the effectiveness of services to protective clients." Social workers also need to assess the total demands that may be placed on any one family and the family's capacity for meeting those demands. In addition, the social worker should be aware of the socio-emotional and financial resources available to the family or changes in relationships which may influence their ability to care for the older dependent elder.

Professional Orientation:
- Unidentified

Type of Exposition:
- Survey Research

Substantive Issues:
- General

063 Hageboeck, Helen, and Brandt, Karen. "Characteristics of elderly abuse." Report from Iowa Gerontology Model Project. Iowa City, Iowa: University of Iowa Gerontology Center, 1981. 12p. (0 References).

TOPIC: The authors report on the nature and scope of elder abuse in one Iowa county. The study is the outcome of a demonstration project funded by the Administration on Aging.

OBJECTIVES: The fundamental objectives were to document the cases of elder abuse found in Scott County, Iowa, and to recommend policy changes in protective services for older persons to the Iowa state legislature.

METHODS: The Iowa Gerontology Model Project program was established as a community-based program for functionally dependent elderly. Multidisciplinary assessments were made through in-home interviews in the community. Seven hundred and ten clients were served by the project from 1978 to 1981. Cases of abuse were referred either from hospitals, the department of social services or through discovery in the in-home assessment conducted by the Iowa Gerontology Model Project team. In 1980, 41 cases out of 238 were suspected cases of elder abuse. These 41 cases or 17.2% of the total number assessed in 1980 constituted the sample from which the data were gathered for this report.

FINDINGS: Abuse was classified as physical, psychological, neglect and financial abuse. The data on elder abuse was similar to that gathered in other states. The results of the survey were also similar. Abuse tended to occur more than once, took place in family settings, and the abusers tended to be close relatives. Most of the victims were older elderly females who lived with the abuser, and appeared to suffer from some type of physical impairment or some other dependency. Two patterns of abuse were noted. The first pattern was the consequence of a general history of family violence. The second pattern was the result of well-meaning relatives who experienced stress with the increasing disability of the older person and manifested that stress abusively. Four cases were reported in order to demonstrate these patterns and to show the method of in-home assessment used by the Iowa Gerontology Project Team.

CONCLUSIONS: In May of 1981, the staff of the Iowa Geronotology Model Project presented the Iowa state legislature with a list of 5 barriers to the provision of services to victims of elder abuse and their families, and 5 recommendations for intervention. The first list citing the barriers included (1) the problem of the elder's denial of abuse, (2) the issue of the anonymity of witnesses of abuse, (3) the absence of guardian in several cases, (4) the difficulties with nursing home placement, and (5) the perpetrators denying service workers access to the home in which the elder victim resides. The recommendations for change in legislation included (1) the proposal for more counties in the state to assess the nature of elder abuse in their areas, (2) the need for mandatory reporting laws which would contain established guidelines for intervention, (3) the recommendation that there be mandatory intervention for elders in danger or those requesting help, (4) the need for greater support for families who are involved in in-home elder care, and (5) the proposal that the caregiver's well-being ought to be looked at more closely.

Professional Orientation:
- Medicine

Type of Exposition:
- Report

Substantive Issues:
- Information
- Types
- Identification

064 Ham, Richard. "Pitfalls in the diagnosis of abuse of the elderly." In: Crouse, Joyce S.; Cobb, Deborah C.; Harris, Britta, B.; _et al._ _Abuse and neglect of the elderly in Illinois: Incidence and characteristics, legislation, and policy recommendations_, Appendix B. Springfield, Illinois: Sangamon State University and Illinois Department on Aging. June 30, 1981. 7p. (0 References).

TOPIC: The author explains why elder abuse is so difficult to detect from a medical perspective.

METHODS: Drawing on his experience and knowledge about the aging process, the author illustrates how normal aging could be interpreted as abuse and; on the other hand, how the label of abuse may be inappropriately applied to normal aging.

CONCLUSIONS: Certain physical conditions related to aging such as bruising and fractures may be false positives with regard to elder abuse. The elder's vulnerability to a variety of traumas, including the tendency to fall more easily than at an earlier age, create a circumstance in which elder abuse may be overly identified. On the other hand, one needs to be suspicious of head injuries, blunt injuries to the abdomen, dehydration, and elimination problems. While these might be construed as factors in aging, they may also have been the consequences of neglect and abuse.

Psychological abuse poses the same dilemma. Dementia and paranoia may be assessed by the professional as an actual case of elder abuse. Conversely, since it is likely that memory loss, confusion, and poor judgment accompany aging, it is difficult to identify psychological abuse. Furthermore, fearful of institutionalization, older persons deny or ignore the abuse rather than confront the prospects of moving out of the household into an institution. In light of the possibilities for false positives and false negatives in elder abuse, greater efforts should be made to facilitate prevention and reporting of cases.

Professional Orientation:
- Social Work

Type of Exposition:
- Review

Substantive Issue:
- General

065 Heflin, Susan. "Elder abuse: The national scene." In: Schultz, Leroy G. ed. Elder abuse in West Virginia. Morganton, West Virginia: West Virginia University, 1983. 15p. (5 References).

TOPIC: The author focuses on the need for national legislation on elder abuse.

OBJECTIVE: The goal of this review is to examine current information on elder abuse and provisions for adult protective services, and to evaluate West Virginia's elder abuse legislation.

METHODS: Literature on the scope and treatment of elder abuse are examined. Reports on elder abuse from the House Select Committee on Aging, five empirical studies on elder abuse, information gathered from the first National Conference on Abuse of Older Persons, and elder abuse legislation in West Virginia are reviewed.

CONCLUSIONS: Elder abuse is an area that Congress and the states have been slow to deal with. However, various studies have shown that four kinds of abuse exists: physical, psychological, negligence, and financial exploitation. On the basis of their own and other studies and information received informally, the Select Committee has come to a number of general conclusions about elder abuse and formulated a number of policy recommendations for preventing it. These conclusions and recommendations should be useful to those states which look to Congress for guidance in this area. The recommendations include the enactment of the Elder Abuse and Treatment Act which, if it were adequately funded and implemented, would provide policy for the prevention of elder abuse at nominal levels. West Virginia needs to do more than what it is now doing -- merely acknowledging that a problem exists. It needs to have a central reporting agency to enforce mandatory reporting, to adequately provide for the treatment of the abused, and to protect everyone involved in the process of identification and treatment of the abused.

Professional Orientation:
- Public Health

Type of Exposition:
- Survey Research

Substantive Issues:
- Definitions
- Scope
- Treatment
- Causal Factors
- Types

066 Hickey, Tom, and Douglass, Richard L. "Mistreatment of the elderly in the domestic setting: An exploratory study." AJPH 71(5):500-7, May, 1981. (7 References).

TOPIC: The article presents some results of an exploratory study of professionals' and practitioners' perceptions of elder abuse based on their experiences through direct services with older persons.

OBJECTIVES: The goal of the study was to test four causes of elder abuse and to use elder services professionals as resource persons for information on the prevalence and the dynamics of abuse in families caring for older persons. Explanations for abuse include (1) elder dependency, (2) situational or life crisis, (3) developmental disorders in socialization, and (4) factors in the social environment.

METHOD: A convenience sample of 228 participants from 10 categories of direct services to older persons were interviewed on the subject of elder abuse. The interviews were taped and the resulting information was both pre-coded and open-ended. These participants worked in five geographical areas in the state of Michigan each of which exhibited ethnic and socio-economic diversity in the population.

FINDINGS: Four types of data from the interviews were analysed. These include (1) the respondents' experience with neglect and abuse, (2) respondents' perceptions of causes for neglect and abuse, (3) the experiences respondents have had with reporting and follow-up of cases, and (4) case illustrations of elder neglect and abuse with which respondents' were directly involved. The data collected on respondents' experience with neglect and abuse show that neglect was more frequent than abuse, passive neglect more prevalent than active, and emotional abuse more frequently reported than physical abuse. Structured responses to causes for abuse varied among both respondents as a whole and among the professions they represent. Unstructured responses show that the prevalent response is "caretaker inability" (mentioned 328 times) with "crowded living conditions" mentioned the fewest number of times (3 times). Case-reporting and follow-up also varied among individuals and professions. However, most reported that follow-up of cases was almost non-existent in their experience. Finally, when respondents were asked for illustrative cases, 89 were described, providing a wealth of details about actual cases.

CONCLUSIONS: The neglect of older persons by their families is "a somewhat 'normal' phenomenon in our society." In addition, respondents did not seem to be troubled by this manifestation of the stereotype of the aging process. Since 60% of the respondents had had some experience with either neglect, abuse or both, we may say that these forms of mistreatment are a part of their work experience. Two conclusions are very clear from the data collected from these 228 respondent. Elder abuse is "no small problem" and, with the lack of identification and follow-up procedures, it appears to be "a problem without known solutions." The article concludes with recommendations. First, workers in adult protective service units of departments of social service are asked to change the focus of their interest so that they include the family setting as a source of the problem of elder mistreatment in addition to those who are homeless or with no families. Second, there may be a fate worse than the nursing home. It may be to live in the community with family and be abused and/or neglected. Finally, the authors conclude the article by calling for the development of "standardized procedures" for the management of elder neglect and abuse cases from identification to follow-up.

Professional Orientation:
- Public Health

Type of Exposition:
- Survey Research

Substantive Issue:
- General

067 Hickey, Tom, and Douglass, Richard L. "Neglect and abuse of older family members: Professionals' perspectives and case experiences." Gerontologist 21(2):171-76. April, 1981. (17 References).

TOPIC: This article focuses on mistreatment of older people by family members.

OBJECTIVE: The authors wish to provide a framework for understanding why older people are sometimes mistreated by family members.

METHODS: Professionals who work in direct service to older adults responded to an interview questionnaire designed to determine their experiences with elder abuse. The 228 respondents represented five Michigan communities of socio-economic and ethnic diversity. The questionnaire used passive and active neglect in addition to verbal, emotional, and physical abuse as categories of abusive behavior. Respondents rated case experiences of domestic mistreatment on a five-point scale and were encouraged to describe experiences in detail. They were also asked to identify causes of mistreatment based on four etiologies suggested by child, spouse, and family violence literature.

FINDINGS: Most respondents had experience with neglect and abuse of the elderly. Passive neglect was experienced first-hand by nearly all of the respondents. Of the 228 respondents, only 77 had no regular experiences with physical abuse. No single cause for neglect or abuse was identified. The multiple or overlapping causes identified seemed to reflect the respondents' professional biases. Respondents' detailed comments often identified sudden or unwanted dependency of an older person as a key factor in mistreatment of the elderly.

CONCLUSIONS: The primary cause of mistreatment of the elderly by family members is found in the flawed development of the abuser, with situational crises or negative environmental conditions acting as triggers for abuse or neglect. Thus, dysfunctional socialization patterns from childhood become the underlying cause for later mistreatment of others.

While the findings from the questionnaires do support the existence of mistreatment of the elderly by family members, an in-depth study of victims and their families is needed before conclusions can be drawn.

Professional Orientation:
- Other

Type of Exposition:
- Discussion

Substantive Issues:
- Characteristics
- Professional Responsibility
- Treatment

068 Hoback, Janet. "New domestic violence studies: The battering of older women." Ms 10(1):17, July, 1981. (0 References).

TOPIC: The focus of this article is on elder abuse in domestic settings.

OBJECTIVES: The author reviews current data on elder abuse and particularly the abuse of elderly women as reported by researchers in the field.

METHODS: Information on elder abuse is presented from the work of researchers and counselors in the field. Included in this report is a case report and a summary of results of studies in this area.

CONCLUSIONS: The incidence of abuse seems to be increasing. Abuse is not usually a one-time phenomenon but tends to be recurrent. Any family caring for an elderly individual is at risk for being overwhelmed by the task unless adequate services are provided. Factors that favor abuse include the pervasive presence and tolerance of violence in our society. Recommendations for the control of abuse include abused and protective legislation for victims.

Professional Orientation:
- Social Work

Type of Exposition:
- Other

Substantive Issues:
- Community Responsibility
- Social Structure
- Identification
- Treatment

069 Hooyman, Nancy R. "Elderly abuse and neglect: Community interventions." In: Kosberg, Jordan I., ed. Abuse and maltreatment of the elderly: Causes and interventions. Littleton, Massachusetts: John Wright, PSG Inc., 1983. 376-90. (35 References).

TOPIC: This chapter considers ways families involved in elder abuse may utilize support from community resources to ameliorate stress and conflict.

OBJECTIVE: "This chapter will define ways to use existing community resources creatively and effectively in both the prevention of abuse and in intervention with abusers and victims."

METHOD: The role and stresses of families' elder care and the value of social support for these stressed families are discussed. Finally, strategies are suggested which use the family social support system to prevent, detect and intervene in high-risk cases of abuse.

CONCLUSIONS: Research shows that caregivers experience considerable emotional strain in the task of elder caregiving. Family routines are altered and caregivers experience constraint on both time and mobility. In addition, families have limited knowledge of the aging process and are usually unskilled in the type of caregiver role they are called to perform for the elder member. All of these frustrations and limitations promote caregiver stress.

Professional intervention can help strengthen natural helping support and assistance to the family through chore services, respite care and similar programs. Three support programs in various parts of the country illustrate how families can be relieved of caregiver stress. Services include financial assistance, self-help groups and emergency back-up for elder care. Educational programs on elder care, socio-emotional management, community resources, and problem solving methods can also be helpful in primary prevention of elder abuse. Prevention strategies used in child abuse offer another option to help families who care for elders reduce stress.

With regard to detection of elder abuse, natural helping systems can play an important role. Persons who routinely interact with elderly such as postal carriers, cab drivers, bank tellers, etc., are in a good position to detect abuse. Therefore, they need to be trained to identify signs of abuse and to know where to go for help. These kinds of "gatekeeper" programs are already operating in some cities. Friends, neighbors or other family members also need to be trained to know the signs of abuse and be prepared to offer support. Some models of mutual help with elderly supporting elderly have begun to form around the country. In one such program, "neighbors were able to identify physical and emotional changes, quickly pinpoint people needing service, and use peer pressure to encourage individuals to seek help."

In these times of scarce resources for help for professional intervention, natural helping networks can aid professionals in elder abuse prevention and identification. Informal helpers should be viewed as partners with the professional with each building on the strengths of the unique services they both provide.

Professional Orientation:
- Social Work

Type of Exposition:
- Advocacy

Substantive Issues:
- Treatment
- Professional Responsibility
- Community Responsibility

070 Hooyman, Nancy R. "Mobilizing social networks to prevent elderly abuse. Phys Occ Ther Ger 2(2):21-35, Winter, 1982. (55 References).

TOPIC: The author proposes a model for elder abuse prevention using informal helping networks.

OBJECTIVES: The model examines how professionals could (1) mobilize, (2) utilize, or (3) create helping networks in order to prevent elder abuse.

CONCLUSIONS: A review of the literature on causes for elder abuse reveals that fundamentally there is a "lack of congruence between the elderly's needs and the family's resources for providing care." Informal helping networks could be of use to both the older person and the family. With regard to strengthening family resources, natural helping networks could provide assistance, information, substitute care and emotional support to high-risk families. The elderly can also avail themselves of the natural helping system. Such individuals as "postal carriers, cab drivers, local merchants, medical office receptionists, beauticians, bank tellers, bus drivers, pharmacists, and ministers" can offer emotional support, practical aid and information to the older person. Neighbors can also be used as natural helpers.

There are some problems attached to this informal support network. The participants may become burned out or meet resistance and criticism by professionals who find their services inappropriate. In this time of financial cutbacks in services to the elderly and their families, professionals need to develop strategies to utilize and work with informal helping networks in the community.

Professional Orientation:
- Social Work

Type of Exposition:
- Position

Substantive Issues:
- Laws
- Identification
- Treatment

071 Hooyman, Nancy R.; Rathbone-McCuan, Eloise; Klingbeil, Karil; et al. "Serving the vulnerable elderly: The detection, intervention and prevention of familial abuse." Urb Soc Change Rev 15(2):9-13, Summer, 1982. (28 References).

TOPIC: The authors emphasize the need for a multidimensional approach to the problem of elder abuse.

OBJECTIVE: Research and legislative developments are reviewed and linked with programs in "detection, intervention, and prevention of elder abuse."

METHOD: The authors assess the current state of research on elder abuse, legislation, clinical treatment, detection and victim, family and community interventions, pointing out problem areas and proposing solutions.

CONCLUSIONS: It is difficult to develop programs on the basis of research findings on elder abuse since that literature has serious methodological flaws. Therefore, further research should be undertaken in order to determine the nature, scope and causes for abuse.

Family violence is multidimensional; therefore, services must be multidimensional also. Those who are involved in legislation to protect older persons present two views. On the one hand, some propose mandatory reporting of elder abuse for all states. Advocates of this position contend that "they serve the dual purpose of documenting the existence of elderly abuse and neglect, and of establishing an effective response system." On the other hand, those who advocate voluntary reporting are concerned that adequate preventive and protective measures and services will not be forthcoming with mandatory intervention, thus worsening conditions of elder abuse.

In the clinical setting, practitioners should utilize a family-oriented assessment in order to match needs/problems with services for intervention in elder abuse. The elder, the caregiver and other family members must be interviewed and observed over several sessions and treatment goals must be tailored to the particular family dynamics involved. However, provisions for family counselling are often tied to legislation making it difficult to pursue this kind of treatment.

Community programs should include a wide range of services including informal networks and should be well coordinated. Detection and intervention are the fundamental objectives of community elder abuse programs. Detection may be difficult because victims are reluctant to report abuse and services suffer from a variety of inadequacies. When abuse is brought to the attention of authorities, verification of abuse must be established. Social service workers and medical personnel need training in detection. A detection protocol developed at the Haborview Hospital in Seattle involves considerable training in its use and provides a multidimensional assessment tool for the detection of elder abuse.

Intervention in elder abuse should operate on three levels--with the victim, the family and the community. In addition, professionals need to acknowledge that elder abuse does exist among their clients and develop "clear" procedures for identifying cases and better services "for the victim, the abuser, and the family." An important aspect of the treatment of victims is their willingness to agree to plans of care. If they do consent to professional help, there is a wide range of options for helping. In addition, the family must be involved in the treatment plan with intergenerational family counselling and given the opportunity for support group activity and educational programs on the aging process. Caregiver stress has been found to be an important factor in elder abuse; and if professionals focus on this circumstance rather than abuse, family members will be much more willing to accept help. In the community, natural helping networks should be established and carefully trained to help in elder abuse. These networks include persons like mail carriers, beauticians, ministers and neighbors. The objective is not to have this natural helping network take the place of professionals, but to work as a partner with the professional in order to strengthen intervention.

Professional Orientation:
- Nursing

Type of Exposition:
- Training Guide

Substantive Issues:
- Professional Responsibility
- Identification
- Treatment

072 Humphreys, Janice; Campbell, Jackie; Barrett, Sara. "Clinical intervention with the abused elderly and their families." Paper presented at thirty-sixth annual meeting of the Gerontological

Society of America. San Francisco, California: November, 1983. 24p. (13 References).

TOPIC: Some principles to use in the identification and treatment of elder abuse victims and their families are proposed from a nursing prospective.

OBJECTIVE: The authors state that "the purpose of this paper is to describe an approach to clinical practice with abused elderly persons and their families."

CONCLUSIONS: Professional intervention in cases of family violence is a multidimensional undertaking. A first step in successful intervention is for the professional to examine his/her attitudes toward family violence. When the professional observes that the phenomenon exists, has dealt with negative feelings toward aging, or acknowledges that abuse is possible in any family, then effective intervention can take place.

Assessment of the family situation is the next phase. Building trust between the professional and elderly client is an important requisite for accurate assessment. Some strategies for building trust include a non-judgemental position on the part of the professional, confidentiality, sincerity of purpose, and a genuine interest in the concerns of the elder client. While tools of identification are still being refined, there are some indicators in the history of the client which point to the abuse potential. These may be discerned through both a medical history and a social history.

With regard to intervention, the nursing perspective involves three levels - primary, secondary, and tertiary. Primary prevention focuses on keeping the family functional by strengthening conditions which maintain the health of its members. Secondary prevention assumes that dysfunction has occured. Professionals need to be especially concerned about forming a trusting relationship and developing a plan of care which is comprehensive and well-coordinated with other health care professionals. Family therapy is especially appropriate at the secondary level. Day care or home health care could be used in conjunction with therapy. The third level of intervention is tertiary prevention. This type of prevention is the most difficult assignment for the professional. It means that the "defect or disability is fixed, stabilized, or irreversible." With long-term abusive patterns, separating the abused from the abuser by means of alternative living arrangements may be the most effective treatment.

More research is needed in a number of areas in elder abuse. These include theory-building to explain causes for abuse, selecting more non-clinical samples for a more objective picture of family violence, the refining of measurement techniques in identification, and obtaining more data upon which to base intervention strategies.

Professional Orientation:
- Psychology
Type of Exposition:
- Research Methods
Substantive Issue:
- Identification

073 Hwalek, Melanie; Sengstock, Mary C; Proctor, Vernon. "The development of an index of elder abuse." Paper presented at the thirty-sixth annual meeting of the Gerontological Society of America, San Francisco, California: November, 1983. 16p. (17 References).

TOPIC: The presenters discuss some of the problems involved in developing a valid and reliable index for measuring elder abuse.

OBJECTIVES: The goal of this presentation "is to identify the optimum characteristics of an index of elder abuse, to discuss potential pitfalls to its development and suggest a method for its construction."

METHODS: The traditional psychometric methods of (1) content validity, (2) criterion-related validity, (3) construct validity, and (4) reliability are proposed in the development of an index on elder abuse.

CONCLUSIONS: Past studies on elder abuse have only limited utility. Research has been flawed by the lack of definitions, untested measures of abuse, secondhand information, inadequate sampling of cases of elder abuse and measures which "fail to distinguish clearly between abuse and normal aging." An index on elder abuse is needed in order to produce meaningful research. A good index for elder abuse should have content validity, criterion-related validity, construct validity and reliability.

Content validity requires that the index include a complete list of items pertinent to abuse and neglect. There are six dimensions of elder abuse which should be contained in the index. These include physical abuse, physical neglect, psychological abuse, psychological neglect, material abuse and violation of personal rights. The index must insure truthfulness of the elderly and caretaker; it should have indirect, direct, and risk indicators; it should address intentionality and should be able to detect abuse even when older persons are unable to respond to questions.

Criterion-related validity is another method of validation. There are two kinds - predictive validity and concurrent validity. Predictive validity is determined by the degree to which "scores on the index correlate with future abusive behaviors." Concurrent validity is determined by how well scores on the index correlate with current conditions of abuse and neglect. Both forms of validation pose problems since we have yet to determine what constitutes abuse.

Construct validity is determined by how well the index of abuse correlates with other scales measuring the same phenomenon. Like criterion-related validity, construct validity cannot be obtained because so little has been done thus far in the testing of theories of elder abuse.

In addition to validity, reliability must also be achieved. The fundamental type to be considered in the index of abuse is inter-rater reliability or the extent to which two or more raters agree on the client evaluation. While ANOVA has been used to test variations, results can be inaccurate. Coefficient Kappa is another method. However, Kappa is an involved measure and may not be an option with some software programs.

In view of all of these problems there are, nevertheless, some strategies which can be used in developing an index. Content validity may be achieved through a number of steps. These include: defining abuse, developing the items for each type of abuse based on expert input, making sure that service providers can observe items in question, and assuring that service providers who are called on to assess the items in the index represent a range of agencies and elders.

Construct validity may be obtained by collecting additional data on the elderly after the index is administered. And, finally, inter-rater reliability requires that "more than one service provider should use the index on the same group of elderly clients."

The development of a valid and reliable index of elder abuse can only be accomplished through the joint committment of researchers and service providers. The uses of such an index are multiple, ranging from accurately determining which resources are the most appropriate in helping the abused to establishing the incidence and prevalence of elder abuse.

Professional Orientation:
- Nursing

Type of Exposition:
- Review

Substantive Issue:
- Varieties

074 Johnson, Douglas G. "Abuse and neglect: Not for children only!" J Geront Nurs 5(4):11-13, July/August, 1979. (10 References).

TOPIC: This study compares elderly abuse with child abuse.

OBJECTIVE: The purpose of this article is to contrast a conceptual model of elder abuse with an established child abuse model.

METHODS: The author mentions her work as a public health nurse in a home health service agency as one source of information on elder abuse and neglect, but the article's conclusions are largely based on review of child and elder abuse literature.

CONCLUSIONS: Conclusions drawn from a child abuse model that may apply to elder abuse are (1) an abuser who was neglected or deprived as a child, (2) a victim of abuse who is seen by the abuser as "different" or handicapped, and (3) a crisis which triggers the abuse.

Professional Orientation:
- Nursing

Type of Exposition:
- Training Guide

Substantive Issues:
- Identification
- Treatment

075 Johnson, Douglas. "Abuse of the elderly." NP 6(1):29-34, January/February, 1981. (7 References).

TOPIC: The author presents a screening protocol for the detection of abuse and neglect of the elderly.

OBJECTIVE: The goal is to make a detection protocol available to health care providers who may not have "learned" the signs of neglect and abuse in the elderly.

METHOD: The screening instrument is based on review of the literature on elder neglect and abuse and on related literature in child abuse.

CONCLUSIONS: The interview-type instrument is designed to be administered to both the older person and the caretaker separately. Subjective observations by the health care provider are requested along with objective questions for the patient and caretaker. Objective questions move from those that are neutral to those that are likely to be threatening. All the while the interviewer is looking for discrepancies between the patient's response and those of the caretaker, indications of support outside the family, and the nature of the interaction between patient and caretaker.

The plan of intervention is the next step. Health care providers should be well-informed about services in the community and be prepared to make referrals. The "plans" component in the screening protocol refers to secondary and tertiary prevention -- what needs to be done after neglect and abuse have occurred. Primary prevention poses the greatest problem because our education and research are not adequate at this point to effectively prevent neglect and abuse from occurring altogether.

Professional Orientation:
- Law

Type of Exposition:
- Discussion Paper

Substantive Issues:
- Scope
- Causal Factors
- Laws
- Varieties

076 Katz, Katheryn D. "Elder abuse." J Fam Law 18(4):695-722. 1979-1980 (approx 31 References).

TOPIC: This report reviews child abuse and elder abuse statutes.

OBJECTIVE: The intent of this discussion is to caution against hasty legislation as a response to the little understood problem of elder abuse. Data from the child abuse literature is used to support this argument.

METHODS: This paper opens by examining the definitions and causes of abuse cited in the research literature on elder abuse. A detailed look at the child abuse reporting statutes of the 1960's then precedes the paper's examination of the problems posed by elder abuse reporting statutes. Concluding remarks discuss the disparity between the legal position of a child and an elderly adult, especially in terms of the legal rights given to each party.

CONCLUSIONS: The past eighteen years of experience with child abuse reporting statutes have revealed some inherent problems. Among the problems identified are the lack of a clear definition of child abuse, invalidity of child abuse reports, and the practice of assigning child abuse cases to only one caseworker who is often inexperienced and who acts in a mutually exclusive role as supporter to both the legal system and the child abuse family. The assumption that effective treatment exists for child abusers and their children is not true. In addition, the elimination of child abuse is not possible by legislative action.

Mandatory reporting of elder abuse presupposes that services are available to deal with the problem when it is identified. This appears to be inaccurate. A report of elder abuse can trigger an incompetency proceeding if the victim refuses protective services. The end result may be a loss of autonomy and freedom. Despite some similiarities, the status of the abused elder differs significantly from that of the abused child. The law states that the status of children is incompetency because of their age, whereas the elderly do not lack decision making power because of their age. The state, in its zeal to protect, may intervene in the lives of those who want to be left alone and by "protecting" may deprive the individual of dignity, autonomy, and self-esteem. Currently, elder abuse reporting laws are another avenue to institutionalization which is the least desirable solution for most elderly victims.

Professional Orientation:
- Medicine

Type of Exposition:
- Review

Substantive Issues:
- Types
- Characteristics
- Definitions
- Attitudes

077 Kimsey, Larry R.; Tarbox, Arthur R.; Bragg, David F. "Abuse of the elderly -- the hidden agenda. I. The caretakers and categories of abuse." JAGS 29(10):465-72, October, 1981. (28 References).

TOPIC: The authors present an overview of elder abuse and neglect by formal and informal caretakers.

OBJECTIVE: The goal of this article is to provide a profile of caretakers and the types of neglect and abuse elders may encounter in order to clarify issues and guide future research in elder mistreatment.

METHOD: The authors reviewed literature on abuse and neglect of the elderly including literature on attitudes toward the elderly. Information from a special task force study on nursing homes in Texas was also included in the review.

CONCLUSIONS: Little is known about the causes of abuse thus far. However, there does seem to be a societal and professional prejudice toward older persons which makes the elderly more vulnerable to neglect and abuse. Family abusers may not be able to deal with intergenerational conflicts. On the other hand, formal caretakers may be abusive to older persons because of the stress of the job, a negative attitude toward aging, or a desire for institutional or personal gain. Older persons in institutional settings tend not to complain because of fear of further abuse by staff if the abuse is reported, a lack of awareness of their legal rights or the elder's general apathy.

Four types of abuse are identified and illustrated. These include physical, psychological (conditions of the facility, diet, grooming, benign neglect, verbal abuse and infantilization), material abuse and fiscal abuse (embezzlement, improper charges, improper record-keeping, mishandling of billing for medication and medicaid fraud). Elder abuse is a multidisciplinary problem; however, little has been done to solve this situation either among disciplines or within them.

Professional Orientation:
- Unidentified

Type of Exposition:
- Review

Substantive Issues:
- Definitions
- Characteristics
- Causal Factors

078 King, Nancy. "Exploitation and abuse of elder family members: an overview of the problem." Response, 6(2):1-2, 13-15, March/April, 1983. (7 References).

TOPIC: The nature and scope of elder abuse in American society are explored.

METHOD: Four early studies by O'Malley et al., Block and Sinnott, Douglass, Hickey and Noel, and Lau and Kosberg are reviewed. Their results are supplemented by other research on violence.

CONCLUSIONS: The literature does not provide conclusive evidence for the incidence of elder abuse. This is due to the fact that definitions of abuse vary and cases of elder abuse are underreported. Victims as well as outsiders (sometimes even professionals) fail to report the abuse to the proper authorities.

The four early studies in Michigan, Massachusetts, Maryland and Ohio show that most abuse is in the form of neglect. Abuse is both recurrent and manifest in multiple forms. These four studies go on to describe the typically abused as female, over age 75, suffering physical impairment and living with the abuser who is a family member. The abuser tends to be the caregiver and appears under stress "and may have suffered from alcoholism and/or mental illness."

Causes which appear to contribute to abuse include the demographic trend of long-term aging which will result in elder physical, financial and emotional dependency of elders. These kinds of dependencies make older persons more vulnerable because of the stresses they create for caregivers. Elder care may be too exhausting or may compete with other family aspirations. "It is increasingly likely that impaired elders will be dependent upon their children for extended periods, perhaps longer than their children were dependent upon them." Caregivers also must face the financial burden in caring for older persons. Some researchers claim that abuse is intergenerational. According to some studies, children who are abused by parents are more likely to abuse them when they get older than children who are not abused. Finally, personal problems of abusers have been cited as causes for abuse.

At the present time, 16 states have mandatory reporting laws. The increase in the number of cases in two of those states. (Connecticut and South Carolina) show an increase in reporting. Better research efforts are needed in order to know the most effective strategies to resolve the problems of elder abuse.

Professional Orientation:
- Social Work

Type of Exposition:
- Other

Substantive Issues:
- Family Dynamics
- Causal Factors
- Treatment

079 Kosberg, Jordan I. "The cost of care index: A case managment tool for predicting family abuse of the aged. Paper presented at the Gerontological Society of America thirty-sixth annual meeting. San Francisco, California: November, 1983. 13p. (15 References).

TOPIC: The author introduces a rating scale to help informal caregivers assess the impact of elder care on the family. This instrument may be used by case management professionals to determine the appropriateness of residential placement for older persons.

METHOD: The Cost of Care Index (CCI), a 27 item Likert-type, four-point range rating scale, is compared with two other self-report indices intended to be used by caregivers to assess their responses to the care of older persons. The CCI differs from the others which are identified as the Zarit et al., Burden Index and the Robinson Caregiver Strain Index, in that it proposes that the instrument be used as a case management screening instrument. The CCI index scores are intended to target families who are at risk for elder neglect and abuse. In addition, it may help families as well as professionals determine the most appropriate placement when older persons need the care of others.

CONCLUSION: The stress of elder care on informal care providers has been documented in a number of studies. This kind of pressure may manifest itself in neglect and abuse of elderly relatives. Even though there is increasing evidence that "informal care providers caring for an elderly person can engage in abusive behavior" professionals turn to family members for elder care.

The Cost of Care Index was designed to detect the level of stress for the informal care provider who cares, or may be expected to care for an older relative. It consists of 6 dimensions. These include (1) social disruptions, (2) personal restrictions, (3) economic costs, (4) values, (5) care recipient as provocateur and (6) psychosomatic consequences. The index could be used in a number of ways. At the case management level it could provide an indicator of how wholesome the family relationship might be if the older family member is placed in the informal care provider's home. In addition, it could target problem areas which families may work on privately or as a part of support groups for care providers. Researchers could also utilize the data from the CCI to determine families at risk for elder abuse. Items in the index could be prioritized vis-a-vis the level of risk.

The instrument is currently being pretested with an Alzheimer's Disease Support Group in Tampa, Florida. It is also being used by the Department of Health and Rehabilitative Services in Pinellas County. It is hoped that its use will minimize "the risks of inappropriate placements and referrals."

Professional Orientation:
- Social Work

Type of Exposition:
- Review

Substantive Issues:
- Causal Factors
- Family Dynamics
- Professional Responsibility
- Community Responsibility
- Treatment

080 Kosberg, Jordan I. "The special vulnerability of elderly parents." In: Kosberg, Jordan I., ed. Abuse and maltreatment of the elderly: Causes and interventions. Littleton, Massachusetts: John Wright, PSG Inc., 1983. 263-75. (35 References).

TOPIC: This chapter focuses on abuse of the elderly by family members.

OBJECTIVE: The author discusses reasons for the special vulnerability of the elderly to abusive behavior by children and grandchildren.

METHOD: Pertinent literature on causes for elder abuse by family members is reviewed. This is followed by the author's recommendations for prevention and treatment.

CONCLUSIONS: The elderly are vulnerable to abuse from anyone because of their declining health, living arrangements, transportation usage and general negative status in the community. On the other hand, the family is viewed as a "panacea" for the elderly and is called upon for the care and protection of its older members. However, families may not be equipped to take on the role of caregiver. Because the family is perceived as protective of its members, it is hard to imagine hostility. The family is a closed system, and abuse is difficult to detect and even harder for victims to report because of the nature of this closed family relationship.

Factors which make older persons vulnerable to abuse by children and grandchildren are the following: patterns of violence present in the home which began with the elders' earlier treatment of the child; the intergenerational cycle of unresolved parent-child conflicts because of personality differences or problems which occur when middle-aged parents are required to care for both their children and their parents at the same time; the social, psychological and financial cost of caring for the elderly; personal problems and special needs of the caregivers; and the problems accompanying a redefinition of parent-child roles.

In order to help prevent abuse, service providers should (1) make an assessment of the suitability of families when elders are in need of their care, (2) be supported by legislation enabling them to monitor situations in which elders are cared for by their families, and (3) intervene where there is conflict. The community needs to provide more supportive services to families, and legislation ought to be passed to provide financial assistance to families who care for the elderly. Finally, there should be more public exposure of the problem of elder abuse so that elders, family caregivers and human service workers may be more prepared to manage frustrations which both precede and follow elder abuse.

Professional Orientation:
- Unidentified

Type of Exposition:
- Review

Substantive Issue:
- General

081 Langley, Ann. "Abuse of the elderly." Human Services Monograph Series. Washington, D.C.: U.S. Government Printing Office, September, 1981. 29p. (18 References).

TOPIC: The author reviews the literature on studies, causal theories, laws, and services related to elder abuse.

OBJECTIVE: The goal is to provide an overview of elder abuse based on the concerns of policymakers, lawmakers, and service providers.

METHODS: Summary statements are largely based on research studies on elder abuse by family members conducted by the University of Maryland, Massachusetts Legal Research and Service for the Elderly, Cleveland Chronic Illness Center, the University of Maryland, and by various service agencies in the states of Maine and New Hampshire. In addition, research studies at the UCLA/USC Long Term Care Gerontology Center, the House Select Committee on Aging, and the Senate Special Committee on Aging support the discussion on developing laws and services for the elderly.

CONCLUSIONS: Family violence may be present in 10 to 20 percent of the households in the United States. Child abuse was brought to our attention first. Then spouse abuse was recognized. Service providers have not responded to this form very quickly. In recent years elder abuse has surfaced. Data on this latter form of family violence is very limited. Some researchers have estimated that 500,000 to 1,000,000 older persons are abused each year nationwide representing a variety of people. A summary of research studies indicates that the most common form of abuse seems to be physical abuse, but several forms of abuse often occurred in systematic, repeated incidences. The majority of elderly abuse victims were females over 75 years of age who had a physical or mental impairment. The abuser, likely to be the victim's relative, usually lived with the elderly person and frequently suffered from some form of stress.

Although various theories of elder abuse were identified, the most commonly found "precipitating factor" was stress. Other factors identified by the House Select Committee on Aging related to elder abuse included revenge by an adult who was mistreated as a child, patterns of family violence as a way of life, lack of close family ties, lack of financial or community resources, resentment of the adult child towards his dependent parent, increased life expectancy, a history of mental problems, alcohol or drug abuse by the abuser, and poor living conditions.

Services to elder abuse victims were hampered by limitation in identification and the victim's not reporting the abuse. The abused are often unwilling to report abuse for a number of reasons. Professionals are sometimes unaware that the problem exists and are not prepared to recognize the signs. Protective service workers may also find legal and intervention options absent, ineffective or inadequate.

Major problems in providing services to the elderly were (1) the lack of service providers' ability to intervene because of the victim's unwillingness to report the abuse or to prosecute, (2) the lack of adult protective laws, and (3) the lack of services appropriate to manage the problem once it has been identified. A key problem related to establishing mandatory reporting laws is that these laws do not establish services for the abuse victims once they are identified.

Professional Orientation:
- Social Work

Type of Exposition:
- Case Studies

Substantive Issues:
- Scope
- Characteristics
- Theory
- Treatment
- Policy

082 Lau, Elizabeth E., and Kosberg, Jordan I. "Abuse of the elderly by informal care providers." <u>Aging</u> 299-301: 10-15, September/October, 1979. (14 References).

TOPIC: This article presents data on elder abuse by informal caretakers.

OBJECTIVE: The authors in the study propose to document the incidence and nature of abuse.

METHODS: This study involved case record review for the detection of elder abuse among all clients 60 and over referred to the Chronic Illness Center in Cleveland, Ohio, over a period of one year.

FINDINGS: The record review yielded 39 cases of elderly abuse out of a total sample of 404 persons which represented a prevalence of 9.6%. Four specific areas of abuse were identified including physical and psychological abuse, misuse of property, and violation of rights. Certain characteristics of abuser and abused are described. Outcomes from intervention include institutionalization, refusal of intervention and assistance, and acceptance of help and support.

CONCLUSIONS: The authors examine the legal and policy implications of elderly abuse including how much responsibility a family should have in abuse and neglect cases, and how the protective laws for older persons should be developed.

Professional Orientation:
- Social Work

Type of Exposition:
- Survey Research

Substantive Issue:
- General

083 Levenberg, Judi; Milan, Judith; Dolan, Mary; *et al*. "Elder abuse in West Virginia: Extent and nature of the problem." In: Schultz, Leroy G. ed. *Elder abuse in West Virginia: A policy analysis of system response*. Morgantown, West Virginia: West Virginia University, 1983. 17p. (0 References).

TOPIC: The authors conducted a survey on the nature and scope of elder abuse in West Virginia.

METHODS: A mailed questionnaire was sent to 385 individuals and agencies who were believed to be involved with elder abuse cases. The questionnaire asked for information on experience with actual cases, types of abuse, reporting, procedure, policy and treatment recommendations. Eighty questionnaires were received for a response rate of 20%.

FINDINGS: A number of conclusions were drawn from this survey. First, the results showed that there was no one agency in West Virginia to which suspected cases of elder abuse were reported. With regard to prevalence, 280 cases had been reported in the last six months. Most citings were in hospitals and Departments of Welfare. Projecting on the basis of the 20% responses, as many as 2,800 elderly could have been victims of abuse. The data also showed an unequal number of staff working with elder abuse cases, and mixed responses regarding the adequacy of services, reporting procedures and treatment. A number of causes for elder abuse were reported by the respondents. The most frequently cited cause was caregiver stress. Most respondents believed that the state should have mandatory reporting. Five types of abuse were identified. In order of frequency from greatest to lowest, they included neglect, mental cruelty, economic abuse, medication abuse and physical abuse. Most of the abusers were children, followed by spouses and other relatives. Among those answering questions on characteristics of the abused, most observed that they tended to be females who were between 60 and 75.

CONCLUSIONS: Several recommendations emerged from the survey: the need for a clear definition; continuous in-service training for professionals who are involved in elder abuse; the need for one agency in the state to oversee cases; a "hotline" for reporting elder abuse cases; publicizing services for elder abuse victims in community settings; and further research on elder needs in West Virginia, especially methods of intervention in elder abuse.

Professional Orientation:
- Nursing

Type of Exposition:
- Case Studies

Substantive Issues:
- Barriers
- Characteristics
- Policy

084 Long, Clara M. "Geriatric abuse." Issues in Men Health Nurs 3:123-135. January/June, 1981. (10 References).

TOPIC: The central issue is family dynamics of elder abuse.

OBJECTIVE: The goal is to outline the factors which inhibit documentation of elder abuse cases and to define the components of elder abuse victim, abuser, and violence.

METHOD: The author gathered information for this article from conversations with persons involved in providing services to elderly persons in family settings.

FINDINGS: Key factors that complicate documentation of elder abuse are the physiological changes associated with the aging process, the sterotypical view of the elderly as confused and forgetful, the inclusion of elder abuse in the general category of family violence, the lack of mandatory reporting laws, and the elderly victim's fear of retaliation or of nothing being done. Key characteristics of the components of abuse are a victim who is vulnerable, a caretaker who is "caught in the middle" of family generations or roles, and a family context that accepts violence under certain circumstances.

CONCLUSIONS: Specific resolutions, such as legislation for public funds and economic incentive to keep the elderly at home are needed. This is particularly true as our society moves away from the nuclear family to the extended family which includes the elderly as family members. Household management will change with the return to the extended family. For example, new roles and responsibility will be taken on as the older person is included in the family. It is unclear, at this point, whether the older person's becoming a member of the household will increase or decrease abuse.

Professional Orientation:
- Unidentified

Type of Exposition:
- Survey Research

Substantive Issue:
- General

085 ______. Maine elderly abuse survey. Augusta, Maine: Maine Committee on Aging and Bureau of Maine's Elderly, Department of Human Services. December, 1980. 11p. (0 References).

TOPIC: This study investigates non-institutionlized elder abuse in the state of Maine.

OBJECTIVE: The purpose of this study was to collect descriptive information on the status and scope of elder abuse in Maine and to promote public discussion on the subject of elder abuse.

METHODS: Data were collected by mailing survey questionnaires to 250 social service workers, police, and various legal, support, and medical personnel. The Maine Committee on Aging and Bureau of Maine's Elderly Department of Human Services chose the survey instrument used by Legal Research and Services for the Elderly in Boston, Massachusetts. Eighty-three or 33% of the questionnaires were completed and returned.

FINDINGS: The survey was based on two theories: that the victim of abuse is very old and disabled, physically or mentally, and that the abuser is under stress which is the result of something other than that produced by the abusive situation.

The results show that 36% of the returned surveys indicated a case of elder abuse occurring in the past eighteen months. Police officers, emergency room supervisors, and home health aides reported no cases. Those reporting the most cases were social workers. In 88% of the cases, abuse occurred more than twice. Incidences of abuse were reported by someone outside the family in 60% of the cases. Over 50% of the abusive situations were not easily detectable and, thus, hard to identify.

The majority of the victims were females who had some physical or mental disability and lived with a relative who was the abuser. The survey results showed that most of the abusers were experiencing some kind of stress, with over half the reports indicating that the victim was the source. Other forms of family violence were noted in 67% of the cases.

Approximately half of the professional respondents took some form of direct action in the elder abuse case, while the other half referred cases to the appropriate community service agency. Among those respondents who reported barriers to services for the victim, 69% noted that it was the victim who refused the help for some reason. Only 39% of the respondents reported that the problem creating the situation of elder abuse had been resolved.

Professional Orientation:
- Law

Type of Exposition:
- Advice-Giving

Substantive Issues:
- Laws
- Treatment

086 Mancini, Marguerite. "The legal side: Adult abuse laws." Am J Nurs 80(4):739-40, April, 1980. (2 References).

TOPIC: This article looks at the ways older persons may be protected from abuse and neglect.

OBJECTIVE: The goal is to consider the substance of adult protective laws to determine how they may be used to protect the elderly against abuse and neglect.

METHODS: The author briefly reviews the scope of adult protective laws in several states.

CONCLUSIONS: While coverage may differ from state to state, overall, the purpose of these laws is twofold -- elders' survival needs and their right to live comfortably. Reporting of cases varies as does the penalty for failure to do so. In addition to reporting, the laws provide for different kinds of treatment options according the state in which one resides. The community health nurse is encouraged to carry out the law in those states in which intervention procedures are in place by reporting cases of neglect and abuse. In states where protocols are not yet in place, they would need to utilize their own resources and work toward adult protective services legislation in their state.

Professional Orientation:
- Law

Type of Exposition:
- Review

Substantive Issues:
- Laws
- Reporting

087 Meyers, Karen J., and Bergman, James A. An analysis of the laws concerning elder abuse in Massachusetts. Boston, Massachusetts: Legal Research and Services for the Elderly, June 20, 1979. 30p. (0 References).

TOPIC: Elder abuse reporting and protective service laws are analysed.

OBJECTIVES: The goal of this study is to analyze domestic violence laws in Massachusetts and to summarize and examine abuse reporting and protective services statutes in other states.

METHODS: Under a grant from the Massachusetts Department of Elder Affairs, the staff of Legal Research and Services for the Elderly (LRSE) studied and analyzed legal and social service responses to elder abuse cases as well as incidence. This report represents a section of this larger study. Massachusetts General Laws, The Older American Act, Title III, Title XIX and XX of the Social Security Act; and various state statutes on abuse document the discussion on the legal aspects of elder abuse.

The appendix contains 28 definitions and recommendations related to state protective service. Reporting laws conclude this review.

CONCLUSIONS: Under the criminal justice system in Massachusetts, an abuse complaint may eventually lead to the removal of the abuser, but little or nothing is done to address the cause(s) of abuse or to provide protective and support services for the abuse victim. In many areas of Massachusetts, no supportive services exist to protect the elderly once a court order removes an abusive caretaker. In addition, LRSE found that coercion was often used to provide protective services when available and that confidentiality was not respected in some case referrals and interagency discussions. Under the judicial system, Massachusetts established three alternatives to assist the elderly: conservatorship, guardianship, and civil commitment (involuntary placement in a mental institution). Other alternatives outside of the judicial system do exist. Restricted bank accounts, representative payee for Social Security, joint bank accounts, and power of attorney are some of the additional options available to the elderly. While the 24 states that LRSE studied did have statutes to protect victims of domestic violence, elders were given even less protection than in Massachusetts largely because of weak enforcement provisions.

The results of the LRSE show that in a large number of abuse cases, there were barriers to services. State intervention and protective services laws that supposedly respected the right of the abuse victim to refuse services were often unclear, outdated, and even unconstitutional. State intervention laws which considered the functional ability of a victim were more likely to provide for appropriate intervention. Even though 11 of the states studied had reporting laws, the effect of sanctions for failure to report abuse is not yet known. This is due to the fact that these provisions often are not enforced. The most controversial aspect of intervention and protective services laws is the victim's rights in emergency intervention cases. Both Alabama and Florida statutes allow the court to intervene without due process of law and do not require proof of the abuse victim's capacity or lack of capacity to give consent for services. Moreover, when involuntary removal from the home was considered for an abuse victim, only one state had a geriatric team who evaluated cases for the least restrictive alternative for placement outside of the home. Both consultations with a professional team and community-based placement, rather than institutional placement, contribute to the least restrictive alternative by protective services.

This review demonstrates that current statutes are inadequate. While the law can spell out conditions for abuse and signify intervention strategies, it stops short of services. There is a need to consider elder rights and to broaden the social service network in order to deal with the problem of elder abuse.

Professional Orientation:
- Social Work

Type of Exposition:
- Position Paper

Substantive Issue:
- Policy

088 Mick, Rebecca E. "Legal interventions: Modes or deterrents to protecting the abused elder?" In: Schultz, Leroy G. ed. <u>Elder abuse in West Virginia: A policy analysis of system response.</u> Morgantown, West Virginia: West Virginia University, 1983. 41p. (39 References).

TOPIC: The article discusses the serious deficiencies in the modes of legal intervention currently being employed in cases of non-consenting victims of elder abuse in West Virginia.

OBJECTIVE: The stated objective is to alert an unsuspecting public about the destructiveness of the current system in order to promote pressure for change.

METHODS: The author uses data gathered from a survey responded to by Adult Protective Services Supervisors, by other professionals and by 16 County Commissioners. In addition, interviews with practicing West Virginia attorneys, existing West Virginia statutes and policies and professional literature are included to show that legal intervention as it is currently practiced in West Virginia is not only unhelpful, but frequently destructive.

CONCLUSIONS: There are currently five modes of legal intervention being employed in West Virginia: (1) involuntary commitment, (2) appointment of a committee, (3) order of attachment, (4) appointment of a guardian, and (5) injunctive relief. The first four of these are used overwhelmingly to the exclusion of the fifth, which the author believes holds great untapped potential. The first four, however, are themselves forms of abuse (albeit unwitting) which the state's employees and cooperating persons inflict on the abused elderly -- ostensibly to protect them from being abused.

It is not the case, as one might assume it to be, that such right-and-dignity-stripping measures are employed only as a last resort for purposes of benevolence or in such a way that the client's rights are protected. Most often, such goals are given lip-service while the elder is stripped of his/her rights and dignity for reasons of economy and efficiency.

For example, involuntary commitment is the method most frequently employed. It is being used in 56% of all legal interventions despite the fact that, according to one study, 20-40% of such persons are dead within six months of commitment. The institutions to which these folks are committed, by their very nature, lend themselves to abuse. Their personnel, as is the case with other major persons deciding on elder's fate, show a great lack of understanding of the aging process, and, hence, they fail to adequately respond to either the needs or the potential of the elderly. Those very individuals whom law and common wisdom assume to have the interests of the abused elderly most at heart are usually inadequately trained or untrained in this area. They do not make contact with those under their charge. Therefore, they would be unable to protect the older person even if they cared to. Frequently, they do not even attempt to do so.

Similarly, guardianship and committeeship also involve the total forfeiting of control of the elder over his/her own life. Nevertheless, each required step toward such a status -- petition, notice, legal representation, hearing -- intended to protect the abused is hamstrung by imprecision, at best, and/or room for totally disregarding the rights of the abused elder, at worst.

Professional Orientation:
- Journalism

Type of Exposition:
- Review

Substantive Issue:
- General

089 Milt, Harry Family neglect and abuse of the aged: A growing concern. New York, New York: Public Affairs Committee, Pamphlet Number 603. May, 1982. 28p. (0 References).

TOPIC: The subject of this pamphlet is elder abuse by family members.

OBJECTIVE: The author proposes to examine the nature, scope, and available services for protection and prevention of elder abuse.

METHODS: This article presents information from a variety of sources including case reports and the results of others' research on the subject.

CONCLUSIONS: This review highlights some of the problems in dealing with elder abuse. These include definitions, causes, and strategies for protection and prevention. Attention is also given to contributing factors. Both the government and relatives have the responsibility of meeting the needs of the elderly. The law regarding elder abuse and the delivery of services need to be reviewed. Legal Research and Services for the Elderly has proposed a model adult protective service plan focusing on the older person's rights and a comprehensive plan of protection. A plan of care would involve a team made up of a variety of health care providers. In the last analysis, there should be a national policy on elder abuse. With this goal in mind, the government should help families who care for their elders through a variety of service options; from hearing aids and walkers to educational programs on the problems associated with aging.

Professional Orientation:
- Psychiatry

Type of Exposition:
- Advice-Giving

Substantive Issues:
- Definitions
- Professional Responsibility

090 Moore, James. "Psychiatry/abuse of the eldery." In: American academy of family physicians. Kansas City, Missouri: 1983. 79-89. (6 References).

TOPIC: This chapter focuses on abuse of the elderly in the home and in institutions.

OBJECTIVES: The author's purpose is to examine various social, environmental, and societal factors related to elder abuse.

METHODS: Professional experience and case presentation supported by a review of the literature provide the basis for discussion.

CONCLUSIONS: Elder abuse appears to be a common yet invisible problem. The major reason for its occurrence seems to be the low value assigned to the elderly in our society. While types of abuse may be related to the personal characteristics of the victim or the environmental setting, most abuse is the consequence of the support person's becoming overwhelmed by elder care.

The physician plays an important role in the prevention of geriatric abuse. As a supporter to both patient and caretaker, the physician should educate them regarding aging and elder needs and offer counsel in cases of problems between the elder and caregiver. Visits to the home offer valuable information about the care for and unmet needs of the elderly patient. In institutional settings, the physician should be visible to and supportive of staff members. The physician should personally examine patients and be alerted to the passive patient who usually denies being abused. If physicians take a constructive tack through educating and supporting caregivers of older persons, many of the causes of elder abuse will be eliminated.

Professional Orientation:
- Other

Type of Exposition:
- Congressional Briefing

Substantive Issues:
- Laws
- Policy

091 Oakar, Mary Rose and Miller, Carol Ann. "Federal legislation to protect the elderly." In: Kosberg, Jordan I., ed. _Abuse and maltreatment of the elderly: Causes and interventions_. Littleton, Massachusetts: John Wright, PSG Inc., 1983. 422-35. (21 References).

TOPIC: This chapter reviews the history of federal legislation on family violence with a focus on current and future legislation on elder abuse.

OBJECTIVE: The goal of this chapter is to provide an account of the kinds of family violence legislation which have been enacted thus far.

METHOD: Circumstances calling attention to various forms of family violence, media reports, the introduction of legislation, congressional hearings, and their results are presented. Three types of family violence are reported. These include child abuse, domestic abuse and elder abuse.

CONCLUSIONS: Child abuse was the first form of abuse brought to the attention of the federal government. It took 100 years (from 1874 to 1974) after the first state society for the prevention of cruelty to children was founded before federal legislation was passed. The Child Abuse Prevention and Treatment Act was designed "to provide federal financial assistance for the identification, prevention, and treatment of child abuse and neglect."

Family violence became the next focus of attention as people became more conscious of child abuse. Legislation was introduced in 1977 for the purpose of establishing an office of domestic violence at the federal level, but the bill failed. Legislation continued to be introduced without success. Presently, a bill proposed in 1981 has been referred to committee but is still awaiting hearings.

Elder abuse came to the attention of Congress in 1978 when Dr. Suzanne Steinmetz presented information on incidences of abuse. Hearings on elder abuse began the following year and over the course of the next two years, from 1979 to 1981, six congressional hearings were held. The results of these hearings culminated in the introduction of legislation "to provide assistance for programs of prevention, identification, and treatment of adult abuse, neglect, and exploitation, and to establish a National Center for Adult Abuse." It was introduced twice, once in 1980 and the second time in 1981. Both attempts were unsuccessful.

Although information is still limited on causes for abuse, caregiver stress appears to be a common characteristic. Therefore, legislation needs to be passed to provide supportive services to families who care for older persons. These services need to be expanded to meet family needs on a number of levels -- financial, socio-emotional, and with the activities of daily living.

Professional Orientation:
- Psychology

Type of Exposition:
- Position Paper

Substantive Issues:
- Causal Factors
- Professional Responsibility
- Attitudes

092 Oliveira, Odacir H. "Psychological abuse of the elderly." In: Tennessee Conference: Abuse of Older Persons, Knoxville, Tennessee, December, 1980. <u>Conference proceedings</u>. Knoxville, Tennessee: School of Social Work, Office of Continuing Social Work Education, 1981. 115-22. (5 References).

TOPIC: The author examines the forms of psychological abuse inflicted on the elderly not only by families, but also by society and professional caregivers.

METHODS: A brief review is provided of typical kinds of psychological abuse by family, society, and professionals along with clarifying examples. General suggestions for change are also given.

CONCLUSIONS: Psychological abuse of the elderly is generally seen as the overt or subtle verbal rejection of, or demeaning of, the elderly which produces psychological stress or trauma in the abused. This is frequently observed in the caretaking family of an elderly parent when the family feels hopelessly confined by the needs of their new addition. They express this in such ways as verbalized desires to return to patterns enjoyed before the parent came to live with them. Society, however, also abuses the elderly by means of its stereotyped views offered in the media, in jokes, and elsewhere. These same negative stereotypes are subscribed to by many professionals who deal (or, perhaps, because of these stereotypes, refuse to deal) with the elderly: psychotherapists, physicians, nurses, and activity therapists in institutions. Thus, the elderly are often perceived as being untreatable and can only be "treated" with psychotropic drugs. Professionals, like the rest of society, often decide what is best for the elderly without considering the particular personality needs of the person, or consulting him or her in the process of determination. In institutions, the elderly are encouraged in subtle and overt ways to shed their individuality and freedom in favor of being conformist and dependent. They are seen more as infants than as other adults with interests appropriate to adults. Not only do we need to recognize the way we train people who work with the elderly, but we also need a thorough-going reorientation of the way that we as a society think about the elderly -- not as those who are hopelessly dying, but as lively persons with potential for growth and change.

Professional Orientation:
- Sociology

Type of Exposition:
- Review

Substantive Issue:
- General

093 O'Malley, Helen C. Elder abuse: A review of recent literature. Boston, Massachusetts: Legal Research and Services for the Elderly. June 1, 1979. 27p. (72 References).

TOPIC: The author provides a literature review of the results of studies on child, spouse and elder abuse.

OBJECTIVES: The purpose of this review is to identify variables in the literature associated with child, spouse and elder abuse and to consider how they may relate to treatment.

METHODS: Reviews of legal statutes, research studies, journal articles, and case records serve as the literature which document definitions, incidences, and causal theories that relate to child, spouse, and elder abuse. A series of questions about elder abuse based on the findings in child and spouse abuse literature conclude the paper's discussion.

CONCLUSIONS: Most definitions of child abuse cited include purposefully inflicted physical abuse. Neglect was most often defined as a withholding of care. In the spouse abuse literature, physical abuse rather than neglect was recognized more often, perhaps, because adults are seen as capable of self-care and thus cannot be neglected. Other literature mentioned the ability to document abuse with radiology as one reason for the enactment of child abuse reporting laws which are now present in all states. Incidence of child abuse ranged from 500,000 to 2,500,000 cases a year. Data supporting several abuse theories frequently conflicted. Additional research focusing on such variables as personality characteristics of parents and children, and environmental or situational stress is needed to comprehend both cause and treatment of child abuse. Agreement concerning the family as the focus of treatment did exist in the literature. Education counseling, financial assistance, and respite home care services are some of the treatment services suggested.

Although data on spouse abuse were sparse, the problem was found to be as widespread as child abuse. One study estimated that approximately 2,000,000 wives were beaten each year. Both husbands and wives commit spouse abuse, but most of the literature examines the abused wife and one study describes her most often as white, married, and in poor physical health. Theories related to spouse abuse include a failure to communicate verbally, established social norms, and learned role models as in the case of an abused wife whose daughter is abused in later years. In addition to legal protection and counseling, it is hypothesized that explanations and the subsequent treatment for spouse abuse will be multi-dimensional just the same as it is for child abuse.

Current literature has largely ignored elder abuse. Most of the available literature has attributed elder abuse to the many stresses involved in caring for an older person. Adult children and other relatives are providing increased care to the elderly as the older population grows. However, as more women enter the job market, and as families have fewer children, family elder care will become more complicated. It will be some time, however, before a sufficient amount of information will be gathered on which to build a theory of elder abuse. In the meantime, many articles have identified support services to caretakers to be vital in preventing elder abuse. The review concludes with a number of questions on elder abuse which still need to be addressed.

Professional Orientation:
- Sociology

Type of Exposition:
- Review

Substantive Issues:
- Treatment
- Barriers
- Policy

094 O'Malley, Helen C.; Segars, Howard; Bergman, James A. An analysis of protective service systems for handling elder abuse cases. Boston, Massachusetts: Legal Research and Services for the Elderly, June 15, 1979. 70-110. (0 References).

TOPIC: The authors examine the nature and implementation of protective services for the abused elderly.

OBJECTIVES: The authors wish to present a model protective services system to describe the protocols which characterize the four basic types of elder abuse situations, and to evaluate three "project sites" which have organized protective services systems.

METHODS: Staff at the Legal Research and Services for the Elderly (LRSE) in Boston, Massachusetts interviewed workers who managed elder abuse cases for Home Care Corporations and for other health services systems. National experts were also interviewed. Literature and statute reviews along with current practices in child abuse protective services provided additional background information.

CONCLUSIONS: Two essential components of any protective services system are a planned protocol for responding to abuse cases with different characteristics and a coordinated interdisciplinary response since elder abuse cases require the services of several agencies. A protective services system should provide the following services: a case worker to coordinate the services of several agencies, a case assessment team to help the case worker, primary health care, legal counsel, a homemaker/home health aid, transportation, meals, financial assistance, police intervention (only when appropriate), emergency shelter, medical care and money, and follow-up case reviews. Additional support services such as counseling for abuse victims and abusers, foster care for the elderly, and day care or recreational centers serve to strengthen a basic protective services system. Although a protective services system varies from state to state, certain elements should be the same in each one. Those elements include standardized record keeping; eligibilty guidelines; case finding, reporting, and referral; confidentiality; training of case workers and state and federal funds for services.

LRSE identified four basic types of elder abuse victims. Some victims were mentally competent and consented to the help of a protective service, while other mentally competent victims of abuse refused the aid of a protective services system.

Clients, both consenting and non-consenting, who were mentally incapacitated were also found. The fourth identified victims were those who were in immediate danger from their abuser.

LRSE examined three project sites, in order to evaluate their protective services systems: Merrimack Valley, Worcester, and Boston Area III Home Care Corporation. While each system was found to use a different approach, none of the systems had a comprehensive protective services system, and all were in operation only until funding stopped. The Merrimack Valley system utilized most of the services available in the 24-community region and followed the principles of the LRSE model. However, this project had no long-term growth plans, limited emergency intervention protocol, an uneven distribution of services to a broader client population, little involvement with physicians, lawyers or police, and no systemized interdisciplinary case review. In Worcester, Elder Home Care Services had a "streamlined" approach to protective services. The professional staff and relatively low costs contributed to community-based, interdisciplinary protective services. Development of an inter-agency referral program working with the community mental health center would enable the Worcester site to identify older abuse victims more effectively. In addition, there should be improvements in inventorying clients' needs along with special support services and financial support from state seed money. The third site examined, Boston Area III, did have almost all services needed by the elderly, but unlike Merrimack Valley and Worcester, these services were not coordinated in one system. There are some options which may resolve the lack of co-ordination. However, Boston's diversity makes a unified protective service system difficult to implement.

Professional Orientation:
- Sociology

Type of Exposition:
- Survey Research

Substantive Issue:
- General

095 O'Malley, Helen C.; Segars, Howard; Perez, Ruben; et al. Elder abuse in Massachusetts: A survey of professionals and paraprofessionals. Boston, Massachusetts: Legal Research and Services for the Elderly, June 1, 1979. 50p. (0 References).

TOPIC: The authors present survey results of a questionnaire on elder abuse in the family setting.

OBJECTIVE: They wish to provide preliminary data on the nature of elder abuse.

METHODS: The information in this study was collected from a survey of medical, legal, social work, and law enforcement professionals in Massachusetts during March and April 1979. Thirty-four percent of the 1044 surveys were returned. Descriptive information on the characteristics of abused elders, their abusers, the incident(s) of abuse, and the professional's response to the abuse incident(s) were provided by 335 respondents.

FINDINGS: One of the most significant findings from the data on the 183 reported citings of elder abuse, which had occurred in an 18 month period, was the tendency for the abuse to be recurring in 70% of the abuse incidents. Seventy percent of these abuse citings were brought to the attention of the professional by an outside, third party. The largest single age group represented in these citings was the group of elders aged 75 years of age or older. In addition, 80% of the citings involved female victims, and, in 75% of the citings, the victim lived with the abuser. Seventy-five percent of the citings included the respondents' statement that the abused elder had a mental or physical disability. This finding supports the survey's premise that the abuser was usually experiencing some form of stress during the abusive incident. When abuse was encountered by a professional, 62% stated that some form of direct action was taken, with placement in a facility such as a nursing home occurring frequently. When service was offered, 70% of the respondents reported some barrier to service.

CONCLUSIONS: The data from this survey do not represent a random sampling of a population, and, of the 183 abuse citings, some citings may represent identical cases. The data are to be viewed as descriptive only. More controlled research is necessary to yield data which could be generalized to the broader population.

Professional Orientation:
- Medicine

Type of Exposition:
- Advice-Giving

Substantive Issues:
- Definitions
- Identification
- Treatment

096 O'Malley, Terrence, A.; Everitt, Daniel E.; O'Malley, Helen C.; *et al*. "Identifying and preventing family-mediated abuse and neglect of elderly persons." *Ann Intern Med* 98(6):998-1005. June, 1983. (35 References).

TOPIC: This article focuses on the physician's role in identifying and managing cases of elder abuse by family members.

OBJECTIVE: The authors present a model for physicians to use in managing cases of abuse.

METHODS: Case histories and studies published in American and British social service and medical journals provide the necessary data to identify characteristics of the elderly victim of abuse and the abuser, and to discuss four frequently cited theories for the cause of abusive treatment. With the above background information as an introduction, this article then proposes a new definition for abuse and offers case management guidelines for the physician and team of other health professionals.

CONCLUSIONS: The terms "abuse" and "neglect" should be replaced by "unmet needs" to avoid unnecessary implications which may contribute to the refusal of case intervention. Each identified case should have a case manager, and the physician should play an active role in a multidisciplinary approach to case management. Effective case management draws from clear guidelines for identification, access and assessment, intervention, follow-up and prevention.

Professional Orientation:
- Unidentified

Type of Exposition:
- Review

Substantive Issue:
- General

097 O'Rourke, Margaret. "Elder abuse: The state of the art." Boston, Massachusetts: Legal Research and Services for the Elderly, 1981. 32p. (15 References).

TOPIC: Findings from studies on elder abuse are reported and a protective services system model is reviewed.

OBJECTIVE: The author wishes to assist policy makers and program developers by summarizing current knowledge on elder abuse in relation to theories of family violence and findings from four research studies. In addition, she presents a detailed model for a protective services system.

METHODS: The paper's review and protective services model are based on elder abuse literature with special attention given to studies conducted by O'Malley et al at Legal Research and Services for the Elderly in Boston, by Block and Sinnott at the University of Maryland, by Douglass, Hickey and Noel at the University of Michigan, and by Lau and Kosberg in Cleveland.

FINDINGS: Causal factors identified as contributing to elder abuse were (1) the physical or mental impairment of a dependent elderly person, (2) the character or personality disorders of the abuser, (3) the pattern of violence learned in a family, (4) the external family stresses such as financial demands, (5) the demographic trends toward a larger elderly population with fewer adult children as caretakers, and (6) the negative attitudes of society about the elderly.

Analysis of the data from the studies revealed that "severe physical and mental impairment as a characteristic of the abused elder" was common to three studies. Two studies that examined age found the abused to be very old and three studies identified them as females with relatives who practiced repeated abuse. Because of the nonrepresentativeness of respondents, the lack of control groups, and the inconsistency in definitions for abuse, no sound estimate of the number of abuse incidences can be made. Three of the four studies, however, did find a "significant level" of physical and psychological abuse. Also, the response of agencies to abuse tended towards removal of the victim from home to an institution.

Nevertheless, past research in elder abuse does increase awareness of the problem. New research should involve intervention, treatment, and prevention."

Based on the findings from this past research, a protective services system model is proposed. It would coordinate the delivery of services to potential abuse victims. It would also include mandatory reporting, responsible guardianship laws, protective intervention and a national policy on elder services.

Professional Orientation:
- Law

Type of Exposition:
- Review

Substantive Issues:
- Identification
- Reporting
- Laws
- Professional Responsibility

098 Palincsar, John, and Cobb, Deborah Crouse. "The physician's role in detecting and reporting elder abuse." J Leg Med 3(3):413-41, September, 1982. (30 References).

TOPIC: The authors review current literature on elder abuse focusing on the medical and legal dilemmas physicians face in their efforts to identify and report cases of elder abuse.

OBJECTIVE: The goal of the article is to communicate to physicians and lawyers the nature, scope, and causes for elder abuse, "and to describe the physician's role in a formal legal response to the problem of the neglect and abuse of elders in informal care settings."

CONCLUSIONS: There are five categories of abuse -- passive neglect, active neglect, psychological abuse, financial abuse, and physical abuse. Although there are no definitive statistics on the scope of elder abuse, most professionals agree that the number of abused elders and the severity of abuse are increasing.

The typical victim is a mentally or physically impaired older female. It is not clear why more women are abused than men. There are both physical and psychological reasons. Mistreatment also tends to be ongoing. Abusers seem to be under stress, impaired by a variety of physical and social-psychological problems, and are often caretaker relatives of the victim. Some researchers say that middle class families are more likely to be abusive to older members because "middle class aspirations suffer more interference from the burden of elder care." However, when the hypothesis is tested, it will probably be the case that more elder abuse will be found among the poor. There are a number of factors cited as causes for elder abuse. These include the losses accompanying long-term aging, financial burden for elder care, inadequate community services for families who care for older members, family conflicts, and negative attitudes toward aging. Since the abused or abuser so seldom reports abuse to some authority, professionals need to do so. The Illinois and Michigan studies show that physicians as a professional group report fewer cases of elder abuse. There are a number of reasons why this might be the case. Some include the fact the physicians may not be aware of the problem, they may feel that it is not their responsibility to go beyond medical treatment, and some may fear legal action from the so-called abuser if they report suspected cases.

Although there are certain conditions under which physicians are protected from a lawsuit when reporting elder abuse cases, they are, nevertheless, not immune in some circumstances. There is yet a further complication in that physicians sometimes may be liable if they do not report cases.

Medical testimony in elder abuse cases must be well-substantiated in order for the case to be verified. Comparing medical documentation of elder abuse with child abuse may be inappropriate. Aging may cause some deteriorating symptoms which would be clear signs of abuse for children but not older persons. This includes both physical and mental changes. There are some signs, such as cigarette burns, which signal abuse no matter how old the victim. Medical testimony may include hospital records, x-rays (as long as they meet certain specifications), photographs, and an assessment of the patient's physical condition and causes for that condition. On the other hand, the physician is not considered competent to identify the abuser, determine the reason for abuse or recommend the proper course of action the society should take.

Adult protective laws in the various states are based on three models - child abuse, family violence, and advocacy. Statutes patterned on the child abuse model render the elder person helpless in making decisions about his/her own fate. The outcome with such a model is often institutionalization. Furthermore, there is likely to be a clause about elder neglect since child abuse statutes tend to include neglect along with abuse. However, there is some question as to whether it is appropriate to include older persons in this category. This raises the question of the degree of elder dependence. Finally, with this type of model, reporting is usually through a central agency. Local state attorneys' offices should know the reporting process. The family violence model assumes all parties are in need of some kind of help. However, this help attempts to avoid criminal prosecution. Since family violence laws are intended to provide short term solutions, they may be of limited value to the elderly victim. The advocacy approach is intended to allow the victim as much independence as possible. This model helps the older person find the least restrictive approach in resolving the problem of abuse and allows that individual the greatest freedom of choice.

A number of tasks will need to be completed before we can solve the problem of elder abuse. These include better research, especially in the areas of theory, nature, and scope of elder abuse; more community services; and more help from the private sector when funds are limited. The legal profession cannot stop elder abuse because a law is passed, but it can facilitate the means to identify cases and support community programs designed to reduce the stress which provokes elder abuse in the first place.

Professional Orientation:
- Sociology

Type of Exposition:
- Review

Substantive Issues:
- Definitions
- Characteristics
- Theory
- Policy

099 Pedrick-Cornell, Claire, and Gelles, Richard J. "Elder abuse: The status of current knowledge." Fam Relat 31(3):457-65, July, 1982. (24 References).

TOPIC: The article consists of a review of current literature on elder abuse with recommendations for new directions for researchers and practitioners.

OBJECTIVES: Three goals are identified in this review. These include a report on the most recent information on elder abuse, an analysis of the limitations of current research and a proposed blueprint for new efforts in information gathering and human service worker intervention.

METHOD: Four studies on elder abuse are the primary focus of this critique. Particular attention is given to their scientific validity. These include the work of Block and Sinnott, Douglass, Hickey and Noel, Lau and Kosberg, and O'Malley et al.

CONCLUSIONS: Elder abuse has become a topic of interest because of a new view of family violence as well as demographic and socioeconomic changes which make its incidence more likely. However, consciousness has "outpaced" research efforts leaving a significant knowledge gap and little information upon which to base policy. Those research studies which do exist do not meet "the normal scientific rules of evidence." Definitions, data on prevalence, characteristics of abusers and the abused and theories of elderly abuse are not based on "quality data" since the research studies have not used a rigorous scientific methodology. Data-gathering and sampling are flawed and, therefore, they are unreliable resources upon which to base programs of prevention and intervention in elder abuse.

In an effort to get the study of elder abuse on more solid footing, a number of recommendations are made to researchers and practitioners. For example, researchers are admonished to use comparison groups from a representative sampling technique. In the other sphere, practitioners are encouraged to locate and actively utilize community resources in order to provide supportive services to families with older members.

Professional Orientation:
- Sociology
Type of Exposition:
- Advice-Giving
Substantive Issue:
- Family Dynamics

100 Pentz, Clyde. "Stress in the extended nuclear family as a precursor for abuse." In: Tennessee Conference: Abuse of Older Persons, Knoxville, Tennessee, December, 1980. Conference proceedings. Knoxville, Tennessee: School of Social Work, Office of Continuing Social Work Education, 1981. 127-32. (4 References).

TOPIC: When an adult child becomes the sole caretaker for his/her aging parent, predictable tensions are created which can result in elder abuse if they are not defused.

METHODS: The author uses material from other studies to illuminate why including an aging parent in the home of an adult child causes stress, and then suggests three ways of alleviating this stress.

CONCLUSIONS: Despite the fact that the extended nuclear family is not the norm in America today, many adults would feel guilty about committing a parent to a nursing home. Taking the now-dependent parent into their home, however, causes increasing stress according to a predictable pattern. Two primary sources of this are the difficulties caused by dealing with "perceived mental deterioration" and experiencing this new arrangement as confining. Though only a minority of families react to this stress through abuse, the stress is still there. It can be dealt with by significantly increasing the information and understanding of the caretaker about needs of the parent, and by increasing government services to the parent such as Meals on Wheels or institutionalizing the parent.

Professional Orientation:
- Other

Type of Exposition:
- Congressional Hearing

Substantive Issue:
- General

101 Pepper, Claude, and Oakar, Rose Mary "Elder abuse: An examination of a hidden problem." Pub. No. 97-277. House Select Committee on Aging, Ninety-Seventh Congress. San Francisco, California: U.S. Government Printing Office, April 3, 1981. 169p. (0 References).

TOPIC: This report represents the first national state-by-state investigation of elder abuse to assess the signficance of the problem.

OBJECTIVES: The major goal of this report is to explore what is known about elder abuse in order to determine the extent of the problem in America. Other secondary goals include determining causes of elder abuse and outlining policy options on the federal, state, and local levels.

METHODS: The House Select Committee's conclusions in this eight-section report represents over a year's work of data gathering which utilized many information sources. Letters and case histories received by the Committee over the past five years were reviewed. Experts in the U.S. General Accounting Office who were exposed to cases of financial abuse were interviewed. In addition, indictment and public court statements were collected. A questionnaire was sent to all State Human Service Departments and follow-up telephone interviews were conducted with over one-third of these departments. Moreover, questionnaires were sent to various metropolitan police chiefs and to the staff of Visiting Nurses Association in Washington, D.C., Maryland, and New Jersey. The Emergency Nurses Association was also contacted. Hearings, reports, books, periodicals and newspaper references on abuse were reviewed. Written communication was conducted with respected authorities on elder abuse and with organizations and service providers. The Committee held hearings to gather additional information in New York, Massachusetts, New Jersey, and Washington, D.C.

FINDINGS: Through the review of hundreds of elder abuse cases Section I, the likely victim was found to be 75 years of age or older, female, dependent on others, and ashamed or unable to report the abuse incident. While the likely abuser was found to be the victim's son (in 21% of the cases) or daughter (in 17% of the cases). The abuser was usually under great stress and possibly an alcoholic, drug addict, or suffering from marital or economic problems. In Section II, 14 categories of support serve to document the Committee's finding that elder abuse is a "widespread, serious and growing problem." No one cause of elder abuse was identified, but several causal theories were offered.

Data from the states support the following findings in Section IV:

- Even though three times as many child abuse cases occur, more money needs to be spent for adult protective services. Most states averaged spending only 6.6 percent of their protective services budget on the elderly, while 86.7 percent has been used for children.

- Twenty-six states have adult protective service laws, 16 of these have mandatory reporting laws, and 10 states do not have any laws concerning elder abuse.

- The majority of states agreed that the needs of the elderly were not being met, and favored legislation for model protective services systems and mandatory reporting requirements.

CONCLUSIONS: Section VIII of this report identifies several recommendations for solving the problem of elder abuse. These recommendations include policy options for states and for the Congress. Among these options are the enactment of the H.R. 769, the Prevention, Identification and Treatment of Elder Abuse Act of 1981, amendments to Title XX, Medicare and Medicaid to assist families better who take care of an elderly person, and enactment of legislation on the state level patterned after H.R. 769.

Professional Orientation:
- Nursing
Type of Exposition:
- Case Studies
Substantive Issues:
- Identification
- Professional Responsibility

102 Phillips, Linda R. "Elder abuse: What is it? Who says so?" Ger Nurs 4(3):167-70, May/June, 1983. (4 References).

TOPIC: This study focuses on the subject of elder abuse in domestic settings and highlights the complexity of the problem of abuse.

OBJECTIVE: The author proposes to identify some of the particular dilemmas for nurses who encounter potential abuse situations by reviewing responses of public health nurses.

METHODS: Thirty-four public health nurses who had participated in a study of 74 frail elderly individuals ages 62 to 92 were asked to select subjects who met the criteria for abuse. A definition and characteristics of abuse derived from the child abuse literature were provided in advance. They were also asked to identify subjects who were believed to have had a good relationship with their caregiver.

The nurses were also asked to document the reasoning behind their group assignments in a short report about each subject. They were then asked to complete the Abuse Report Form which rated the severity of abuse on a five-point scale, with four or more indicating abuse. This paper gives accounts of five cases that were difficult for referring nurses to define as abuse cases. Possible reasons why these cases were difficult to view as examples of abuse conclude the author's presentation of the five case histories.

CONCLUSIONS: Identifying abuse is an extremely difficult task because most elder abuse cases are not examples of outright battering. Few elders will report abuse because of their fear of jeopardizing their current living arrangement.

The home setting itself, the elder's right to a chosen way of life, the referring nurse's value system, and the caretaker's pleasant manner or prominent position all come into play when nurses are presented with the problem of identifying elder abuse cases.

Nurses have a special role in the identification of elder abuse. They have access to about every site where elderly individuals are located. Nurses have a dual obligation to identify their beliefs as to the needs and rights of elders and communicate these beliefs to other caregivers. They should also present the problems of elderly individuals in domestic settings and their families to the public and legislators.

Professional Orientation:
- Unidentified

Type of Exposition:
- Survey Research

Substantive Issues:
- Treatment
- Professional Responsibility

103 Pratt, Clara C; Koval, James; Lloyd, Sally. "Service workers' responses to abuse of the elderly." <u>Soc Casework</u> 64(3):147-53, March, 1983. (approx 17 References).

TOPIC: This study contrasts physician and service providers responses to hypothetical cases of elder abuse.

OBJECTIVE: The goal was to assess intervention responses of social service providers and physicians to hypothetical cases of elder abuse by family members.

METHODS: The study examined the intervention methods chosen by social service agency workers and physicians in response to four vignettes representing hypothetical cases of different types of elder abuse by a male abuser toward a female victim. The age of the victim and the relationship to the abuser (spouse or son) varied in each of the vignettes. Responses were analyzed by content and assigned to thematic categories of intervention and referral.

FINDINGS: The factors having the greatest impact on the respondents' intervention strategy were the severity of the abuse and the respondents' professional position. For example, the more severe the abuse, the greater the likelihood that respondents would refer the case to an outside agency rather than intervene personally. Physicians were more likely than agency workers to refer elder abuse cases to attorneys and clergy. They were also more likely than other professionals to intervene personally or recommend counselling. Agency supervisors and direct service providers tended to make referrals to another agency.

CONCLUSIONS: While the focus of the respondents' intervention strategies was on the victim, successful intervention should also include aid to the abuser who is usually responding to some form of stress in the family. Also, few respondents mentioned the need to coordinate referral of cases so as not to overwhelm or further stress the abused elder and the family. In addition, the initial personal contact with the victim and the victim's family needs to be handled with special sensitivity. Finally, health care providers need to be informed about the elder abuse intervention system in the community as well as the service options.

Professional Orientation:
- Social Work

Type of Exposition:
- Case studies

Substantive Issues:
- Types
- Characteristics

104 Rathbone-McCuan, Eloise. "Elderly victims of family violence and neglect." <u>Soc Casework</u> 61(5):296-304. May, 1980. (5 References).

TOPIC: The subject of this article is the abuse of elderly individuals in non-institutional settings by family members.

OBJECTIVE: The purpose of this study is to describe and analyse situations in which noninstitutionalized aged persons are victims of physical abuse and physically endangering neglect carried out by caregivers.

METHODS: The author briefly reviews the current status of elder neglect and abuse and uses an exploratory framework of intra-family violence to further discuss this subject. Ten cases of intergenerational abuse of the elderly are presented to highlight various aspects of this topic.

FINDINGS: In a majority of cases certain characteristics are present that may help with identification in the future. Many obstacles are identified that hinder intervention and need to be changed. It is apparent that further research in this area is needed, and greater community awareness of the phenomenon needs to occur before significant progress in handling this problem can occur.

Professional Orientation:
- Social Work

Type of Exposition:
- Advice-Giving

Substantive Issues:
- Causal Factors
- Family Dynamics
- Social Structure
- Treatment
- Policy

105 Rathbone-McCuan, Eloise, and Hashimi, Joan. "Elder abuse and isolation." In: Rathbone-McCuan, Eloise and Hashimi, Joan, eds. Isolated Elders, Health and Social Intervention. Rockville, Maryland: Aspen Systems Corporation, 1982. 177-209. (20 References).

TOPIC: Causes, legislation and intervention for elder abuse are reveiwed with a special focus on family and societal isolators which may lead to abuse.

METHODS: Literature on causes, legislation, and intervention are reviewed. Reports from case studies, a House Selection Committee on Aging Hearing, and The Missouri Association for the Prevention of Adult Abuse are also used in order to exemplify some major problems in current policy and intervention in elder abuse.

CONCLUSIONS: A review of the literature on causation identifies possible sources as (1) the revenge framework, (2) the pathological personality framework, (3) the generational transmission framework, (4) the absence of community resources framework, (5) the functional incompetency framework, and (6) the economic exploitation framework. These variations are complex and confusing, but they do "suggest the importance of stress and isolation."

Caregiving roles for elderly family members can create stress for all of the family. The aging process may be accompanied by loss and changing roles in the family. There is a comparison between dependent elder care and caring for schizophrenics living in the household. "Relatives must come to terms with difficult circumstances such as social withdrawal, underactivity, excessive sleeping, and socially embarrassing behavior." A manifestation of the response to stress is isolation from family and from the environment. There is a variety of isolators. Some intrafamily isolators among abused elders include such factors as fear of the caretaker and dependency on others for self-care needs. Environmental isolators may be illustrated by the condition of inadequate reporting laws for elder abuse and inadequate outside financial assistance for families who care for older members. There is no easy resolution to isolation, and sometimes one form of isolation can be corrected but in the process replaced by another. While stress may be inevitable, isolation need not be. Intervention in cases of elder abuse should focus on the elimination of isolators. "Abuse is a problem within a family that can be met by a response from without in the form of resources." Intervention may come from the clinical setting or the legal-political system. At the federal level, the House Select Committee on Aging conducted a Hearing in 1980 to consider the nature and scope of elder abuse laws in the various states. Testimony on behalf of better protection for older persons was presented by a number of members of the House and Senate. One example of state efforts to protect against elder abuse is the program in Missouri. In 1973, approximately 50 social service workers formed a group to work on the problem of elder abuse in Missouri. The two major goals of this newly formed Missouri Association to Prevent Adult Abuse were (1) to seek legislation for adult protective services, and (2) to be prepared in the social service areas to carry out the law. After variations and modifications, Senate Bill 576 passed in 1980. On a local level, the Missouri Association to Prevent Adult Abuse was called upon to implement the final adult protective service bill. In consequence, a number of problem areas have arisen. "The MAPAA faces a series of complex questions on how to implement a viable model in view of a funding scarcity, uncoordinated service components througout the community, and the many uncertainties created by an overall statewide program that performs many administrative and technical functions far beyond the current effort's capabilities."

No type of intervention should be ruled out since there is no research data as yet on the effectiveness of various intervention strategies. There is a need for this kind of evaluation as it relates to the particular form of mistreatment called elder abuse. In addition, there is a need to compare intervention strategies in other forms of family violence with elder abuse.

A number of issues related to elder abuse should be explored. These include (1) learning which types of families are at risk for elder abuse, (2) discovering which factors are present in high risk families, (3) determining which interventions might minimize the risk factors, (4) finding ways to measure the impact of these strategies on the rate and severity of elder abuse, (5) projecting what a national prevention strategy would cost, and (6) deciding which interventions will require a "rethinking of individual rights and societal values toward the family and the aged."

Professional Orientation:
- Social Work

Type of Exposition:
- Clinical Observations

Substantive Issues:
- Family Dynamics
- Treatment

106 Rathbone-McCuan, Eloise; Travis, Ann; Voyles, Barbara. "Family intervention: The task-centered approach." In: Kosberg, Jordan I., ed. Abuse and maltreatment of the elderly: Causes and interventions. Littleton, Massachusetts: John Wright, PSG Inc., 1983. 355-75. (29 References).

TOPIC: This chapter explores the task-centered model in the context of the family-oriented intervention model for elder abuse.

OBJECTIVE: The authors discuss how a family-centered intervention called the Task-Centered Model can be applied to elder clients and their families in an adult protective service setting.

METHOD: The Task-Centered Model has been used in field work in clinical gerontology at the George Warren Brown School of Social Work. In particular, the results of the field experiences of those studies involved in elder abuse intervention in an adult protective services unit will be reviewed.

CONCLUSIONS: Two other family-oriented intervention models have been applied to the counseling of families with older family members besides the Task-Centered Model. The Contextual Family Therapy Model has its roots in psychoanalysis. It is a long-term therapy approach focusing upon the multigenerational family.

The Problem-Centered Systems Family Therapy Model centers upon specific family problems. The family collaborates in the treatment and follows a contract designed to resolve the problem. The Task-Centered approach has been used to deal with the problems of daily living often experienced by older persons and their families. It stresses individualized needs of the family members and personalized intervention.

The application of the Task-Centered Model involves identification of the target problems, formulation of the task and sometimes task modification and facilitation by the worker. Two essential features, however, are that family members are cooperative in carrying out treatment plans and the elder is a partner in formulating a plan of intervention. A case illustration is presented in order to show how the model is implemented. Problems were clearly defined in this case but kept to a minimum. Tasks did not focus on the deviance which some members of the family were experiencing but centered on members mobilizing resources to solve the problem. It must be emphasized that this model of intervention also requires utilizing other community resources such as advocates, self-help groups and ombudsman programs in the problem-solving process.

Professional Orientation:
- Social Work

Type of Exposition:
- Training Guide

Substantive Issue:
- Treatment

107 Rathbone-McCuan, Eloise, and Voyles, Barbara. "Case detection of abused elderly parents." Amer J Psychiat 139(2):189-92, February, 1982. (6 References).

TOPIC: The article contains procedures for in-home human service practitioners to use in the detection of elder abuse.

OBJECTIVES: The material is designed to fill in some of the knowledge gap in the identification of conditions in domestic settings which are "potential indicators" of elder abuse.

METHOD: Drawing on their experiences in case detection, the authors offer a number of personal and relational characteristics of older persons and their adult child caregivers which suggest the presence of elder abuse.

CONCLUSIONS: Two problem areas which have prevented identification in the past are reviewed. First, practitioners have tended to be ignorant of the reality of elder abuse or deny its existence even though other forms of family violence have been acknowledged. Second, there is an absence of information on critical issues in elder abuse which makes detection procedures difficult to construct. Such limitations as the lack of a uniform definition, the lack of understanding on how social-psychological factors might influence abuse and the need to come up with reasons for abuse are barriers to detection.

Despite these limitations, detection guidelines are presented. These guidelines include two types of abuse -- physical and behavioral. Illustrative of the "potential indicators" of elder parent abuse are cigarette burns, the older person being tied to a chair or a locked food cupboard. Behavioral cues may be picked up both through observation and an interview. When the older person shows fear of the adult child caregiver or the adult child caregiver seems indifferent to advice by the clinician on elder care, then there is reason to suspect abuse.

Mental health care agencies should train their staffs in this type of family-oriented detection and assessment so that intervention may be planned more meaningfully.

Professional Orientation:
- Law

Type of Exposition:
- Advice-Giving

Substantive Issues:
- Laws
- Barriers
- Professional Responsibility
- Community Responsibility

108 Redmond, Rosemary. "Hitting the elderly." Fam Advo 2(3):17-9, Winter, 1980. (0 References).

TOPIC: The author explores some of the dilemmas lawyers, victims of elder abuse, and families face when there is a need for adult protective services.

OBJECTIVE: The purpose of this article is to consider the complications in the legal system which make adult protection difficult, and to provide a list of elder support activities which the states and local communities could develop in order to help prevent conditions of abuse, exploitation, and neglect.

METHODS: A case of elder exploitation is used to illustrate some of the legal limitations in attempts to protect older persons from elder abuse. In addition, a program in Dallas, Texas, called Access Center for the Elderly is outlined to show how one community coordinates services to older persons in an effort to minimize problems older persons might experience and, therefore, prevent abuse.

CONCLUSIONS: One complication in protecting the legal rights of older persons occurs when family members are the abusers. For example, it is necessary for the elderly victim of abuse, exploitation, and neglect to request some kind of legal intervention. However, when family members are the abusers, the victims may be reluctant to seek protection under the law. Another option in adult protection is guardianship. But if guardianship is instituted, the older person is in danger of losing a number of rights such as choice of residence, the right to marry, and the right to vote. Power of attorney and conservatorship also have their limitations with regard to protecting the elderly.

As the older population increases, there is a greater need for protective services. The legal profession, in particular, needs more flexible and creative forms of legal services to the elderly in order to insure better protection against abuse, exploitation, and neglect. Sixteen recommendations to states and local communities are presented. Most of these suggestions involve programs to prevent abusive circumstances from developing. These programs include such activities as home visiting programs, telephone services, elder advocacy, family counseling centers, nutritional services, and transportation for older persons.

Professional Orientation:
- Law

Type of Exposition:
- Position Paper

Substantive Issue:
- Laws

109 Regan, John J. "Elder abuse: Legal remedies for the involuntary client." In: First National Conference on Abuse of Older Persons, Cambridge, Massachusetts, March, 1981. Conference Proceedings. Boston, Massachusetts: Legal Research and Services for the Elderly, 1981. 8p. (0 References).

TOPIC: This presentation addresses the issue of where to draw the line between family privacy and public intervention by professionals.

OBJECTIVE: The question is raised about how we can protect the involuntary client who is abused but will not ask for professional help.

METHODS: The assessment of both the rights of the abused and the abuser is presented as well as an assessment of the professional caseworker's rights when dealing with abusive families.

CONCLUSIONS: There are, indeed, federal laws which protect citizens from unreasonable search and seizure and from intrusion. Clients have the right to refuse treatment even if it means death. States, however, can intervene to prosecute abusers even when victims refuse help. Guardians may be appointed in cases of incompetence and incapacity. In addition, there are legal mechanisms available to the caseworker to overcome barriers in providing services. Caseworkers may enter private dwellings with a court order when elder abuse is being investigated, or they may gather evidence of abuse sufficient to warrant a court order; but the dilemma persists that it is an involutary activity. Involuntary programs should be changed to voluntary intervention if we expect to meet the needs of abused older persons. "In elder abuse, therefore, as elsewhere, doing good means not just providing help where needed, but knowing the limits of one's power to help others."

Professional Orientation:
- Law

Type of Exposition:
- Position Paper

Substantive Issues:
- Laws
- Treatment
- Professional Responsibility

110 Regan, John J. "Intervention through adult protective service programs." Gerontologist 18(3):250-54, June, 1978. (15 Referencs).

TOPIC: The author considers the legal provisions for protecting the elderly.

OBJECTIVE: The goal of this article is to examine the forms of legal adult protective services and to assess the degree to which the older person's rights are preserved in the process of implementation.

METHODS: A case report of a frail elderly person in need of assistance from others in the community, a review of the literature, and the author's position on the functioning and effectiveness of adult protective service laws constitute the foundation of the discussion.

CONCLUSIONS: An increasing number of states are adopting service and intervention programs to protect adults. However, the legal provisions have not kept pace in many of these states. The consequence may be changing "well-meaning programs into instruments for oppressive intervention..." The important concern is for the preservation of the civil liberties of the older person. The case of Mrs. D. is an example of a person who was unable to maintain herself in her own home and, at the same time, had no continuous support from friends, family, or community agencies to help her remain in her home. Protective services is a system which focuses on helping older persons to live independently and protects them against abuse and exploitation. These protective service organizations are expected to provide services to the elderly and to have the authority to intervene on the older person's behalf. Sometimes the law permits helping agencies to forego client consent and intervene against the older person's judgement. Legal procedures which culminate in guardianship, conservatorship, and power of attorney do not always protect the elder in the fairest way. These measures tend to be rigid and absolute rather than accommodating to the inevitable individual differences among older persons in need of protective services. Seven guidelines are proposed for the purpose of altering the guardianship law so that they might be more responsive to what is in the best interest of the older person. Some of these guidelines include (1) the need for criteria of incompetency to focus on functional limitations rather than mental illness, (2) the need for a "geriatric evaluation team" to screen cases to determine the least restrictive measures for adult protection, (3) the need to match the level of authority in guardianship with the level of the elder's incompetence, and (4) the need for a special office of public guardian to be instituted to provide for dependent elders who have no place else to turn. Underlying these guidelines is the advocacy client consent for services and an orientation toward the least restrictive measures in order to maintain the elder's personal rights. The legal system needs to be less drastic in its protective measures and more flexible in its provisions for the personal liberty of the older person.

Professional Orientation:
- Medicine

Type of Exposition:
- Position Paper

Substantive Issues:
- Identification
- Treatment
- Family Dynamics

111 Renvoize, Jean. "Granny bashing." In: Renvoize, Jean. <u>Web of Violence</u>. London, England: Routledge and Kegan Paul, 1978. <u>113-27.</u> (Bibliography).

TOPIC: The subject of this discussion is on elder abuse by family members.

OBJECTIVES: The purpose of this review is to discuss elder abuse, the various situations in which it is encountered, and the factors contributing to and increasing the likelihood of abuse.

METHODS: Because of a lack of research on elder abuse, the discussion is largely structured around comments from geriatricians, a pathologist, and a female caretaker of a blind, elderly family member.

CONCLUSIONS: Abuse prevention measures include the need for the older person to maintain good health and strategies for the elder to remain in the community as opposed to hospitalization. If elderly family members would seek medical treatment for problems which have been traditionally attributed to old age such as deafness, incontinence, or locomotion, then the burden to caretaking families could be greatly diminished. Caring for an elderly person is a major undertaking for any family and becomes more difficult with increasing dependency. Many of the caregivers may now be older and be less well-equipped to provide care. The family's burdens and the potential for abuse could be reduced if they had some respite one or two days a week or for a few weeks annually for a family vacation. Older members also need to have comfort and privacy in the family household. Finally, researchers, practitioners, and the public need to plan for the future as the elderly population increases. Making the lives of older persons and their families more meaningful will greatly reduce elder abuse.

Professional Orientation:
- Nursing

Type of Exposition:
- Survey Research

Substantive Issue:
- Treatment

112 Reynolds, Elizabeth, and Stanton, Sheila. "Elderly abuse in a hospital: A nursing perspective." In: Kosberg, Jordan I., ed. Abuse and maltreatment of the elderly: Causes and interventions. Littleton, Massachusetts: John Wright, PSG Inc., 1983. 391-403. (6 References).

TOPIC: The central issue of this chapter is the role of the nurse in cases of elder abuse.

OBJECTIVE: The goal of this chapter is to present the findings of a study of nurses' involvement in cases of elder abuse and strategies nurses can use in order to take a more effective role in the identification and treatment of elder abuse.

METHOD: An exploratory study was conducted in south and central Florida by means of a mailed questionnaire to 500 members of the Emergency Department Nurses Association. Some 206 responses were received which produced a response rate of 40.2%.

FINDINGS: The results of the survey show that 89% of the nurses are aware of the problem of abuse and 83% were able to recognize situations of abuse including its various forms: physical, psychological, material, violation of rights, and others. The survey also shows that while 83% of the emergency room nurses have observed elder abuse, only 36% have reported cases to some other authority.

CONCLUSIONS: Nurses are in a key position to be advocates for the elderly. They can serve as role models of caring as well as educate others about the need to treat the elderly "with dignity and respect." This role can be enacted in a number of nursing settings. In the hospital, the nurse should develop a nursing care plan which involves the patients' total needs rather than just physical problems alone. Interviewing the patient is an important means of gaining information about the social history of the older person. An assessment then can be made about the conditions for and kinds of abuse which may occur. Once the patient is admitted, protective and preventive measures can be used including discharge planning, patient education about health care needs, reporting cases of abuse to the appropriate authority and being informed about community services available to the elderly and their families.

Nurses in community settings such as visiting nurses, those in public health and outpatient clinics are also in a position to identify elder abuse and help families develop preventive measures.

The Association of South Florida Nurse Educators has already begun the task of informing nurses in 13 hospitals about the important role they can play in elder abuse.

Professional Orientation:
- Social Work

Type of Exposition:
- Clinical Observations

Substantive Issue:
- Treatment

113 Riley, Patrick V. "The family approach to abuse." In: First National Conference on Abuse of Older Persons, Cambridge, Massachusetts, March, 1981. Conference Proceedings. Boston, Massachusetts: Legal Research and Services for the Elderly, 1981. (0 References).

TOPIC: The presentation describes a treatment program called Family Service Association of Greater Boston which provides a variety of services to families involved in abuse and neglect of older persons.

OBJECTIVE: The presentation is designed to show just how the Family Service Association of Greater Boston provides help for neglecting and abusing families.

METHOD: The author relates the experiences of this organization in the management of abuse and neglect.

CONCLUSIONS: Intervention strategies to protect older persons are family centered, and staff members respond to both the needs of the victim and the abuser. A common feature in both neglect and abuse cases is the fact that there is "usually" a strong relational bond between the elderly victim and the caretaking abuser. This makes it necessary to work with both parties.

Careful diagnostic assessment must be undertaken, including a medical work-up. Abusers are informed that their actions are being monitored by a network of family, friends, and helping agents; but in the last analysis, the best treatment for the victim is to meet both the needs of the victim and the abuser.

Professional Orientation:
- Medicine

Type of Exposition:
- Survey Research

Substantive Issues:
- Types
- Treatment
- Professional Responsibility

114 Roe, P.F. "Self-neglect." Age and Ageing 6(3):192-4, August, 1977. (1 Reference).

TOPIC: Gross self-neglect cases in a hospital geriatric unit in Britain are discussed.

OBJECTIVE: The purpose of this research is to determine whether hospital admission of elderly self-neglect patients has an adverse effect on their survival and quality of life.

METHODS: Hospital admissions records from a five-year period were reviewed retrospectively to identify patients who met A.A. Baker's definition of self-neglect. Only 25 cases could be found which matched the definition. There were 11 men and 14 women between the ages of 66 and 93 in this sample. Hospital admission was based on a variety of reasons.

FINDINGS: Some 64% of the 25 cases identified were eventually discharged, while 36% died or were still hospitalized and diagnosed as terminally ill. Mortality for the first three weeks was 12% in this study compared with 25% in the Baker research. The quality of life of 15 patients was assessed as good and seven subjects were judged to have a poor quality of life. No clear assessment could be made on the remaining three patients.

CONCLUSIONS: This research tends to contradict the findings of Baker. These discrepancies may be due to the fact that Baker's unit was a psychiatric, not a geriatric unit. The difference in patients and services could account for the contradictory findings.

Although this study was rather unscientific and used a small sample, it shows that the majority of the 25 patients experienced a good quality of life while in the hospital. Some individuals who are self-neglecting, who are not a nuisance to others, and who do not wish to be admitted to the hospital should have the choice not to be hospitalized. However, other self-neglecting persons should be encouraged to be hospitalized because their quality of life may be enhanced.

Professional Orientation:
- Social Work
Type of Exposition:
- Review
Substantive Issue:
- Laws

115 Salend, Elyse; Kane, Rosalie A.; Satz, Maureen; *et al*. "Elder abuse reporting: Limitations of statutes." *Gerontologist* 24(1):61-69. February, 1984. (19 References).

TOPIC: This article includes a review of 16 elder abuse reporting laws in the United States which were passed between 1973 and 1980.

OBJECTIVES: The goals of this report are to compare these 16 laws in the areas of content and implementation, and to evaluate their effectiveness in protecting victims of elder abuse.

METHODS: Data were gathered from three sources: the content of the 16 statutes, telephone interviews with one administrator from each state who was responsible for the implementation of the statute, and telephone interviews with one or more Adult Protective Services supervisors in each state's largest city.

CONCLUSIONS: Each of the 16 states "varied widely in purpose, coverage, implementation agency, registry requirements, mandated reporters and reporting requirements, immunity provisions, confidentiality provisions, and mandated investigation or service components." Target populations were not uniform from state to state, neither were definitions of key terms such as abuse, neglect and exploitation. Reporting procedures varied in the areas of who reported, how the report was made, and whether penalties for non-reporting were institued. However, immunity for reporters and confidentiality of case records were fairly uniform from state to state. Follow-up practices were also dissimilar. Funding, involuntary service, emergency service, and guardianship were among these differential provisions. There was, however, a "least restrictive alternative" clause in most states which guarded against automatic institutionalization of those identifed as abused.

Interviews with those implementing these statutes and supervisors in Adult Protective Services reveal that the methods used to bring elder abuse to the attention of state legislators also varied. In most states, there was no needs assessment conducted. Instead, the reporting of cases prompted Adult Protective Service workers, Offices of Aging, Senior Citizens groups, and similar groups to press for legislation.

A review of the information on cases of elder abuse as a consequence of the reporting mechanism in the various states, produced vague, undeveloped, or incomplete records. Funding, a lack of treatment options, and a lack of procedures to substantiate actual cases played a role in creating barriers to the implementation of statutes. The service delivery system also suffered from lack of resources, underdeveloped legal procedures, uncooperative families and abused elders, and inadequate preparation to deal with cases of elder abuse.

There are conflicting viewpoints in the literature about whether mandatory elder abuse reporting laws are effective in protecting victims. In light of this, "a first step is raising the consciousness of those in a position to observe active problems." Professionals most likely to come in contact with the elderly should be experienced in assessment and treatment alternatives. Since there is the danger that elder abuse laws could lead to more elder vulnerability through infantilization, these statutes need to be more carefully examined for intent and consequence.

Professional Orientation:
- Social Work

Type of Exposition:
- Review

Substantive Issue:
- Laws

116 Salend, Elyse; Satz, Maureen; Pynoos, Jon. "Mandatory reporting legislation for adult abuse." In: First National Conferences on Abuse of Older Persons, Cambridge, Massachusetts, March, 1981. Conference Proceedings. Boston, Massachusetts: Legal Research and Services for the Elderly, 1981. 7p. (0 References).

TOPIC: The presentation summarizes the parameters of elder abuse legislation in both written and tabular form.

OBJECTIVE: The authors wish to point out the variations in elder abuse legislation among the states.

METHODS: The presentation is a review by the Senate Select Committee on Aging, March 1980 report of the essential statutes among those states which have some form of elder abuse legislation.

FINDINGS: Elder abuse reporting and intervention legislation arose out of a need to protect the elders who are incapacitated or incompetent. Most states have adult protective services: 26 states have adult protective legistlation and 16 states have reporting legislation for adult and elder abuse. Most of the reporting legislation has been passed in the last 5 years. Much of the legislation is patterned after child abuse legislation, but the intent in cases of elder abuse is "to identify and protect incapacitated adults and elders who are victims of self-neglect or maltreatment by others." Although domestic violence legislation has increased, the statutes do not necessarily address the special problems of the elderly. There is wide variation among the states in the areas of definitions of abuse, reporting and service delivery.

At this reporting, the UCLA/USC Long Term Care Gerontology Center is finishing a study of designs and implementations of elder abuse legislation. The objective is to provide policy recommendations for improving interventions. In addition, the national legislation proposed in HR 7551 would be a valuable resource to the states, should it pass.

Preceeding the table which specifies the provisions for the 16 states in which there is some form of elder abuse legislation is a brief review of subjects not presented in the chart. These issues include: immunity, report contents, confidentiality, privileged information, other agency involvement, least resistance alternative, geriatric evaluation team, and religious provisions. These eight issues serve as reminders of the complexities in elder abuse legislation.

Professional Orientation:
- Social Work

Type of Exposition:
- Congressional Briefing

Substantive Issues:
- Laws
- Policy

117 Satz, Maureen. Prepared Statement and Attachment, "Mandatory reporting legislation for adult abuse." Physical and Financial Abuse of the Elderly, Appendix 2. Hearing of the Select Committee on Aging, House of Representatives, April 3, 1981. San Francisco, California: U.S. Government Printing Office, 1981. 139-163, (0 References).

TOPIC: This statement reports on the findings of the Long Term Care Gerontology Center at UCLA/USC in a study of mandatory reporting legislation for elder abuse.

OBJECTIVE: The goal of this study was to analyze "the design and implementation of mandatory reporting legislation for adult abuse and protective services in sixteen states."

METHODS: Data were obtained from a survey of state Adult Protective Services department adminstrators, State Departments of Aging, and supervisors of social workers in these departments.

FINDINGS: Data from the survey indicated that the number of reported abuse cases had increased and the service delivery to the victim had improved since mandatory reporting legislation was passed.

Findings from the survey indicate that a model reporting statute should include (1) provisions for a State Agency to implement the law, (2) a clear definition of what an abuse report is to contain and of those individuals whose abuse is protected by the law, (3) mandate-reporting for all individuals, (4) indications about who is covered, (5) guaranteed immunity for reporters who act in good faith, (6) confidentiality for all persons involved in the case, (7) penalties for those identified as abusers, (8) clearly defined terms such as abuse and the nature of protective services, (9) a central state registry provided to maintain all records, (10) additional provisions for emergency intervention, (11) due process safeguards to protect the victim's right to refuse services, (12) assessment by a geriatric evaluation team, and (13) funding for a protective services system which is also important for a successful mandatory reporting system.

CONCLUSION: The statute must be tied to adult protective service programs in order to be effective. Also, adult protective service systems can only be effective if the agency is equipped to respond to cases. Finally, effectiveness in implementation can be increased by professional and public education.

Professional Orientation:
- Sociology

Type of Exposition:
- Survey Research

Substantive Issues:
- Identification
- Scope
- Barriers

118 Sengstock, Mary C. and Barrett, Sara. "Techniques of identifying abused elders." Paper presented at the twelfth meeting of the International Congress of Gerontology, Hamburg, Germany: July, 1981. 12p. (15 References).

TOPIC: This paper focuses on ways professionals identify elder abuse and what problems may arise in the identification process.

METHODS: A questionnaire was mailed to 302 service agencies in the Detroit metropolitan area in order to determine the prevalence and characteristics of elder abuse. Some 100 responded, 25 of which had active cases during February, 1981 (the designated time). There were 258 cases reported during a one-month period which could represent a total of 1,032 elder abuse cases each year.

FINDINGS: Following a review of the literature which pointed out some of the problems in identification, the results of the survey were reported. The data showed that agencies used several means for identification from victim self-report to referrals from dentists. Most of the agencies observed that at least two symptoms were present in cases which were identified as elder abuse.

It was also determined that "agencies often overlook abusive situations among their aged clients." There were six reasons given for this problem. First, victims can be successful in preventing discovery even when the professional has been involved with the family for some time. Second, agencies reported what is also found in the literature, that elders do not report abuse because of their attachment to and dependence on abusers. A third problem in identification comes from the fact that "victims themselves often fail to recognize their predicament." Fourth, there is the problem of awareness of abuse on the part of the agency worker. The focus may be on correcting a problem such as malnutrition without looking for the source of the problem. A fifth barrier to identifying elder abuse is the consequence of agency specialization. Not only do agencies tend to see only a small number of older persons, but they also tend to focus on their area of expertise -- the medical profession on physical abuse and social work on financial abuse. And sixth, a fear of litigation against the professional or agency should they misidentify a case of elder abuse prevents some from identifying suspected cases. As a consequence of these limitations, we must conclude "that abuse of the elderly is a much more pervasive problem than available data would lead us to believe."

Professional Orientation:
- Sociology

Type of Exposition:
- Survey Research

Substantive Issues:
- Varieties
- Treatment
- Family Dynamics
- Social Structure

119 Sengstock, Mary C; Barrett, Sara; Graham, Robert. "Abused elders: Victims of villains or of circumstances?" Paper presented at the thirty-fifth annual meeting of the Gerontological Society of America. Boston, Massachusetts: November, 1982. 18p. (17 References).

TOPIC: The authors report on victims' assessments of causes for elder abuse.

METHODS: The Wayne State University Institute of Gerontology collected data on elder abuse from Detroit Metropolitan Area social service and health agencies. The project was supported by the NRTA-AARP Andrus Foundation. Mailed questionnaires and interviews were used. From the 77 cases which were identified, 20 victims of elder abuse were interviewed. Trained interviewers asked questions about demographics of the older person, family relationships, and attitudes toward stress and conflict. The Holmes and Rahe Social Readjustment Rating scale was used to measure victim and family stress.

FINDINGS: Most victims were older females. Half were black and half were white. Most were victims of psychological abuse, although they also suffered from other forms of abuse. Most of the abusers were sons or daughters of the victim. Victim and family stress was confirmed by the fact that most came from settings in which there were many problems. Scores from elder abuse victims were compared with the Justice and Justice study on child abuse which contained both abusing and non-abusing parents: The results showed that there was a significant difference in stress between non-child abuse families and child-abusing families. However, the scores for abused elders were even higher than abused children, but not significantly different. When asked to indicate three of the most serious problems the victims had experienced in the last month, most did not mention the abuse. It may be that victims realized that the abuse was simply a symptom of even greater problems which provoked the abuse. Problems mentioned included having no friends, a dirty house, and a critical landlord.

CONCLUSIONS: Resolution of the problem of elder abuse cannot be achieved by blaming the abuser. Abusers are often victims of circumstance who need as much help as the abused. Better intervention procedures are needed to protect the abused, to counsel the abuser, and to develop methods to help the family deal with problems which seem to lead to abuse. Finally, it is important to maintain a service delivery system which is able to keep pace with environmental circumstances which may create more problems for families during certain periods.

Professional Orientation:
- Sociology

Type of Exposition:
- Research Methods

Substantive Issues:
- Types
- Varieties
- Identification
- Family Dynamics

120 Sengstock, Mary C; Hwalek, Melanie; Barrett, Sara. "Content analysis of measures for identification of elder abuse." Paper presented at The Gerontological Society of America thirty-sixth annual meeting, San Francisco, California: November, 1983. 30p. (5 References).

TOPIC: The authors analyse the nature, scope and clarity of items used in several current elder abuse identification instruments.

METHODS: A content analysis of seven elder abuse identification indices is performed in order to statistically and qualitatively analyse how each item taps a particular form of elder abuse. These indices are supplemented by 12 child abuse indices and four sources from the legal literature. A panel of judges made up of staff members from the Institute of Gerontology at Wayne State University rated items from these sources in the following areas: (1) type of abuse measured, (2) the degree to which the item was an important indicator of abuse, (3) whether the item was clearly understood, and (4) other limitations as identifiers of elder neglect and abuse.

CONCLUSIONS: Elder abuse items are divided into seven types of abuse: physical abuse, physical neglect, psychological abuse, psychological neglect, material abuse, violation of rights, and risk indicators.

Overall, most items in both the elder abuse and child abuse literature identification measures represent risk indicators rather than specific determinants of abuse. The summary data on the item by item comparisons on types of abuse show that physical neglect and abuse are the most frequently represented items although these constitute less than 20% of the items for both elder abuse and child abuse measures. The remaining four categories of elder abuse and child abuse are negligible. Researchers like Block and Sinnott have found that psychological abuse and neglect is the most prevalent type of abuse. However, the identification items developed thus far have not tapped this type of abuse.

Qualitative analysis of the items in the identification measures show that the meaning of items is not clear and that items do not always focus on a single variable. In the area of physical abuse of elders, some major limitations in the items involve the absence of items on sexual abuse, the heavy dependence on the elder for indentification of the abuse, and the failure to clearly distinguish physical abuse from signs of normal aging. The major problem with items on psychological abuse is their lack of specificity. It appears that service providers would need to know much more about family interaction before psychological abuse could be identified. The same limitations may be found in psychological neglect. Here, too, psychological neglect may be confused with normal aging. Material abuse and violation of rights are not very clearly distinguished from one another and even harder to assess using those few items which do appear in elder abuse identification measures. Finally, risk indicators are evaluated. These types of items comprise more than half of the items among the identification indices. These indicators use family situations and characteristics of possible victims and caretakers.

In sum, current identification measures reveal the need for better techniques in (1) better identification of the types of abuse, (2) distinguishing types of abuse, (3) clarity of meaning of the items, (4) techniques for identifying the source of information, (5) identifying key information from case histories and observations, and (6) separating the phenomena of normal aging from actual elder neglect and abuse.

Professional Orientation:
- Sociology

Type of Exposition:
- Survey Research

Substantive Issues:
- Characteristics
- Family Dynamics
- Identification
- Treatment
- Professional Responsibility

121 Sengstock, Mary C. and Liang, Jersey. Identifying and characterizing elder abuse. Detroit, Michigan: Institute of Gerontology, Wayne State University, February, 1982. 144p. (81 References).

TOPIC: The authors conducted a study on elder abuse in Detroit, Michigan by interviewing service delivery agencies and victims.

OBJECTIVES: Five research questions comprised the objectives. In summary form, they include profiles of abused, abusers and family situations; dynamics of elder abuse; methods of identification; treatment; and prevention.

METHODS: Data were gathered in five phases. First, questionnaires were mailed to 302 agencies in the Detroit area which might have been involved in elder abuse cases. There were 108 agency responses, representing a response rate of 36%. Second, interviews were conducted with the 25 agencies which reported having had cases of elder abuse. These 25 agencies suggested an additional 20. Therefore, a total of 45 agencies were contacted and asked to describe their experience with elder abuse cases. The third phase consisted of securing information from these agencies on 77 cases of elder abuse. The fourth phase involved interviewing 20 of the 77 victims of elder abuse. The remaining 57 were not interviewed for a variety of reasons ranging from confidentiality to refusal to be interviewed. Finally, 50 persons age 60 or older who had not been abused were interviewed and served as a control group.

FINDINGS: Interviews with agencies involved with elder abuse cases were used to establish characteristics of the abused, abusers and family circumstances. Most of the victims lived in the central city with one other person or alone, had limited social contacts, were female, had low incomes, and were Protestant. They were evenly divided between blacks and whites and distributed fairly evenly in age. Abusers tended to be either sons or daughters in middle age or older. Sexes of the abusers were fairly evenly divided. The results suggest "the tensions of intergenerational living and caring for an aged parent" may be a major cause for elder abuse.

In looking for abuse incidents in particular, the most frequently reported type was psychological. Physical abuse and neglect were least frequently reported. There was also a correlation between the type of abuse and the relative involved. For example, sons were more likely to be engaged in direct abuse, while daughters were reported to have been involved in psychological abuse. Overall, abusive families seemed to be multi-problem families, and violence in the past had been common. These families did not wish to seek outside help, although their problems seemed to merit it. Typical of family situations were mental illness, substance abuse and financial problems.

With regard to agency involvement with cases of elder abuse, services were uneven. Reporting tended to be higher for workers who considered elder abuse a major problem. Priority of issue was correlated with the number of cases reported. There was also a correlation between the type of agency and the kind of abuse reported. Cases came to the attention of the agencies most frequently through the self-report of the victims. However, there were several barriers to identification of elder abuse. These ranged from inadequate staff to a reticence of staff to infringe on family privacy.

CONCLUSIONS: There are four recommendations for ways agencies can improve services to victims of elder abuse. There is a need to define a clear set of symptoms which characterize abuse, better preparation by workers in the areas of identification, awareness of the spectrum of services available, and standardization of agency services, both within agencies and among them.

Professional Orientation:
- Drama Director

Type of Exposition:
- Plays

Substantive Issues:
- Type
- Family Dynamics

122 Shroeder, Judith D. "Can you help me, Hannah?" Five plays presented by the OWLS Theatre group in connection with the Elderly Abuse Program, Providence, Rhode Island. 1981. 12p. (0 References).

TOPIC: The central focus of the plays is elder abuse by family members.

METHOD: Through the medium of drama, the plays point up five illustrations of elder abuse.

CONCLUSIONS: The first vignette entitled "Can You Help Me, Hannah?" depicts an older woman whose adult child takes her social security checks, confines her to the attic, isolates her from contact with others, and is physically abusive when the older woman attempts to assert herself. The short play called "Ed and Grace" describes a self-abusive elderly husband who has not been able to manage some of the losses he has experienced and has turned to alcohol. His wife is also a casualty. During his bouts of drinking, he is psychologically and physically abusive toward his wife. Vignette three entitled, "The Patient" is about an elderly parent who is threatened with physical abuse by her son if she does not help him maintain his drug habit. The fourth short play entitled "The Park" describes non-family abuse by teenagers in the community. The elder relates that he is living alone, his children live elsewhere, and he now needs the support of friends or acquaintances in the community to protect him against these kinds of attacks by strangers. Finally, the play called "The Parents" concludes the vignettes. An older couple have given their daughter their home and have turned over their bank account to her. In return, they suffer from her family's neglect and psychological abuse.

Professional Orientation:
- Social Work

Type of Exposition:
- Discussion

Substantive Issue:
- Laws

123 Smith, Sharon. "Domestic violence act: Application and implications towards elder abuse." In: Schultz, Leroy G. ed. Elder abuse in West Virginia: A policy analysis of system response. Morgantown, West Virginia: West Virginia University, 1983. 6p. (3 References).

TOPIC: Current West Virginia laws are insufficient to insure that services are being provided to all the abused elders who need them and who are legally entitled to them.

OBJECTIVE: The author wishes to promote filling the "cracks" that now exist in the current system of providing services to abused elders.

METHODS: The essay looks at the laws pertaining to elder abuse and explains how current procedure often circumvents those needy persons the law intends to help. The author then recommends a number of ways of dealing with this problem.

CONCLUSIONS: The Domestic Violence Act of the State of West Virginia gives authority to provide services to all abused elders; but this is not being done because (1) criteria for services apply primarily to incapacitated elders and it is not clear who is responsible for capacitated elders, and (2) Domestic Violence Centers can choose whom they will and will not admit. They tend to favor abused women and their young children because they assume they do not have the facilities required for the "special" needs of the elderly. To remedy this situation (1) these centers should be mandated to service all victims of domestic violence as the Domestic Violence Act states, (2) the Department of Welfare should be required to serve both capacitated and incapacitated elder abuse victims, (3) Domestic Violence Centers should provide counseling to all types of abusers, (4) where the problem is alcohol-related, the abuser should be referred to the relevant state agency, (5) places should be provided for both male and female victims of elder abuse in existing shelters provided by the Y.M.C.A., the Salvation Army, and other facilities, and (6) the Domestic Violence Centers should be required to do further research on the needs of the elderly abused and how they can be met.

Professional Orientation:
- Medicine

Type of Exposition:
- Training Guide

Substantive Issues:
- Treatment
- Attitudes

124 Solomon, Kenneth. "Intervention for the victimized elderly and sensitization of health professionals: Therapeutic and Educational Efforts." In: Kosberg, Jordan I., ed. Abuse and maltreatment of the elderly: Causes and interventions. Littleton, Massachusetts: John Wright, PSG, Inc., 1983. 404-21. (58 References).

TOPIC: This chapter focuses on the role of the health care professional and the management of therapeutic needs of victims of elder abuse and their families.

OBJECTIVE: The goal is to make health care providers aware of therapeutic treatment options for the victim and family, and then raise consciousness about the abusiveness of ageism.

METHOD: This chapter is organized as a training guide for health care providers, offering step by step programs and educational courses.

CONCLUSIONS: Whether just the victim or the family is involved, the crisis intervention process is similar. In addition to pharmacological treatment which may be indicated for the victim, victims are encouraged to talk about difficulties, reverse the helplessness they feel, learn mastery of the situation, and then begin to remove the stress. The same prescription can be used with family members. In long-term intervention, older persons are often more motivated than younger individuals to change because of life-experience and the recognition that the number of years they have left are declining.

Geriatric and gerontological curricula are needed to teach health care providers, including adult protective service workers, about normative aging disorders which may occur among the elderly and methods for handling these cases; also ways to counteract the negative images of aging current in the society. A number of programs designed to understand aging and identify problems are reported. All of these programs provide some evidence that negative stereotypes of older persons can be changed through the educational process. In order to demonstrate what health care providers need to know in order to effectively serve victimized elderly, a five module training course is thoroughly outlined.

Professional Orientation:
- Social Work

Type of Exposition:
- Position Paper

Substantive Issues:
- Treatment
- Professional Responsibility
- Laws
- Policy

125 Sophos, Julie. "The practice of protective services: Definition and issues." In: Crouse, Joyce S.; Cobb, Deborah C.; Harris, Britta B,; _et al_. _Abuse and neglect of the elderly in Illinois: Incidence and characteristics, legislation, and policy recommendations_, Appendix A. Springfield, Illinois: Sangamon State University and Illinois Department on Aging. June 30, 1981. 16p. (14 References).

TOPIC: The author focuses on strategies adult protective services may use in helping victims of elder abuse and neglect.

OBJECTIVES: The goal is to examine the meaning of protective services and consider the application of protective services for abused older persons.

METHODS: The author proposes strategies to use to maximize protection under the law and prevention in the community. To support her position, she draws on literature in the field of adult protective services, elder abuse and neglect programs, and her own experiences in adult protective services.

CONCLUSIONS: Protective service workers should be advocates for the elderly as well as case managers and work with older persons as partners to develop treatment plans. Legal procedures with regard to elder abuse need to be carefully questioned. Under conditions which involve police in elder abuse cases, considerable care should be used so as not to threaten the family or jeopardize the service worker-client relationship. Also, caution ought to be used when considering removal of the elder from the home or whether guardianship should be used. The least restrictive alternative to treatment should be used whenever possible whatever the circumstances.

The literature suggests that the largest number of cases fall within the category of self-abuse/neglect and neglect by others. Therefore, it is important to focus on prevention of neglect. Alternative housing arrangements such as foster homes, shared homes, and emergency shelters need to be available to the elder victim of neglect and abuse. Other protective strategies include informed legal counsels who can respond appropriately to abuse, public awareness that the problem exists and places persons might go for help.

Model programs for protection and prevention of elder abuse and neglect have been developed in Illinois, Wisconsin, San Diego, Georgia, and Connecticut. While other states and cities could be included, those mentioned here provide examples of the varieties of programs which have been enacted.

Professional Orientation:
- Sociology

Type of Exposition:
- Survey Research

Substantive Issues:
- Family Dynamics
- Cultural Patterns
- Treatment
- Social Structure

Steinmetz, Suzanne K. "Dependency, stress, and violence between middle-aged caregivers and their elderly parents." In: Kosberg, Jordan I., ed. Abuse and maltreatment of the elderly: Causes and interventions. Littleton, Massachusetts: John Wright, PSG, Inc., 1983. 134-49. (24 References).

TOPIC: The chapter focuses on problems experienced by both older persons and their caregiving adult children as they confront the aging process and elder care.

OBJECTIVE: The purpose of the study reported in this chapter was to determine the "stresses, conflicts, abuse and maltreatment experienced in families who cared for an elderly parent."

METHOD: Adult child caregivers were solicited through the media, through information packets sent to agencies serving elder persons, and by means of personal contact with aging services which work with minority groups. This search for volunteers produced a non-representative sample of 77 adult children who cared for 103 dependent elders. Respondents were interviewed on tape by students and a medical social worker. Questions were designed to elicit three pieces of information: (1) a description of tasks performed for dependent elders, (2) caregiver stress assessments of those tasks, and (3) techniques used by elders and caregivers to resolve interpersonal problems.

FINDINGS: Increased life expectancy impacts on the whole family life cycle. When the aging process causes elder dependency, caregiver stress is likely to occur. Unless resources are available to counteract the stress, it may manifest itself in elder abuse or neglect. Analysis of the data from the 77 interviews shows the relationship among dependency, stress and elder mistreatment.

Both caregivers and carereceivers tend to be women, most caregivers are older (i.e., age 55+), and violence is directed both ways -- from the caregiver to the dependent elderly and from the dependent elderly to the caregiver. Finally, caregivers are caught in the middle between two generations and find it hard to set priorities on which generation needs them the most.

Interviews revealed considerable dependence on adult caregivers by their elders with instrumental household tasks being the least stressful for the caregiver to perform. On the other hand, expressive tasks such as social-emotional support were the most stressful. When conflicts arose between the adult child and the dependent elder, the most frequently used techniques by the caregiver was talking, which included a loud voice and shouting. Older persons were most likely to use pouting and withdrawal as their way to resolve conflicts. An interesting finding regarding physical abuse showed that older persons are 18 times more likely to use physical abuse toward their caregivers than the caregiver is to use this form of conflict resolution on the older person.

CONCLUSIONS: The media may distort the profile of the abuser by characterizing that individual as wanting to deliberately abuse or neglect the older person. It may be that the demands of a multigenerational family militate against adequate elder care. Another factor which produces stress for the elder is the value the society places on independence. Dependence signals failure. When the aging elder experiences dependence, it is hard to adjust to this condition. In some cases adjustment is also difficult because parent-child conflicts from former times (when the child was in the dependent role) have still not been resolved.

Service providers are needed to help elders adjust to their dependent role, to help caregivers learn how to "parent" their dependent elders, and to provide services which will reduce caregiver stress. While instrumental assistance like chore services are helpful, the data show that social-emotional and mental health services, such as the friendly visitor and respite care, are even more important in reducing caregiver stress.

Professional Orientation:
- Sociology

Type of Exposition:
- Survey Research

Substantive Issues:
- Family Dynamics
- Types

127 Steinmetz, Suzanne K. "Elder abuse." Aging 315-16:6-10, January/February, 1981. (12 References).

TOPIC: The author describes abuse of the elderly by their caregiver children.

OBJECTIVE: The goal of the research was to gather information on the circumstances promoting elder abuse by interviewing adult child caregivers of older family members.

METHODS: Data were gathered in the spring of 1980 from 60 adult child caregivers of older persons by means of in-depth structural interviews. They responded to newspaper ads and notices at senior centers. A snowball technique of asking respondents to suggest others who might be eligible was also used. Therefore, respondents constituted a volunteer, non-representative sample who were diverse in economic backgrounds and social class.

FINDINGS: A number of problems unique to elder abuse were highlighted in the interviews. First, older people were reluctant to acknowledge abuse because of the stigma and guilt they expressed about their own children abusing them. A second dilemma involved the fact that women bear the major role in caregiving and are also found to be the most vulnerable to abuse, thus experiencing a kind of double jeopardy, because they are female. Third, there was a tendency for adult caregivers to be elderly themselves which, in turn, made elder care more difficult and problematic. A fourth dilemma rested with the fact that violence in the family can be double-directional. Parents can be just as abusive to their adult caregiving children as their children are to them. Finally, caregivers often faced double demands when they were involved in intergenerational family maintenance, such as child care and elder care at the same time.

CONCLUSIONS: Family care for older members may arise from love or responsibility. The growing dependency of the elder, increased caregiver strain and a lack of family support services leads to frustration and greater vulnerability of older persons. Elder abuse may be the consequence. Understanding this form of family violence is a problem which most of us will have to address at some point. Therefore, national attention needs to be focused on elder abuse so that researchers and practitioners can gather data, share knowledge, and move toward developing policy for comprehensive elder care.

Professional Orientation:
- Sociology

Type of Exposition:
- Congressional Briefing

Substantive Issues:
- Varieties
- Family Dynamic

128 Steinmetz, Suzanne K. Prepared statement for the Select Committee on Aging, U.S. House of Representatives, Ninety-Sixth Congress, First Session. June 23, 1979, Boston, Massachusetts. Elder abuse: The hidden problem, Washington, D.C.: U.S. Government Printing Office, 1980. 7-10. (0 References).

TOPIC: The author discusses family dynamics and elder abuse.

OBJECTIVE: The author's goal is to emphasize the need to examine the interpersonal relationships between the generations involved in caretaking for an elderly family member.

METHODS: Case histories of elder abuse and parallels with spouse and child abuse substantiate this statement's discussion.

CONCLUSIONS: Similarities between child and elderly parent abuse are discussed. Also discussed is the assumption that in our society families love and support all family members. However, families must face the stresses that a dependent child or elderly adult places on them. This stress can lead to abuse. The probability for abuse is further increased by the recent growth in the elderly population who live beyond economically productive years.

Even if the relationship between a caregiving child and a dependent parent is a positive one, caretaking families need resources to aid them in meeting the demands of caring for the elderly. Resources suggested include meals on wheels, homemakers, day care, financial assistance, education, counseling, and support groups.

Professional Orientation:
- Sociology

Type of Exposition:
- Survey Research

Substantive Issues:
- Causal Factors
- Family Dynamics

129 Steinmetz, Suzanne K., and Amsden, Deborah J. "Dependent elders, family stress, and abuse." In: Brubaker, Timothy H., ed. Family Relationships in Later Life. Beverly Hills, California: Sage Publications, Inc., 1983. 173-92. (38 References).

TOPIC: The authors examine the nature of caregiver and carereceiver relationships when elders become dependent in order to determine the level of stress, the assessment of caregiver burden, and the likelihood of abuse.

OBJECTIVES: There are three objectives in this chapter. "The goal of this study is to ascertain the relationship between dependency measured by the frequency with which tasks or services need to be provided for the elder, stress as perceived by the caregivers, and the abusive techniques utilized to gain or maintain control."

METHODS: A "snowball technique" was used to secure a nonrandom sample of 119 adult respondents. Print media was used to ask for volunteers who were middle-aged "child" caregivers living with and caring for an elderly parent. Out of the total, 104 were interviewed by means of structured and semistructured questions.

FINDINGS: Families are faced with a new form of intergenerational relationships -- generationally inverse relationships. Adult and older caregivers are caring for elderly and very old relatives who are dependent upon the family in some way. The care of dependent older family members can be stressful. Issues such as personal time, privacy, medical care of the elderly and financial strain illustrate the kinds of stressors families experience. However, there is another variable which must be included before abuse can be considered a possibility. Burden is defined as the subjective perception of the situation and can be an ameliorator of caregiver stress. How the individual perceives the dependency may be a more important predictor of abuse than stress itself. Finally, abuse in family settings can be in both directions -- caregiver abuse and carereceiver abuse.

The study of dependency, stress and abuse represented a sample in which 91% of dependent elders were 70 years or older, 94% were cared for by women, and about 66% of the caregivers were above age 50. With regard to dependency, the elderly were dependent on family for (1) household management (99% of elderly), (2) grooming (70%), (3) mobility (61%), (4) financial management (90%), (5) social-emotional needs (98%), and (6) mental health needs, (94%). Fifteen stressors were presented to adult caregivers. The least stressful condition was the older person's trying to maintain an authority role in the family and the most stressful was the elder's loneliness. Respondents were also asked whether they felt burdened or not. The results show that neither the tasks performed for the dependent elder nor the stress produced by the task were necessarily correlated with burdensomeness. "In fact, many more families report being stressed by some aspect of caregiving than they are burdened."

Conflict resolution techniques differed between caregivers and carereceivers. While adult children used talking as their major strategy (83%), older relatives pouted or withdrew (60%). Nineteen other strategies fall somewhere in between.

Drawing the four variables of dependency, stress, burden and abuse together, social-emotional and mental health dependency were the most stressful, burdensome and were "strongly (and significantly) correlated" with abuse.

CONCLUSION: Dependency can lead to stress, burden and abuse. Families need to understand the aging process in order to make the adult/elder communication process more effective. Caring for the dependent elderly is not an easy task. "There is a point when even the most dedicated, loving child is ill-equipped to deal with personal grooming, physical, social-emotional, and mental health needs of an elderly parent." Support services in the community can help relieve stress and burden and, create better communication between the caregiver and carereceiver.

Professional Orientation:
- Psychologist

Type of Exposition:
- Review

Substantive Issues:
- Causal Factors
- Theory
- Family Dynamics
- Professional Responsibility
- Characteristics

130 Steuer, Joanne L. "Abuse of the physically disabled elderly." In: Kosberg, Jordan I., ed. <u>Abuse and maltreatment of the elderly: Causes and interventions</u>. Littleton, Massachusetts: John Wright, PSG Inc., 1983. 234-50. (42 References).

TOPIC: The author discusses why the physically impaired elderly may be victims of elder abuse.

OBJECTIVE: This discussion of elder disability looks for possible causes for abuse in a variety of contexts - the characteristics of the illness, the individual, the caregiver and the society.

METHOD: Several disabling illnesses are reviewed and individual and family responses are evaluated in order to identify factors which may lead to abuse.

CONCLUSIONS: Some physical events likely to lead to disability are stroke, diabetes, arthritis and various kinds of injuries. Responses to disability come both from the victims and the caregivers and, therefore, practitioners need to consider the adaptability of both parties. The most important factor in the individual's response is one's perception of the loss of functioning which, in turn, is determined by demographic characteristics such as sex, age and socio-economic status. Data on families' responses concerning disabled elders are limited. However, what is available points to the kinds of stresses on caregivers which may errupt into violence. These include lack of social support, "changes in the homemaking, recreational, and vocational activities of the caregiver," and the overall changes in their life style as a result of the caregiving function. It is important to note that disability is not necessarily correlated with stress in the caregiver. The critical factors are the level and stress reduction through external family support.

Some of the social circumstances which contribute to elder abuse are that women are likely to be both the abused and the abuser. Other factors such as the cycle of violence, unresolved conflict from the past, role reversal so that adult children care for their dependent parents, and the loss of power in the aging process point to the potential for abuse.

What is needed to help counteract abuse is in-depth research on abusing families and caregiver stress. In addition, for primary prevention, public information on community support programs and services for elder care needs to be made available, as well as information about how families could better care for their elder. Counseling should be offered to families who are considering care of older persons in order to assist them in making decisions.

More facilities should be offered to support caregivers, and social and medical health care professionals need to learn the signs for potential abuse. At risk families need to be counseled as well as families wherein the abuse has occurred. Legal intervention is also an option. However, family rights to privacy often prevent intervention.

Professional Orientation:
- Psychologist

Type of Exposition:
- Survey Research

Substantive Issues:
- Characteristics
- Types

131 Steuer, Joanne, and Austin, Elizabeth. "Family abuse of the elderly." <u>JAGS</u> 28(8):372-6, August, 1980. (8 References).

TOPIC: The authors describe the abuse of the disabled elderly by family members.

OBJECTIVE: The goal is to bring the problem of elder abuse by family members to the attention of health professionals and to offer possible methods of intervention and prevention.

METHOD: Findings were reported from a study of 12 cases of abuse of elderly victims identified as victims when they were hospitalized for an acute medical problem or who were visited by a social worker at the request of a home-care nursing service.

FINDINGS: The majority of the abused victims were women, ages 76 to 86, who had some form of physical or mental disability. Abuse tended to be either physical or verbal/psychological. Neglect was the most common form of abuse. In four of the cases, financial problems and established family conflicts or long-term strained family relationships appeared to contribute to the abuse.

CONCLUSIONS: Additional research is needed on elder abuse in the community and at the agency level. A major goal of that research should be to set standards of care for the elderly which are acceptable to private families, service agencies and local communities. Another focus for future study should be to establish guidelines for prevention which include public dissemination of resources available to the elderly. In addition, more facilities are needed for temporary relief for home caretakers.

Professional Orientation:
- Unidentified

Type of Exposition:
- Review

Substantive Issue:
- General

132 ______. "The elderly: Newest victims of familial abuse." JAMA. 243(12):1221-25. March 28, 1980. (0 References).

TOPIC: This review focuses on elder abuse by family members.

OBJECTIVE: This review summarizes findings on elder abuse research presented in a symposium at the Gerontological Society meeting in Washington, D.C. in 1979.

METHODS: The article reviews the results of findings from studies completed by Block & Sinnott at the University of Maryland's Center on Aging, Lau and Kosberg at Case Western Reserve University, and Douglass, Hickey and Noel at the University of Michigan.

FINDINGS: Block and Sinnott's findings agreed with Kosberg's that the abused elderly are often physically impaired and poor in health. However, Block and Sinnott found more cases of psychological abuse while Lau and Kosberg identified more physical abuse cases. Some reasons for abuse of the elderly shared by many symposium members were reverse abuse (child abuse changed to retaliation by adult child against the elder), the pressure that a family caretaker may feel being positioned between a dependent, elderly parent and demanding children, and unsolved parent/child conflicts. Discussion at the symposium also included methods to detect and intervene in elder abuse cases. Both of these areas are fraught with difficulties. Detection is not easy and intervention is not clear-cut.

Professional Orientation:
- Clinical Gerontologist

Type of Exposition:
- Clinical Observations

Substantive Issues:
- Types
- Professional Responsibility

133 Thibault, Jane M. "A developmental research design for the clinical treatment of indirect life-threatening behaviors in elderly patients." Paper presented at the fifth annual meeting of the Southern Gerontological Society. Knoxville, Tennessee: May, 1984. 11p. (1 Reference).

TOPIC: The author defines, illustrates, and explains the behavior known as indirect self-destructiveness in the elderly.

OBJECTIVES: The goal of the presentation is to alert health care professionals to the nature of the problem and to propose some techniques for therapeutic intervention.

METHODS: Patients who exhibited indirect self-destructive behavior, or ISDB, were observed by the author in a family practice setting in 1982. Three specific cases are used to illustrate varieties of ISDB.

FINDINGS: Some patients exhibit configurations of behavior which the author has identified as ISDB. Patients appear to be self-neglecting or present a history of ISDB, manifest an acute response to a chronic condition, have worried their families and friends, and tend to be relieved when hospitalized.

However, hospitalization as a result of the same acute condition (exacerbated by noncompliance with the physician's plan of care) may occur several times over the course of a year. Rehospitalization and the patient's resistance create a negative attitude toward the patient on the part of the hospital staff.

The hypothesis that the ISDB patients are suicidal was tested. Comparing interviews and psycho-social testing, the results showed that while this kind of behavior may lead to death in the patient, the underlying motive is not suicidal. This type of behavior may be nothing more than a problem-solving behavior where there are no other options, as illustrated by the two case examples of Mrs. A and Mr. C. On the other hand, ISDB may be an attempt to avoid a problem, as illustrated by Mrs. B. Or, finally, this behavior may be a way to call others' attention to one's problem. Instead of trying to destroy oneself, ISDB is a survival tactic.

CONCLUSIONS: Five therapeutic interventions which should be used by physicians include (1) the need to inquire about the reasons for the patient's noncompliant behavior, (2) the need to implement changes in the physical setting when the patient seems powerless to do it himself or herself, (3) the need to use other support persons to help the patient learn how to confront problems, (4) the need to encourage nursing personnel to offer positive reinforcement to the patient, and (5) the need to recognize that if the patient cannot constructively solve the problem, death may result.

Professional Orientation:
- Social Work

Type of Exposition:
- Training Guide

Substantive Issues:
- Identification
- Treatment

134 Tomita, Susan K. "Detection and treatment of elderly abuse and neglect: A protocol for health care professionals." Phys and Occ Ther Ger 2(2):37-51, Winter, 1982. (11 References).

TOPIC: The author describes an elder abuse protocol which may be used in a variety of settings by a variety of health care providers.

OBJECTIVE: The goal of this article is to show one group of health care providers (physical and occupational therapists) how they can detect elder abuse and educate patients and caregivers in order to reduce the incidence of abuse.

METHOD: The author describes how physical and occupational therapists might use the detection protocol developed at the Harborview Medical Center in the unit called the Harborview Senior Care Program.

CONCLUSIONS: The detection protocol developed by and used at the Harborview Medical Center is intended to improve "detection, assessment and documentation" of families at risk for elder abuse and families actually involved in elder abuse. A second value of the protocol is to help design intervention strategies. Referrals at Harborview come from emergency room chief of services, inpatient social workers, and communication with other staff who may have observed or have been told about the abuse. "This protocol is designed for use by all disciplines in geriatrics: physical therapy, occupational therapy, social work, nursing, and medicine." Physical therapists and occupational therapists are in an important position to detect abuse and can do so in a number of ways. However, the protocol assumes that three barriers must be surmounted (1) the professionals' denial that elder abuse is actually occuring among their patients, (2) the lack of a written case detection instrument, and (3) the absence of treatment options for the victim, perpetrator and the family.

Interventions may be either direct or indirect. Physical and occupational therapists can refer the patient to other agencies or carefully document abuse on the patient's chart as illustration of indirect intervention measures. Other staff involved in the care of the elderly must also record observations of suspected physical abuse. Direct interventions can only take place when the patient acknowledges the need for help. When this occurs, a number of plans of care can be developed, from assertiveness training to alternative living arrangements. Since family members are often the abusers, intervention must also involve them. After repeated visits to gather information about the family, a needs assessment is made. After the assessment is made, there are three types of family intervention -- a therapeutic plan, educational plan, resource linkage, or combinations of these three options.

Following the article is a sample of the detection protocol used at Harborview Medical Center including instructions for administering it.

Professional Orientation:
- Social Work

Type of Exposition:
- Training Guide

Substantive Issue:
- General

135 Tomita, Sue. Elder abuse and neglect training package. Seattle, Washington: Harborview Medical Center. 1983. 22p. (18 References).

TOPIC: The author presents a workshop outline to be used in the management of cases of elder abuse.

OBJECTIVES: In particular, workshop foci include (1) an awareness of the meaning and scope of elder abuse, (2) an understanding of how one diagnoses elder abuse, and (3) ways one might treat cases of elder abuse.

CONCLUSIONS: Six types of abuse are identified. These include physical abuse, psychological/verbal abuse, material abuse, neglect/omission, sexual abuse/assault, medication abuse and misuse. In addition, six studies are reviewed on the nature and scope of elder abuse. Most present a profile of the victim as female, over 75 and physically or mentally impaired. On the other hand, abusers tend to be relatives, especially spouses and children. Several causal factors are then reviewed.

Diagnosis should involve a check for some likely signs/symptoms of abuse, functional assessment of the patient, a physical exam, and observation of patient-caregiver relationship. Caregivers should also be interviewed to detect signs/symptoms of potential abuse such as stressors, lifestyle or behavior toward the patient. Then, the data from both the patient and caregiver are compared and an assessment is made. When abuse is diagnosed, a care plan includes further diagnosis, an educational plan for both victim and caregiver, and a therapeutic plan for both which is directed toward abuse resolution. Besides professional intervention, there are a host of natural helpers in the community who can provide various kinds of support. These include postal workers and grocery clerks as well as a number of others whose work brings them into contact with older members of the community.

Professional Orientation:
- Law

Type of Exposition:
- Training Manual

Substantive Issue:
- General

136 Villmoare, Edwin, and Bergman, James "Elder abuse and neglect: A guide for practitioners and policy makers." <u>Physical and Financial Abuse of the Elderly</u>. Appendix 1. Hearing of the Select Committee on Aging, House of Representatives, San Francisco, California: U.S. Government Printing Office, April 3, 1981. 57-134. (18 References).

TOPIC: This article serves as a manual for service providers and policy makers concerned with intervention protocol, protective services systems and legislation, and training for handling elder abuse cases.

OBJECTIVE: The current literature on elder abuse is reviewed in order to offer practical guidelines for practitioners and policy makers concerned with elder abuse case managment.

METHODS: A review of the current literature concentrating on four major studies conducted in Massachusetts, Michigan, Ohio, and Maryland, and a survey of state statutes related to elder abuse serve as the major sources for the information in the article.

FINDINGS: This article presents findings in four parts. Part I reviews the literature on elder abuse. Part II offers practical guidelines for handling elder abuse cases. Part III details suggestions for protective services systems and legislation, and Part IV discusses training and public education. Each part is further divided into chapters which address specific topics.

Chapter 1 reports the findings from the four major research studies on elder abuse conducted in Massachusetts, Maryland, Michigan, and Ohio. Although these studies lack common definitions for abuse and neglect, and use small or non-representative samples, comparative conclusions can be drawn. Three of the studies identified the majority of abuse victims as dependent because of a physical or psychological impairment and as females who lived with relatives who abused them. Two studies that investigated age found the victims to be very old (over 75). Three of the studies identified significant levels of both physical and psychological abuse. The usual response towards the identified abuse was removal of the victim from home to an institution.

The major causal theories for elder abuse summarized in Chapter 2 include (1) the physical and psychological impairment of the dependent elderly person, (2) personality or character disorders of the abuser, (3) learned behavior patterns of family violence, (4) external stresses such as low income, (5) demographic trends towards an increasing elderly population, and (6) negative attitudes about the elderly.

Chapter 3 summarizes the key points of Behind Closed Doors which is the first national study of family violence in American that used a large random sample. This study also used measurement devices to predict family violence and compared findings from spouse, child, sibling, and parent abuse cases.

Part II's discussion (Chapters 4, 5 and 6) on handling elder abuse cases follows six principles: (1) "the client's right to self determination," (2) "the use of the least restrictive alternative in treatment and placement," (3) "maintenance of the family unit whenever possible," (4) "the use of community-based services rather than institutionalization wherever possible," (5) the avoidance of blame," and (6) "inadequate or inappropriate intervention may be worse than none at all." With these principles in mind, this part of the article outlines specific guidelines for identifying, assessing, and managing elder abuse cases, in addition to identifying legal issues and detailed protocols for handling abuse cases. These protocols deal with four types of abuse clients: (1) competent, consenting clients; (2) competent, non-consenting clients; (3) incompetent clients; and (4) emergency care clients.

Part III's discussion includes information found in Chapter 7 on general characteristics and types of services available in a protective services system. Chapter 8 follows with a discussion of abuse and protective services laws.

Part IV on training of service workers and educating the public devotes Chapter 9 to a discussion of a training design and format for professionals. Suggestions in Chapter 10 for the use of the media to alert the community about the problem of elder abuse conclude the article. Strategies are outlined on how one presents a talk on elder abuse in the most effective way.

Professional Orientation:
- Social Work

Type of Exposition:
- Clinical Observations

Substantive Issues:
- Definitions
- Treatment
- Characteristics
- Policy

137 Walker, Jacqueline C. "Protective services for the elderly: Connecticut's experience." In: Kosberg, Jordan I., ed. Abuse and maltreatment of the elderly: Causes and interventions. Littleton, Massachusetts: John Wright, PSG Inc., 1983. 292-302. (0 References).

TOPIC: The author reports on the operation of the ombudsman office for the state of Connecticut which is oriented to protect "the lifestyle and well-being of Connecticut's elderly citizens."

OBJECTIVE: The goal in this review is to demonstrate how reports are received and investigated by the state ombudsman's office.

METHOD: The ombudsman program is explained by presenting a number of cases of abuse and neglect in which it has been involved.

CONCLUSIONS: The ombudsman's office consists of one state director, six regional directors, and ninety volunteers who must go through a three-day training program. Connecticut requires mandatory reporting of all cases of abuse within five days of the observation and failure to do this results in a $500 fine.

Following the report, the regional ombudsman makes an investigation. If the ombudsman determines that the case is valid, the protective service worker becomes involved, reporting to the ombudsman's office after 10, 45 and 90 days. Connecticut uses four categories of abuse (1) abuse, physical or mental, which is willfully perpetrated by a caretaker, (2) neglect which is either the result of the individual's failure to provide "services necessary to maintain physical and mental health" or another's failure to provide these services, (3) abandonment, including "desertion or willful forsaking" of an older person, and (4) exploitation which refers to "taking advantage of an elderly person..."

The ombudsman program in Connecticut reveals that most of the abused are women, are over 80, and come from all types of economic and residential settings. Abusers tend to be family members; and when they are elderly themselves or experience alcoholism or psychiatric problems, this affects the way they care for dependent elderly.

Other phases of the ombudsman program include arranging for needed services for the elderly and monitoring the client's progress through contact with the protective service worker. In addition, in cases in which clients refuse assistance but are deemed incompetent by the ombudsman, the referral for treatment is made anyway.

Professional Orientation:
- Medicine

Type of Exposition:
- Discussion

Substantive Issues:
- Causal Factors
- Social Structure

138 Walshe-Brennan, Kieran. "Granny bashing." Nurs Mirror 145:32-34. December 22, 1977. (10 References).

TOPIC: The author discusses elder abuse by family members.

OBJECTIVE: The goal of the article is to expose the problem of elder abuse by family members as it relates to current socio-cultural trends in the British society.

METHODS: The author draws on professional experiences, conference addresses and newspaper articles to substantiate the article's major points.

FINDINGS: The problem of granny bashing appears multifaceted. Causes are associated with alcoholism, congested, multi-level living units in urban areas, rising crime, psychiatric and psychopathological illness, and changing cultural values that support the avoidance of responsibility and perpetuate a lack of affection for others. These results suggest that the State should take the lead in encouraging community and individual responsibility.

Professional Orientation:
- Social Work

Type of Exposition:
- Report

Substantive Issues:
- Law
- Treatment

139 Whalen, Marilyn. "Adult protective services in Tennessee," In: Tennessee Conference: Abuse of Older Persons, Knoxville, Tennessee, December, 1980. Conference proceedings. Knoxville, Tennessee: School of Social Work, Office of Continuing Social Work Education, 1981. 67-72. (1 Reference).

TOPIC: The presenter outlines the provisions included in the Tennessee law on elder abuse and neglect.

CONCLUSIONS: In 1980, Tennessee changed its law to include protection of all adults explicitly including the elderly. Funding for protective services is provided by Title XX of the Social Security Act as well as other resources. Anyone can report a case of neglect, abuse, or exploitation. Those persons reporting cases are protected from liability. When T.C.A. Counselors receive calls, they are instructed to ask the caller to identify the nature of the abuse, the parties involved and themselves. There are clear guidelines for follow-up of cases. For example, those persons eligible for adult protective services must be unable to protect themselves "and <u>must</u> be harmed or threatened with harm." Services include investigation and assessment of needs as well as appropriate services to meet the older person's needs. Under some circumstances, the Department of Human Services can request legal intervention.

Professional Orientation:
- Social Work

Type of Exposition:
- Position Paper

Substantive Issues:
- Causal Factors
- Treatment

140 Wilks, Carl. "Past conflicts and current stress: Factors in the abuse of the elderly." In: Tennessee Conference: Abuse of Older Persons, Knoxville, Tennessee, December, 1980. <u>Conference proceedings</u>. Knoxville, Tennessee: School of Social Work, Office of Continuing Social Work Education, 1981. 103-114. (15 References).

TOPIC: The author examines four primary factors giving rise to abuse of the elderly.

METHODS: Previous studies as well as the author's own experience are drawn upon to establish the primary sources of elder abuse. Methods of dealing with these causes are offered by the author.

CONCLUSIONS: There are four primary sources of elder abuse: (1) unresolved conflicts between the now-dependent parent and the caretaker child, (2) unresolved issues of sibling rivalry between the caretaker child and favored but non-caretaking brothers and sisters, (3) in cases where therapy is involved, parent/child conflicts the therapist encountered which have never been resolved and which are, hence, imported into the therapy relationship to the detriment of the elderly client, and (4) societal abuse generated by the relatively low status that the elderly have in our society. It is important that therapists be aware of and able to deal with the first three of these problems so that they can help their clients deal with such crucial issues as how the change in the dependency relationship brings out memories of earlier decision-making conflicts; how the elderly parent's continuing favoritism toward a brother or sister of the caretaker (especially when the favored one is not taking his/her share of responsibility for the parent) creates intolerable stress on the caretaker; and how the therapist's own unresolved problems may contribute to his/her abuse of the client through the inadequate provision of services. These problems can best be dealt with by group therapy along the lines laid out by Housman. The fourth source is, as the name suggests, a social rather than an individual problem and must be dealt with by re-educating people about the elderly, and by insuring that the elderly have adequate financial resources to deal with the various problems they have to face.

Professional Orientation:
- Other

Type of Exposition:
- Survey Research

Substantive Issues:
- Characteristics
- Causal Factors

141 Wills, Michelle, and Walker, Jacqueline C. "Abuse of the elderly: A preliminary report." In: First National Conference on Abuse of Older Persons, Cambridge, Massachusetts, March, 1981. <u>Conference Proceedings</u>. Boston, Massachusetts: Legal Research and Services for the Elderly, 1981. 7p. (10 References).

TOPIC: This is a presentation on the results of a study of physical abuse of older persons in the state of Connecticut.

OBJECTIVE: The goal of the study was "to develop a first picture of the characteristics of the abuse, the abuser, and the abused and to suggest some causal hypotheses for later research."

METHODS: The study was an exploratory pilot study of 22 selected victims of elder abuse in the state of Connecticut. In-depth interviews were conducted with these 22 people during the summer of 1980.

FINDINGS: Most physical abuse reported involved the head, neck and upper extremities. Eleven of the twenty abusers were over the age of 60; 11 were male; 10 were the children of the older person and the remainder were other relatives; 14 had a history of psychiatric problems. On the other hand, the abused profile indicates that most of the victims were over the age of 70; 17 were female; 12 lived with their children; 17 had no mental impairment, but most had some kind of physical impairment. These results may point to reasons for physical abuse.

CONCLUSIONS: Since 11 of the caregivers ranged in age from 60 to 84, caregiving itself may be stressful. If one is old himself or herself and manifests psychiatric or substance abuse problems, the danger for physical abuse is increased. In addition to the age factor and psychological problem, economic and social problems affect the caregiver's attitude toward the older persons. Although it is difficult to predict the future, elder abuse may increase along with increased longevity.

Professional Orientation:
- Social Work
Type of Exposition:
- Discussion Paper
Substantive Issue:
- Definitions

142 Wineman, Lonnie. "Elder abuse: A matter of definition." In: Schultz, Leroy G. ed. Elder abuse in West Virginia: A policy analysis of system response. Morgantown, West Virginia: West Virginia University, 1983. 8p. (2 References).

TOPIC: The author presents evidence for a lack of agreement in West Virginia about the meaning of the term elder abuse.

METHODS: Drawing from both existing policy definitions and from responses to questionnaires and interviews, the author documents the lack of a consistent operational definition of "elder abuse" in West Virginia.

CONCLUSIONS: A major barrier to providing effective elder abuse services in West Virginia has been the lack of a consistent definition of terms. This lack is obvious not only when the existing terminology of relevant legislation is compared with that of the Department of Welfare's Policy Manual, but it also can be implied by the imprecise language used in many of the responses to a questionnaire survey.

Until a standard definition can be agreed upon by service-givers, there is "little hope of developing a uniform, consistent and comprehensive service system within the state."

Professional Orientation:
- Social Work
Type of Exposition:
- Review
Substantive Issue:
- General

143 Wineman, Lonnie. "West Virginia's current condition and response to elder abuse: An overview." In: Schultz, Leroy G. ed. Elder abuse in West Virginia: A policy analysis of system response." Morgantown, West Virginia: West Virginia University, 1983. 4p. (12 References).

TOPIC: The author discusses the current lack of co-ordination of anti-elder abuse programs and the need for a co-ordinated effort.

OBJECTIVE: The objective is to illustrate the lack of coordination in treatment by describing the various bodies and issues involved in all or part of the response to elder abuse and to urge study of other systems with an eye toward developing a comprehensive, functional program.

METHODS: The author briefly reviews the historical and situational reasons for the lack of co-ordination, points to the range of services provided and discusses hopeful existing policies, as well as guidelines for developing a more functional system.

CONCLUSIONS: Government concern with elder abuse is a relatively recent phenomena; and, thus, it has been lumped together with other related problems for treatment that have, as a result, frequently been inadequate. There are a wide range of public and private bodies which respond to the problem; however, their responses "are as diverse as the systems themselves." And when this diversity is complicated by "the unique features of the elder abuse system itself," one can understand the lack of co-ordination and communication and even the impenetrability to thorough analysis that this creates.

Two existing West Virginia policies represent a movement toward an effective response to elder abuse. The present period of interest and ferment is an ideal time for studying other state systems in order to use their experience in developing an effective West Virginia system.

Policy makers attempting a centralized approach should also take into account the needs of all those "with a stake in the efficiency of these services."

Professional Orientation:
- Psychology

Type of Exposition:
- Survey Research

Substantive Issues:
- Identification
- Treatment
- Characteristics
- Theory

144 Wolf, Rosalie S.; Strugnell, Cecile P.; Godkin, Michael A. <u>Preliminary findings from three Model Projects on elder abuse.</u> Worcester, Massachusetts: University of Massachusetts Medical Center, University Center on Aging, December, 1982. 99p. (23 References).

TOPIC: The authors present preliminary findings on an evaluation of the programs of Three Model Projects on Elderly Abuse funded by the Administration on Aging.

OBJECTIVES: Three goals are mentioned. These include (1) the nature and scope of elder abuse, (2) an assessment of learning activities disseminated by the Model Project program, and (3) an assessment of the interventional model.

METHODS: A community survey was undertaken at the end of 1981 which included four research sites - Worcester, Massachusetts; Boston, Massachusetts; Onodaga County, New York; and Rhode Island. Two hundred and eighty agencies responded which represented a response rate of 48%. Both agency responses and individual case reports were gathered.

FINDINGS: While all agencies responding to the survey were familiar with elder abuse, it was difficult to get firm data on prevalence from the four sites because of incomplete information and differing agency interpretations. When asked to whom they would turn or to whom they actually did turn in cases of elder abuse, agencies varied as well, reflecting different structures for managing elder affairs. Each site reported that it did not use a standard protocol in identifying cases and lacked adequate information on local resources for dealing with elder abuse cases, although they believed that resources were adequate.

Individual case reports were used to look at the nature and scope of elder abuse. Most elderly abuse victims were physically and mentally impaired white females ages 70 and older. They also presented a picture of multiple abuses which tended to be recurrent. Most victims lived with relatives and were not socially isolated. Perpetrators tended to be adult children of the victim, especially males who suffered from some kind of impairment -- physical, financial, and social. Victims and abusers seemed to exhibit mutual dependence in some way which, in turn, made it difficult for them to receive outside help. There is still insufficient evidence to explain elder abuse by means of an established theory. However, common features of these abusive families are that they are living at poverty level with limited support and seem to experience increasing stress. For these reasons, social-cultural theories may be most useful in the protection and prevention of elder abuse.

B. UNANNOTATED BIBLIOGRAPHY

1. SELECTED PROFESSIONAL BIBLIOGRAPHY

145 _____. "Abuse of the elderly." Gerontopics 3(2):319, 1979.

146 Amato, Mia. "Spotting and handling elder abuse." Coord July, 1983.

147 Ascoli, Marian L., and Hadley, Frances. "Preventive/protective services for our nation's elderly." In: National Conference on Social Welfare, Chicago, Illinois, 1977. Official Proceedings. Columbus, Ohio: Columbia University Press, 1978. 129-141.

148 _____. "Black holes of boarding care homes." Fifty Plus 19, 9, February, 1979.

149 _____. "Conditions 'tragic' in adult care homes." Aging 24-29, January/February, 1980.

150 Dix, Gretchen. "Nursing assessment for elder abuse and neglect." Paper presented at the thirty-sixth annual meeting of the Gerontological Society of America. San Francisco, California, 1983.

151 Eastman, Mervyn and Sutton, Margaret. "Granny battering." Ger Med November, 1982.

152 _____. "Elder abuse reporting laws." Gerontopics 3(6):410, 1980.

153 _____. "Elderly abuse." Gerontopics New England Gerontology Center: 3(6):398-399, 1980.

154 Emener, William G., Jr.; Stilwell, William E.; Witten, Barbara J. "Delivering human services for abused clients: A systems and individual approach." Fam Comm Health 4(2), August, 1981.

155 Finn, Jerry. "Elder abuse in a rural community." Paper presented at the fifth annual meeting of the Southern Gerontological Society meeting, Knoxville, Tennessee, 1984.

156 Fulmer, Teresa T. "Data on referrals, assessment and actions." Paper presented at the thirty-sixth annual meeting of the Gerontological Society of America, San Francisco, California, 1983.

157 Fulmer, Teresa T. "Elder abuse assessment in a hospital setting." Paper presented at the thirty-sixth annual meeting of the Gerontological Society of America, San Francisco, California, 1983.

158 Gresham, Mary L. "The infantilization of the elderly: A developing concept." Nurs Forum 15(2):195-210, 1976.

159 Griesel, Elma L. "Testimony on elder abuse in nursing homes." In: First National Conference on Abuse of Older Persons, Cambridge, Massachusetts, March, 1981. Conference Proceedings, Boston, Massachusetts, Legal Research and Services for the Elderly, 1981. 5p.

160 Haggerty, M. "Elder abuse: Who is the victim?" Gray Pan Net 171-176, 21, January/February, 1981.

161 Halamandaris, Val J. "Fraud and abuse in nursing homes." In: Kosberg, Jordan I., ed., Abuse and mistreatment of the elderly, causes and interventions, Littleton, Massachusetts: John Wright, PSG, Inc., 1983. 104-14.

162 Kastenbaum, Robert. "Abuse of the elderly in mental institutions." In: First National Conference on Abuse of Older Persons, Cambridge, Massachusetts, March, 1981. Conference Proceedings. Boston, Massachusetts: Legal Research and Services for the Elderly, 1981. 12p.

163 Kosberg, Jordan I. "Family conflict and abuse of the elderly: Theoretical and methodological issues." Paper presented at the thirty-second annual meeting of the Gerontological Society of America, Washington, D.C., 1979.

164 Matlaw, J. "Community relations and elder abuse." Paper presented at the thirty-sixth annual meeting of the Gerontological Society of America, San Francisco, California, 1983.

165 Minaker, K. "Physician's responsibility in assessment and reporting." Paper presented at the thirty-sixth annual meeting of the Gerontological Society of America, San Francisco, California, 1983.

166 Newbern, V.B. "A study of patient abuse: Ramifications for the elderly." Paper presented at the thirty-sixth annual meeting of the Gerontological Society of America, San Francisco, California, 1983.

167 _____. Old age abuse. Report of a Conference Age Concern, Greenwich, England, 1983.

168 O'Malley, Terrence A. "Elder abuse and neglect: Interventions, outcomes, and categories." Paper presented at the thirty-sixth annual meeting of the Gerontological Society of America, San Francisco, California, 1983.

169 Ornstein, Sheldon, M.S.W., R.N. "Abuse and neglect." New York State Nurs Asso 6(3):35-38, November, 1975.

170 Pelton, L. "The politics of abuse and neglect." Unpub Man, Princeton, New Jersey, 1980.

171 Pillemer, Karl A., and Wolf, Rosalie, S. "The role of dependency in physical abuse of the elderly." Paper presented at the thirty-sixth annual meeting of the Gerontological Society of America, San Francisco, California, 1983.

172 Regan, John J. "Protective services for the elderly: Commitment, guardianship, and alternatives." William Mary Law Rev 13(3):569-622, Spring, 1972.

173 Regan, John J. "The legal dimension of protective services for the elderly." In: National Conference on Social Welfare, Washington, D.C., 1976. Official Proceedings. Columbus, Ohio: Columbia University Press, 1977. 163-71.

174 Schwartz, Steven J. and Fleischner, Robert, Jr. "Elder abuse in mental health institutions." In: First National Conference on Abuse of Older Persons, Cambridge, Massachusetts, March, 1981. Conference Proceedings, Boston, Massachusetts: Legal Research and Services for the Elderly, 1981. 11p.

175 _____. Second National Conference for Family Violence Research, Durham, New Hampshire, August 7-10, 1984. Durham, New Hampshire: New England Center for Continuing Education, University of New Hampshire, The Family Violence Research Program and the Department of Sociology and Anthropology at the University of New Hampshire.

176 Shapiro, M. "Trauma assessment in the elderly." Paper presented at the thirty-sixth annual meeting of the Gerontological Society of America, San Francisco, California, 1983.

177 Solomon, Kenneth. "Victimization by health professionals and the psychologic response of the elderly." In: Kosberg, Jordon I., ed., Abuse and Mistreatment of the Elderly, Causes and Interventions, Littleton, Massachusetts: John Wright, PSG, Inc., 150-171, 1983.

178 Stannard, Charles I. "Old folks and dirty work: The social conditions for patient abuse in a nursing home." Soc Prob 20(3):329-42, Winter, 1973.

179 Star, Barbara. Helping the abuser. New York: Family Service Association of America. 1983. 262p.

180 Stathopoulos, Peter A. "Consumer advocacy and abuse of elders in nursing homes." In Kosberg, Jordon I., ed. Abuse and Mistreatment of the Elderly, Causes and Interventions, Littleton, Massachusetts: John Wright, PSG, Inc., 335-54, 1983.

181 Steinmetz, Suzanne. "Politics of aging, battered parents. Society 15(5):54-55, July/August, 1978.

182 _____. "Suffering in silence." A Conference on Elder Abuse, Washington, D.C., September 21, 1982. Conference Proceedings. Washington, D.C.: D.C. Commission for Women, 1984.

183 _____. "The battered elder syndrome: Violence begins at home." Encore 54-57, March, 1980.

184 _____. The judmentally impaired elderly: Issues of abuse and victimization, New York City, May 10-11, 1984. New York, New York: The Brookdale Institute on Aging and Adult Human Development, Columbia University and the New York City Long-Term Care Ombudsprogram of the Community Council of Greater New York.

185 Wescott, K. "Elder abuse: A descriptive study of factors associated with elder abuse in families." Unpub Master's Thesis, University of Maryland, 1980.

186 Wetle, Terry. "Ethical consideration in elder abuse." Paper presented at the thirty-sixth annual meeting of the Gerontological Society of America, San Francisco, California, 1983.

2. NEWSPAPER ARTICLES ON ELDER ABUSE*

187 "A New Troubling Social Concern: Our Elderly Are Being Mistreated." J.C. Borden. (Times News Service) Rutland Daily Herald, Rutland, Vermont. July 31, 1981.

---

*This list contains a sampling of newspaper articles on elder abuse. Newspapers which are more available to the national public may have more than one entry.

188 "Abuse in Families Tied to Crime and Violence in Streets." Richard A. Gelles. The New Haven Register, New Haven, Connecticut, April 8, 1981.

189 "Abuse of Aged is often Ignored." New York Times, p. 9, (Section III), July, 13, 1983.

190 "Abuse of the Aged: A Growing Problem." Mark Starr. Chicago Tribune, p. 25, (Section 1), July 5, 1981.

191 "Abuse of the Aged Largely Unreported." Sandra Gardner. The New York Times, p. 1, (Section 11), August 7, 1983.

192 "Abuse of the Elderly: A Secret Shame." Eleanor Roberts. Boston Herald American, p. 3, (Section A), May 27, 1979.

193 "America's Neglected Elderly," Didi Moore. New York Times, p. 30, (Section 6), January 30, 1983.

194 "Battered Grandparents: Hidden Family Problem." Robert M. Press. Christian Science Monitor, p. 9, December 5, 1979.

195 "Battered Parent Problem Rises." Washington Post, p. 13, February 16 1978.

196 "Boothbay Mother, Son (39) Found Living in Squalor: State and Local Agencies are Vague as to their Responsibility." Boothbay Register, March 26, 1981.

197 "Chicago Area Emergency Room Physicians Report on Abuse of Aged." Chicago Tribune, p. 13, (Section 3), January 28, 1979.

198 "Child Abuse in Reverse: Elderly Victims of 'Parent Abuse'." S. Gallaghen. Detroit Free Press, April 13, 1975.

199 "Congress Panel Hears of Physical Abuse of the Elderly." Ari L. Goldman. The New York Times, p. 4, (Section B), April 22, 1980.

200 "Domestic Violence; Study Favors Arrest." Philip M. Boffet. New York Times, April 5, 1983.

201 "Elder Abuse Widespread, Report Says." Charlotte Observer, p. 2, (Section A), April 3, 1981.

202 "Elderly Abuse Cases Soaring." Tom Fahey. Union Leader, Manchester New Hampshire. August 16, 1982.

203 "Elderly Abuse: Old Problem Comes our of the Closet." George Esper. Portland Press Herald, March 15, 1982.

204 "Elderly Tell of Abuse by Family and Relatives." Bangor Daily News, Bangor, Maine. June 2, 1980.

205 "Forum Examines Parent Abuse." Betty Potter. Kennebec Journal, Kennebec, Maine. September 9, 1980.

206 "Granny Bashing, Parent Abuse, Seen as Major Problem." Los Angeles Times, p. 1, (Section IA), November 7, 1980.

207 "Growing Problem of Neglect and Abuse of the Elderly." Chicago Tribune, p. 1, (Section 2), March 3, 1980.

208 "House Panel Finds Widespread and Growing Abuse of the Elderly." New York Times, p. 12, April 3, 1981.

209 "Howland Murder Trial." Thomas Sabolik. Foster's Daily Democrat, Dover, New Hampshire, May 31, June 15, June 17, August 3, August 23, 1977; January 24, 25, 26, 27, 28, 1978.

210 "L.A. Council Committee Hears Testimony on Abuse of the Elderly." Los Angeles Times, p. 1, (Section II), December 20, 1980.

211 "Legislators Told Elders Face Neglect, Abuse, Legal Woes." Alfred B.G. Emonds. Manchester Journal Inquirer, Manchester, Connecticut. August 21, 1980.

212 "More than Law Needed to Curb Elderly Abuse." William R. Cash. Boston Globe, April 15, 1981.

213 "Need for Adult Abuse Reporting Bill." John J. Fay, Jr. New York Times, p. 28, (Section XI), May 10, 1981.

214 "Old and Beaten." Jane M. Littleton. Cleveland Plain Dealer, p. 25, (Section 1), March 5, 1978.

215 "On Beating Grandmother." Russell Baker. The New York Times, p. 41, November 16, 1976.

216 "Panel to Study Violence in Family Announced by Reagan and Smith." Leslie M. Werner. The New York Times, p. 27, (Section A), September 20, 1983.

217 "Parent Abuse - A New Plague." Lewis Koch and Joan Koch. Parade, January 27, 1980. The Washington Post, pp. 14-15.

218 "Parent Abuse May Be Common Problem." Sue Smith. Ithaca Journal, Four Part Series, August 20-23, 1979.

219 "Plight of Abandoned Aged Persons in Private Georgetown Hospital Eyed." Washington Post, p. 1, (Section A), March 22, 1975.

220 "Relative Backs Son's Effort to Evict Parents in Wichita, Kansas." Chicago Tribune, p. 16, (Section 1), June 10, 1981.

221 "Reported Abuse of Maine's Elderly is on the Rise." Tammy Eves. Lewiston Daily Sun, Lewiston, Maine. July 18, 1980.

222 "Social Scientists Discuss Abuse of Elderly." New Orleans Times - Picayune, p. 5, (Section 2), January 7, 1979.

223 "State Finds Abuse of Elderly by Kin." Andree Brooks. The New York Times, p. 1, (Section 23), September 19, 1982.

224 "Stonington Couple Beaten: 44 Year Old Son Arrested." Pat Flagg. Ellsworth American, Ellsworth Maine. March 19, 1981.

225 "Study Finds Aged Abuse Widespread." Pacific Stars and Stripes. December 5, 1979.

226 "Survey Results on Care of Elderly Parents by Children Released." Los Angeles Times, p. 2, (Section V), January 7, 1982.

227 "The Shocking Plight of Abused Parents." Susan S. Long and Harold Feldman. Family Weekly, pp. 21 and 23, March 14, 1982.

228 "Thousands Face Abuse at Their Children's Hands." Charlotte Observer, p. 2, (Section A), June 12, 1980.

229 "U.S. Congres Begins to Tackle Problem of Elder Abuse." Christian Science Monitor, p. 11, June 20, 1980.

230 "U.S. Probe Opens on Elderly Abuse." Bill Dooley. Boston Herald American, March 24, 1981.

231 "U.S. Report Reveals Growing Problem of Abuse of the Elderly." Chicago Tribune, p. 7, (Section 1), April 3, 1981.

232 "Violence in the Family Assessed at Conference." New York Times, p. 18, (Section N), July 26, 1981.

233 "When Abuse Adds to the Woes of the Old." Ward L. Matthew. New York Times, August 24, 1980.

3. STATE PUBLICATIONS ON ELDER ABUSE

ALABAMA

234 Family Violence, A Comprehensive Approach to the Community Problem. University of Alabama Law Center, 1980.

ALASKA

235 An Act Relating to Protection of the Elderly. HCS CSSB 122 (HESS), Chapter 36, June 30, 1983.

ARIZONA

236 Decents' Estates, Guardianships, Protective Proceedings, and Trusts. House Bill 2134, Chapter 127, 1980.

ARKANSAS

237 Investigation Policies and Procedures. Protective Services for Adults.

238 Protective Services. Advocacy Assistance Program Description, Project Overview. September 15, 1980.

239 Protective Services. Implementation of Act 166. Department of Human Services, Office of Aging. July 13, 1980.

CALIFORNIA

240 A Report on the Abuse of Elders in San Francisco. A Project of the Coalition of Agencies Serving the Elderly Conducted by the Elder Abuse Task Force. April 1, 1983.

241 Domestic Violence. California Department of Justice. Information Pamplet No. 11, U.S. Department of Commerce, National Technical Information Services. April, 1978.

CONNECTICUT

242 Abuse of the Elderly, A Preliminary Report. Department on Aging. February, 1981.

243 An Act Concerning Appointment of Conservators. Substitute House Bill No. 7895, Public Act No. 77-446.

244 Elder Abuse Reporting Laws. Gerontopics: 3(6), 410, 1980.

245 Forms for Mandatory Reporting.

246 Protection of the Elderly. Title 46a, Chapter 814.

247 Protective Services for the Elderly. Pamphlet W2052. July, 1978.

248 Protective Services for the Elderly. Form W2052. July, 1978.

249 Protective Services for the Elderly. Department of Social Serivces Bulletin No. 3071. August 8, 1978.

250 Protective Services for the Elderly. Manual Vol. 8, Chapter 11 and Statutes.

DISTRICT OF COLUMBIA

251 Proposed Strategies: Elder Abuse. D.C. Commission for Women, Government of the District of Columbia, Washington, D.C.

FLORIDA

252 Abuse, neglect, or exploitation of aged or disabled persons. Sentate Bill No. 124, Chapter 83-82. July 1, 1983.

253 Adult Services Programs. The Department of Health and Rehabilitative Services, HRS Manual. January 1, 1982.

HAWAII

254 Elderly Abuse or Neglect (Chapter 349C). Hawaii Revised Statutes, 1981 Supplement, Vol. 4.

IDAHO

255 Elderly abuse, exploitation, neglect, and abandonment regulations. Idaho Code Sections 39-5201 (39-5301) establishing the Department of Health and Welfare as the official agency of the state government to handle cases of elderly abuse, exploitation, neglect, and abandonment.

256 Protection of the Elderly. Senate Bill No. 1417. Amended by Judiciary and Rules Committee.

IOWA

257 Elder Abuse Reporting Law. S.F. 541, Spring, 1983.

KANSAS

258 Reporting Abuse Senate Bill No. 590. Adult Care Homes, 80th General Assembly, page 6. April, 1980.

KENTUCKY

259 "Adult Services." Policy and Procedure Manual, Chapter II, Department of Social Services. December, 1982.

260 "Protection of Adults." Cabinet for Human Resources, Chapter 209, Department of Social Services.

MAINE

261 Adult Abuse Manual. Compiled by the Abuse Task Force, Department of Human Services. August, 1982.

262 Adult Abuse, Neglect, or Exploitation, brochure. Department of Human Services. October, 1982.

263 Adult Service Plan. Department of Human Services. August 27, 1979.

264 Adult Services Plan (1984-85). Department of Human Services.

265 Cooperative Administration Agreement. Bureau of Social Services - Division of Adult Services and the Bureau of Maine's Elderly. August, 1982.

266 Elderly Abuse Forum Proceedings. Maine Committee on Aging and the Bureau of Maine's Elderly. September 8, 1980.

267 Elderly Abuse: Summary of Follow-Up Survey of Area Agencies. Report prepared by Natalie Dunlap for Bureau of Maine's Elderly, Department of Human Services. November 3, 1981.

268 Long Term Care for Adults, Testimony on: Regional Hearings, by Larry Gross, Portland, Maine. April 10, 1980.

269 Summary of Area Agency Survey on Abused Elderly. Report prepared by Natalie Dunlap for Bureau of Maine's Elderly, Department of Human Services. June 24, 1980.

270 Supportive Services for Adults. Paper prepared for the Blaine House Conference on Aging by George Odencranz, Director Adult Protective Services, Department of Human Services. October, 1980.

271 Title XX Services to Adults: Comprehensive annual services Program Plan, p. 111, 123, 153, 156-7, Department of Human Services.

272 Victimization of the Elderly. Paper prepared for the Blaine House Conference on Aging by Ginnie Norman, Executive Director, Maine Committee on Aging. September 30, 1980.

MASSACHUSETTS

273 An Act Providing Further Protection of Elderly Persons. The Commonwealth of Massachusetts, Acts and Resolves, Chapter 604, 1982.

274 Elder Abuse Project, Center on Aging/Worcester University of Massachusetts Medical Center, National Clearing House on Aging. June, 1981.

275 Massachusetts Files Bills to Protect Elders From Abuse. Gerontopics: 3 (6), 410, 1980.

276 Protective Services for the Elderly, Legislation H 4112, S 5640 and H 617, H 3448.

277 Regulations Governing the Elder Abuse Reporting and Protective Services Program. Department of Elder Affairs, 651 CMR 5.00.

278 The Implementation of Chapter 604: Protective Services for Massachusetts' Elders. Prepared for House and Senate Committees on Ways and Means by Lillian Glickman, Chet Jakubiak, and Kent Boynton, Department of Elder Affairs. October, 1983.

MICHIGAN

279 Building a Community Based Network for Adult Protective Services by Claudia Wink-Bosing, School of Social Work, Western Michigan University, Kalamazoo, Michigan. October, 1980.

280 Kalamazoo Adult Protective Services, Community Network Project; Final Report. October, 1980.

MINNESOTA

281 Minnesota Strengthens Protections for Vulnerable Adults. Collation: No. 16, p. 65-65. July, 1980.

282 Reports of Maltreatment of Vulnerable Adults. Minnesota Department of Public Welfare, Social Services Division, Monitoring and Reporting Section. April, 1983.

MISSOURI

283 Protective Service Law.

284 Protective Service Law to help Missouri Elderly. Newsletter, Missouri Division of Aging: 2 (2), 1, 1980.

MISSISSIPPI

285 Adult Protective Services Manual. Department of Public Welfare, Social Services Department. July 1, 1982.

286 Mississippi Adult Protective Services Act of 1982. Senate Bill No. 2280. April 23, 1980.

NEW JERSEY

287 A Bill To Protect Elderly Residents. OARS. February 11, 1983.

NEW YORK

288 Model Adult Protective Services Laws: Ad hoc committee on Adult Homes, Council on Aging, Nassau Division, New York State Chapter, National Association of Social Workers. January 19, 1982.

289 New York Issue, Patient Abuse Report. Collation: No. 16, page 64. July, 1980.

290 New York State Statistical Analysis, Patient Abuse Reporting. New York State Department of Health, Office of Health Systems Management. April 15, 1979.

291 New York State Statistical Analysis, Patient Abuse Reporting. July 31, 1979.

292 New York State Statistical Analysis, Patient Abuse Reporting. October 15, 1979.

293 New York State Statistical Analysis, Patient Abuse Reporting. January 15, 1980.

294 Nursing Home Patient Abuse: Realities and Remedies by Deputy Attorney General for Medicaid Fraud Control.

295 "Protective Services." Consolidated Laws Service, 362-364, 1981.

296 Protective Services for Adults. Department of Social Services, Bulletin 194. September 29, 1981.

297 Protective Services Risk Assessment: A New Approach to Screening Adult Clients, by Sol Daches, Ph.D., Research Director, Project Focus, Human Resources Administration of the City of New York, Family and Adult Services. February, 1983.

298 Reporting Abuses of Patients in Residential Care Facilities; New York State Public Health Law 2803-d.

299 Requirements Governing Reporting of Patient Abuse in Residential Health Care Facilities. Fourth Annual Report to the Governor and Legislature. New York State Department of Health Office of Health Systems Management. March 15, 1981.

300 Risk Assessment: A Guide for Adult Protective Workers by Sol Daches, Ph.D., Research Director, Project Focus, Human Resources Administration of the City of New York, Family and Adult Services. January, 1983.

301 "Short-term Involuntary Protective Services Orders." Consolidated Laws Service, 365-367, 1981.

302 Testimony on Domestic Violence vs the Elderly, by Lou Glass. Presented to subcommittee on Human Services of Select Committee on Aging. April 21, 1980.

OHIO

303 Protective Services for Adults. Sections 5101.60 to 5101.71. Effective November 15, 1981.

OKLAHOMA

304 Protective Services for the Elderly Act of 1977. 1979 Supplement Oklahoma Statutes, Vol. 1.

OREGON

305 Alleged Abuse in SNFs and ICFs. Protective Services. June 1, 1983.

306 "Alleged Elderly Abuse." Oregon Administrative Rules, Chapter 411, Division 21 -- Senior Services Division. August, 1982.

307 "Protective Services -- General." Oregon Administrative Rules, Chapter 411, Division 20 -- Senior Services Division. May, 1982.

308 Report to 62nd Legislative Assembly on Implementation of HB-2865. Department of Human Resources, Senior Services Division. March 8, 1983.

PENNSYLVANIA

309 Protection of the Elderly Act, Protective Service Legislation.

310 Survey Marks Start of Elderly Abuse Study by Department on Aging. Department on Aging News: 1, 4. October, 1980.

311 The Protection of the Elderly Act, a Briefing Paper, proposed by Senator F. Joseph Leoper.

312 What type of Protective Services Legislation will the Department on Aging Support? Department on Aging Prospectus, 42-43. April, 1980.

RHODE ISLAND

313 Mandatory Reporting Law.

314 Protective Services for the Elderly. Legislation H 5089.

SOUTH CAROLINA

315 Elder Abuse: A guide for Model State Policy and Programs. Paper prepared for the National Round Table Conference of the American Public Welfare Association by Tim Cash, Director of Adult Protective Services, South Carolina Department of Social Services. November 29 - December 2, 1983.

316 Major Revision of Chapters 700 and 2000 of the Manual of Adult Services. October 21, 1980

317 "Protective Services for Developmentally Disabled and Senile Persons," Chapter 29 from Code Laws of South Carolina 1976 with the 1979 amendments enacted by J 2254. July 1, 1979.

318 Revision of Appendix of Manual of Adult Services. Department of Social Services. July 6, 1979

UTAH

319 Three Year Plan (July 1983 - June 1986) For Adult Protective Services in Utah. Utah's Adult Protective Services Task Force on Aging. May, 1983.

VERMONT

320 Conference on Elderly Abuse. Program Resume, Participants and copy of the Senior Herald. Vol. 2, No. 7. September, 1981.

321 Elderly Protection Program: Reports received July, 1981, March, 1982.

322 Elderly Protection Program Annual Report. Prepared by Martha Schultz, Elderly Protection Program Coordinator. September 1, 1983.

323 Regarding a Reporting Law for the Protection of the Elderly. Public Acts. 1979, No. 150. An Act to Add 18 V.S.A. Chapter 22 H 282. Chapter 22 Reports on Abuse, Neglect, and Exploitation of Older Vermonters.

324 The Elderly Protection Program, brochure. Vermont Department of Health. September, 1981.

325 The Elderly Protection Program. Regulations. Vermont Department of Health, Medical Care Regulation.

WASHINGTON

326 Adult Protective Services Survey. Prepared by Helen G. McLeod, Jinny Hart, Alice Wing Jordon, Bob Patton, Dorothy Hoyt, and Lynda

Jensen, Bureau of Aging, Department of Social and Health Services. February, 1981.

WEST VIRGINIA

327 Protective Services for the Elderly. Legislation SB 121. State Health Notes: Intergovernmental Health Policy Project, George Washington University, No. 18. April, 1981.

328 Social Services for Adults. Article 6 of Senate Bill 121. April 11, 1981.

329 West Virginia Adult Protective Services. Prepared by Sylvia Giese Casey in cooperation with the West Virginia Commission on Aging.

WISCONSIN

330 Abuse Incident leads to Public Scrutiny of Wisconsin Enforcement System. Collation: No. 16, page 58, State Legislation and Regulatory Activities. July, 1980.

WISCONSIN

331 Battered Elderly Need Protection: Aging in the News, Bureau of Aging: No. 64, pages 7-8. May, 1980.

332 Respite Care Projects Approved. Aging in the News, Bureau of Aging: No. 64, pages 9, 10. May, 1980.

WYOMING

333 Protective Services for the Elderly. Legislation Chapter 155, Laws of 1981-m HB 49A.

4. FEDERAL PUBLICATIONS ON ELDER ABUSE

334 Abuse of older persons. Hearing, House Select Committee on Aging, Cambridge, Massachusetts, Committee Publication 97-289, March 23, 1981.

335 Crimes against the elderly, part I. U.S. Congress: House Joint Hearing Select Committee on Aging and the Committee on Service and Technology. Committee Publication 95-122. Government Printing Office, Washington, D.C., 1978.

336 Domestic violence versus the elderly. U.S. Congress: Select Committee on Aging, Subcommittee on Human Services, Hearing. Series House SCoA 96-233, New York and Washington, D.C., April 21, 1980.

337 Domestic violence: Elder abuse. Janice Fowler. Education and Public Welfare Division, Library of Congress, Congressional Research Service, Washington, D.C., February 6, 1981.

338 Elder abuse. U.S. Congress: Joint Hearing Special Committee on Aging, U.S. Senate and the Select Committee on Aging, U.S. House, Government Printing Office, Washington, D.C., June 11, 1980.

339 Elder abuse. U.S. Department of Health and Human Services: Office of Human Development Services, Administration on Aging. Publication Number OHDS-81-20152, May, 1980.

340 Elder abuse (An examination of a hidden problem). A report with additional views. U.S. Congress: House Select Committee on Aging. Committee Publication 97-277, April 8, 1981.

341 Elder abuse: An overview. U.S. Senate: Select Committee on Aging. Developments in Aging Part I, 1980.

342 Elder abuse: The hidden problem. U.S. Congress: House Select Committee on Aging. A Briefing, Boston, Massachusetts. June 23, 1979. Committee Publication Number 96-220. Government Printing Office, Washington, D.C., 1980.

343 Family violence: Intervention strategies. U.S. Department of Health and Human Services: Office of HHS Administration for Children, Youth and Families, Children's Bureau, National Center on Child Abuse and Neglect by Ellen Barnett, Carla B. Pittman, Cynthia K. Ragan, Marsha K. Salus, DHHS Publication Number (OHDS) 80-30258, May, 1980.

344 Fraud versus the elderly. U.S. Congress: House Select Committee on Aging, Hearing and Response, New York City, New York, October 23, 1980.

345 Non-stranger violence, the criminal court's response. Barbara E. Smith. A publication of the National Institute of Justice, U.S. Department of Justice, Washington, D.C., 20531, January, 1983.

346 Nursing home care in the United States: Failure in public policy. Introductory report prepared by the Subcommittee on Long-Term Care of the U.S. Senate Special Committee on Aging. Report Number 93-1420, November, 1974.

347 Physical and financial abuse of the elderly. House Select Committee on Aging. Hearing, San Francisco, California, Committee Publication 97-297, April 3, 1981.

348 Protective services for adults. A guide to exemplary practice in states providing protective services to adults in OHDS programs; by James J. Burr, Director of Protective, Ombudsman and Legal Services Staff. The Administration on Aging, Office of Human Development Services; DHS Publication Number (OHDS) 82-20505, Spring, 1982.

349 Protective services for the elderly. A working paper: U.S. Congress: Senate Special Committee on Aging, July, 1977.

II. A DIRECTORY OF ORGANIZATIONS PROVIDING SERVICES TO OLDER PERSONS

A. STATE ADULT PROTECTIVE SERVICES

Adult Protective Specialist
Bureau of Adult Services
Department of Pensions and Security
Administrative Building
64 North Union Street
Montgomery, Alabama 36130

Social Services
Department of Health and Social Services
Division of Family and Youth Services
Pouch H-05
Juneau, Alaska 99811

Adult Services Operations
Aging and Adult Administration
Arizona Department of Economic Security
1400 West Washington
Phoenix, Arizona 85007

Adult Protective Services
Donaghey Building, Room 1428
Little Rock, Arkansas 72201

Adult Services Branch
Department of Social Services
744 P Street
Sacramento, CA 95814

Department of Social Services
1575 Sherman Street
Denver, Colorado 80203

State of Connecticut
Department on Aging
80 Washington Street
Hartford, Connecticut 06115

Department of Health and Social Services
New Castle, Delaware 19720

Protective Services for Adults
Room 613
122 C Street, N.W.
Washington, District of Columbia 20001

Abuse Registry Supervisor
1317 Winewood Boulevard
Tallahassee, Florida 32301

Division of Family and Children Services
Georgia Department of Human Resources
878 Peachtree Street, N.E.
Atlanta, Georgia 30309

Social Services Intake Unit
1149 Bethel Street, Room 400
Honlulu, Hawaii 96813

State of Idaho
Division of Welfare
Statehouse
Boise, Idaho 83720

State Agency on Aging
421 E. Capitol Avenue
Springfield, Illinois 62706

Commission on Aging and Aged
Graphic Arts Building
215 North Senate Avenue
Indianapolis, Indiana 46202

Bureau of Adult Services
Hoover State Office Building
Des Moines, Iowa 50319

Adult Services
State Department of Social and
Rehab. Services
2700 West 6th Street
Topeka, Kansas 66606

Adult Protective Services
Department of Human Services
Bureau of Resources
Development, Station 11
State House
Augusta, Maine 04333

Acting Executive Director, SSA
Social Services Administration
Department of Human Resources
State of Maryland
300 West Preston Street
Baltimore, Maryland 21201

Department of Elder Affairs
38 Chauncy Street
Boston, Massachusetts 02111

Office of Adult and Family
Community Services
Adult Protective Services Division
300 South Capitol Avenue
P.O. Box 30037, Suite 707
Commerce Center Building
Lansing, Michigan 48910

Adult Protection Consultant
Social Services, Department of
Public Welfare
Centennial Office Building
St. Paul Minnesota 55155

State Department of Public Welfare
Protective Services Unit
P.O. Box 352
515 E. Amite Street
Jackson, Mississippi 39205

Missouri Division of Aging
P.O. Box 570
Broadway Office Building
Jefferson City, Missouri 65102

Department of Social and
Rehabilitative Services
Social Services Division
Box 4210
Helena, Montana 59601

Division of Social Services
Adult Service Unit
Nebraska Department of Public
Welfare
Lincoln, Nebraska 68509

Department of Human Resources
Welfare Division
251 Jeanell Drive
Carson City, Nevada 89710

Division of Welfare
Bureau of Adult Services
Haven Drive
Concord, New Hampshire 03301

Department of Human Services
Division of Youth and Family
Services
Trenton, New Jersey 08625

Department of Human Services
Adult Services Unit, PERA Building
P.O. Box 8348
Santa Fe, New Mexico 87503

New York State Dept. of
Social Services
Division of Adult Services
40 North Pearl Street
Albany, New York 12243

Department of Human Resources
Division of Social Services
325 N. Salisbury Street
Raleigh, North Carolina 27611

<u>North Dakota</u>
County Social Service Boards

Bureau of Adult Services
Division of Social Services
Ohio Department of Public Welfare
Social Services Intake Unit
30 East Broad Street
Columbus, Ohio 43215

Department of Human Services
Division of Services to Adults
and Families
P.O. Box 25352
Oklahoma City, Oklahoma 73125

Adult and Family Services
Department of Human Resources
400 Public Service Building
Salem, Oregon 97301

Department of Public Welfare
Room 533
Health and Welfare Building
Harrisburg, Pennsylvania 17120

Dept. of Social and Rehab. Services
Providence District Office
111 Fountain Street
Providence, Rhode Island 02903

Adult Protective Services Unit
Adult Services Division
State Department of Social Services
Box 1520
Columbia, South Carolina 29202

Office of Adult Services
Kneip Building, 700 Illinois Street
Pierre, South Dakota 57501

Tennessee Department of
Human Services
Division of Social Services
111-19 7th Avenue North
Nashville, Tennessee 37203

Alternate Car for Aged and
Disabled Adults Division
Texas Department of Human Resources
P.O. Box 2960
Austin, Texas 78769

APS Program Specialist, DoA & AS
Division of Aging
150 West North Temple, Suite 326
P.O. Box 2500
Salt Lake City, Utah 84110

Elderly Protection Service
Coordinator
Department of Health
60 Main Street
P.O. Box 70
Burlington, Vermont 05401

Department of Social Services
Blair Building
8007 Discovery Drive
Richmond, Virginia 23288

Bureau of Aging and Adult Services
OB-43G
Olympia, Washington 98504

West Virginia Commission on Aging
Holly Grove - Capitol Complex
Charleston, West Virginia 25305

Office on Aging
Department of Health and
Social Services
Division of Community Services
1 West Wilson Street
P.O. Box 7851
Madison, Wisconsin 53707

Wyoming Department of Health and
Social Services
Division of Public Assistance and
Social Services
Hathaway Building
Cheyenne, Wyoming 82002

B. STATE AGING SERVICES

Ms. Helen Geesey, Executive Director
Commission on Aging
State Capitol
Montgomery, Alabama 36130

Randall A. McCain, Director
Arkansas Department of Human
Services
Arkansas Office on Aging
Donaghey Building - Suite 1428
Seventh and Main Streets
Little Rock, Arkansas 72201

Jon B. Wolfe
Executive Director
State of Alaska
Older Alaskans Commission
Pouch C, M.S. 0209
Juneau, Alaska 99811

Douglas X. Patino, Director
Aging and Adult Administration
1400 West Washington
Phoenix, Arizona 85007

Alice Gonzales, Director
Director
State of California
Health and Welfare Agency
Department of Aging
1020 19th Street
Sacramento, California 95814

William J. Hanna, Director
Aging and Adult Services Division
Department of Social Services
Room 503
1575 Sherman Street
Denver, Colorado 80220

Mary Ellen Klinek, Director
Department on Aging
80 Washington Street
Room 312
Hartford, Connecticut 06115

Eleanor L. Cain, Director
Department of Health and
Social Services
Division of Aging
1901 North Dupont Highway
New Castle, Delaware 19720

E. Veronica Pace
Executive Director
District of Columbia
Office on Aging
1012 Fourteenth Street, N.W.
Eleventh Floor, Room 1106
Washington, District of Columbia 20005

John Stokesberry, Director
Program Specialist
Aging and Adult Services
Department of Health and
Rehabilitative Services
1323 Winewood Blvd.
Tallahassee, Florida 32301

Randy Oven, Director
Aging Section
Department of Human Resources
618 Ponce De Leon Avenne, NE
Atlanta, Georgia 30308

Renji Goto, Director
Executive Office on Aging
Office of the Governor
1149 Bethel Street, Room 307
Honolulu, Hawaii 96813

Gary H. Gould, Director
Idaho Office on Aging
State House, Room 114
Boise, Idaho 83720

Peg R. Blaser, Director
Illinois Department on Aging
421 East Capitol Avenue
Springfield, Illinois 62706

Jean Merritt, Executive Director
Indiana Department on Aging and
Community Services
Suite 1350
Indianapolis, Indiana 46204

Karen L. Tynes, Executive
Director
Commission on the Aging
236 Jewett Building
914 Grand Avenue
Des Moines, Iowa 50319

Sylvia Hougland
Kansas Department on Aging
610 West 10th
Topeka, Kansas 66612

Peggy T. Mooney, Director
Division for Aging Services
Department for Human Resources
DHR Building, 6th Floor
275 East Main Street
Frankfort, Kentucky 40621

Margaret W. Sloan, Director
Office of Elderly Affairs
P.O. Box 80374
Baton Rouge, Louisiana 70898

Patricia Riley, Director
Bureau of Maine's Elderly
Department of Human Services
State House, Station 11
Augusta, Maine 04333

Matthew Tayback
State Director on Aging
Office on Aging
301 West Preston Street
Baltimore, Maryland 21201

Richard H. Rowland, Secretary
Department of Elder Affairs
38 Chauncy Street
Boston, Massachusetts 02111

Kenneth Oettle, Director
Office of Services to the Aging
300 East Michigan Avenue
P.O. Box 30026
Lansing, Michigan 48909

Gerald A. Bloedow, Executive Director
Metro Square Bldg., Room 204
7th and Robert Streets
St. Paul, Minnesota 55101

Jay Moon, Executive Director
Mississippi Council on Aging
301 Executive Building
802 North State Street
Jackson, Mississippi 39201

Rick Westpal, Director
Division on Aging
Department of Social Services
P.O. Box 1337
Jefferson City, Missouri 65101

Norma Vestre, Administrator
Community Services Division
P.O. Box 4210
Helena, Montana 59604

Heather N. Hong, Executive Director
Department on Aging
P.O. Box 95044
301 Centennial Mall South
Lincoln, Nebraska 68509

S. Barton Jacka, Director
Department of Human Resources
Division for Aging Services
Administrative Office, Kinkead Bldg.
Room 101
505 E. King Street - Capitol Complex
Carson City, Nevada 89710

Stephanie Eaton, Director
Council on Aging
14 Depot Street
Concord, New Hampshire 03301

Eugene S. Callender, Director
N.Y. State Office for the Aging
Nelson A. Rockfeller Empire
State Plaza
Albany, New York 12223

Ernest B. Messer, Director
Division on Aging
708 Hillsboro Street, Suite 200
Raleigh, North Carolina 27603

Larry Brewster, Administrator
Aging Services
Department of Human Services
State Capitol Building
Bismarck, North Dakota 58505

Joyce F. Chapple, Director
Ohio Commission on Aging
50 West Broad Street, 9th Floor
Columbus, Ohio 43215

Jacques O. Lebel, Director
Division on Aging
Department of Community Affairs
P.O. Box 2768
363 West State Street
Trenton, New Jersey 08625

Eugene T. Varela, Administrator
State Agency on Aging
440 St. Michael's Drive
Chamisa Hills Building
Santa Fe, New Mexico 87503

Roy R. Keen, Program
Administrator
Special Unit on Aging
Department of Human Services
P.O. Box 25352
Oklahoma City, Oklahoma 73125

Richard C. Ladd, Administrator
Oregon Senior Services Division
313 Public Service Building
Salem, Oregon 97310

Jacqueline L. Nowak, Director
Bureau of Advocacy
Department of Aging
231 State Street
Harrisburg, Pennsylvania 17101

Anna M. Tucker
Director
State of Rhode Island and
Providence Plantations
Department of Elderly Affairs
79 Washington Street
Providence, Rhode Island 02903

Harry R. Bryan, Director
South Carolina Commission on Aging
915 Main Street
Columbia, South Carolina 29201

Michael Vogel, Administrator
Office of Adult Services and Aging
Department of Social Services
Richard F. Kneip Bldg.
700 North Illinois Street
Pierre, South Dakota 57501-2291

Emily M. Wiseman, Executive Director
Tennessee Commission on Aging
715 Tennessee Building
535 Church Street
Nashville, Tennessee 37219

Chris Kyker, Executive Director
Texas Department on Aging
P.O. Box 12786, Capitol Station
Austin, Texas 78711

Louise Lintz
APS Program Specialist, DoA & AS
Division of Aging
150 West North Temple, Suite 326
P.O. Box 2500
Salt Lake City, Utah 84110

Scott Sessions
State of Wyoming
Department of Health
Social Services
Office on Aging
720 West 18th Street
Cheyenne, Wyoming 82002

Mary Ellen Spencer, Director
Office On Aging
Department of Health
103 Main Street
Waterbury, Vermont 05676

Wilda Ferguson, Director
Department for the Aging
830 E. Main Street
Suite 950
Richmond, Virginia 23219

Charles Reed, Director
Bureau of Aging and Adult
Services
Department of Social and Health
Services
OB-43G
Olympia, Washington 98504

Phillip D. Turner,
Executive Director
West Virginia Commission
on Aging
Holly Grove - Capitol Complex
Charleston, West Virginia
25305

Donna McDowell, Director
Bureau on Aging
1 West Wilson Street
Room 685
Madison, Wisconsin 53707

C. STATE MEDICAID AGENCIES

OFFICIALLY DESIGNATED AUTHORITY	PROGRAM CONTACT
Medical Services Adminstration 2500 Fairlane Drive Montgomery, Alabama 36130 205/277-2710	None

Department of Health and Social
Services
Pouch H-01
Juneau, Alaska 99811
907/465-3030

Department of Human Services
406 National Old Line Building
Little Rock, Arkansas 72201
501/371-1001

Department of Health
714 P Street
Office Building Number 8
Sacramento, California 95814
916/445-1248

Department of Social Services
1575 Sherman Street
Denver, Colorado 80203
303/839-3513

Department of Social Services
110 Bartholomew Avenue
Hartford, Connecticut 06306
203/566-2008

Department of Health and Social
Services
Delaware State Hospital
New Castle, Delaware 19730
302/421-6705

Department of Human Resources
District Building - Room 406
1350 E. Street, NW
Washington, DC 20004
202/629-3079

Department of Health and
Rehabilitative Services
1323 Winewood Blvd.
Tallhassee, Florida 32301
904/488-7721

Division of Public Assistance
Department of Health and Social
Services
Pouch H-07
Juneau, Alaska 99811
907/465-3355

Office of Medical Services
Division of Social Services
Dept. of Human Services
P.O. Box 1437
Little Rock, Arkansas 72203
501/371-1086

Medical Assitance Division
State Department of Health
714 P Street
Sacramento, California 95814
916/322-2334

Division of Medical Assistance
Department of Social Services
1575 Sherman Street
Denver, Colorado
303/839-3031

Medical Care Adminstration
Department of Social Services
110 Bartholomew Avenue
Hartford, Connecticut 06306
203/566-3435

Medical Assistance Services
Department of Health and Social
Services
P.O. Box 309
Wilmington, Delaware 19899
302/571-3130/3131

Department of Human Resources
1329 E Street, NW
Washington, DC 20004
202/347-3512

Medical Services
Department of Health and Rehabilitative Services
1323 Winewood Boulevard
Tallhassee, Florida 32301
904/487-2380

Georgia Department of Medical
Assistance
1010 West Peachtree St., NW
Atlanta, Georgia 30309
404/894-4911

Medicaid Office
Department of Medical Assistance
1010 West Peachtree Street, NW
Atlanta, Georgia 30309
404/894-4911

Department of Public Health and
Social Services
P.O. Box 2816
Agana, Guam 96910
Overseas Operator: 734-9901

Medical Care Services
Department of Public Health and
Social Services
P.O. Box 2719
Agana, Guam 96910
Overseas Operator: 734-9901

Department of Social Services and
Housing
P.O. Box 339
Honolulu, Hawaii 96809
808/548-6260

Medical Care Administration
Department of Social Service and
Housing
P.O. Box 339
Honolulu, Hawaii 96809
808/548-6584

Department of Health and Welfare
Statehouse
Boise, Idaho 83720
208/384-2336

Bureau of Medical Assistance
Department of Health and Welfare
Statehouse
Boise, Idaho 83720
208/384-3556

Dept. of Public Aid
316 South Second Street
Springfield, Illinois 62706
217/782-6716

Division of Medical Program
Services
316 South Second Street
Springfield, Illinois 62706
217/782-1211

Dept. of Public Welfare
State Office Building
100 North Senate Avenue - Room 701
Indianapolis, Indiana 46204
317/633-6650

Division of Medical Services
State Department of Public Welfare
100 North Senate Avenue-Room 701
Indianapolis, Indiana 46204
317/633-5582

Department of Social Services
Lucas State Office Building
Des Moines, Iowa 50319
515/281-5452

Medical Services Section
Department of Social Services
Lucas State Office Building
Des Moines, Iowa 50319
515/281-3386

Department of Social and Rehabilitation Service
State Office Building
Topeka, Kansas 66612
913/296-3271

Medical Services Section
Department of Social and Rehabili-
tation Services
State Office Building
Topeka, Kansas 66612
913/296-3981

Department for Human Resources
DHR Building
Frankfort, Kentucky 40601
502/564-7130

Division for Medical Assistance
Bureau for Social Insurance
Department for Human Resources
Frankfort, Kentucky 40601
502/564-4321

Health and Human Resources Administration
P.O. Box 44215
Baton Rouge, Louisiana 70804
504/389-5796

Medical Assistance Program
Office of Family Services
Medical Assistance Unit
P.O. Box 44065
Baton Rouge, Louisiana 70804
504/389-5035

Department of Human Services
Statehouse
Augusta, Maine 04330
207/289-2736

Medical Assistance Unit
Department of Human Services
Statehouse
Augusta, Maine 04330
207/289-3846

Department of Health and Mental Hygiene
201 West Preston Street
Baltimore, Maryland 21201
301/383-2600

Medical Programs
Department of Health and Mental Hygiene
201 West Preston Street
Baltimore, Maryland 21201
301/383-6327

Department of Public Welfare
600 Washington Street
Boston, Massachusetts 02111
617/727-6190
Massachusetts Commission for the Blind
110 Tremont Street
Boston, Massachusetts 02108
617/727-5580

Medical Assistance
Department of Public Welfare
600 Washington Street
Boston, Massachusetts 02111
617/727-6095/3907
Medical Assistance
Massachusetts Commission for the Blind
110 Tremont Street
Boston, Massachusetts 02108
617/727-5590

Michigan Department of Social Services
Commerce Center Building
300 South Capitol Avenue
Lansing, Michigan 48926
517/373-2000

Bureau of Medical Assistance
Department of Social Services
300 South Capital Avenue
Lansing, Michigan 48926
517/373-1970

Dept. of Public Welfare
Centennial Office Building
658 Cedar Street
Saint Paul, Minnesota 55155
612/296-2701

Medical Assistance Program
Bureau of Income Maintenance
Department of Public Welfare
690 North Robert Street
Saint Paul, Minnesota 55155
612/296-8517

Mississippi Medicaid Commission Third Floor, Dale Building, North 2906 North State Street P.O. Box 5160 Jackson, Mississippi 39216 601/354-7464	None
Department of Social Services Broadway State Office Building Jefferson City, Missouri 65101 314/751-4247	Medical Services Division of Family Services Department of Social Services Broadway State Office Building Jefferson City, Missouri 65101 314/751-2500
Department of Social and Rehabilitation Services P.O. Box 4210 Helena, Montana 59601 406/449-3451	Medical Assistance Bureau Economic Assistance Division Department of Social and Rehabilitation Services P.O. Box 4210 Helena, Montana 59601 406/449-3952
Department of Public Welfare 301 Centennial Mall South 5th Floor Lincoln, Nebraska 68509 402/471-3121	Medical Services Division Department of Public Welfare 301 Centennial Mall South 5th Floor Lincoln, Nebraska 68509 402/471-3121
Department of Human Resources Kinkead Building-Capitol Complex 505 East King Street Carson City, Nevada 89710 702/885-4730	Medical Care Section Welfare Division Department of Human Resources 251 Jeanell Drive Capital Complex Carson City, Nevada 89710 702/885-4775
Department of Health and Welfare Services 8 Loudon Road Concord, New Hampshire 03301 603/271-3331	Office of Medical Services 8 Loudon Road Concord, New Hampshire 03301 603/271-3706
Department of Human Services 135 West Hanover Trenton, New Jersey 08625 609/292-3713	Division of Medical Assistance and Health Services Department of Human Services 324 East State Street Trenton, New Jersey 08608 609/292-7110

Health and Social Services
Department
P.O. Box 2348
Santa Fe, New Mexico 87503
505/827-2371

Medical Assistance Division
Health and Social Services
Department
P.O. Box 2348
Santa Fe, New Mexico 87503
505/827-2401

State Department of Social Services
Ten Eyck Office Building
40 North Pearl Street
Albany, New York 12243
518/474-9475

Division of Medical Assistance
State Department of Social Services
Ten Eyck Office Building
40 North Pearl Street
Albany, New York 12243
518/474-9132

Department of Human Resources
325 North Salisbury Street
Raleigh, North Carolina 27611
919/733-4534

Medical Services Section
Department of Human Resources
325 North Salisbury Street
Raleigh, North Carolina 27611
919/733-2060

Social Services Board of North
Dakota
State Capitol Building
Bismarck, North Dakota 58505
701/224-2321

Medical Services, Social Services
Board of North Dakota
State Capitol Building
Bismarck, North Dakota 58505
701/224-2321

Department of Public Welfare
30 East Broad Street, 32nd Floor
Columbus, Ohio 43215
614/466-6282

Division of Medical Assistance
Department of Public Welfare
30 East Broad Street, 32nd Floor
Columbus, Ohio 43215
614/466-2365

Department of Institutions
Social and Rehabilitative Services
P.O. Box 25352
Oklahoma City, Oklahoma 73125
405/521-3646

Medical Services Division
Department of Institutions
Social and Rehabilitative Services
P.O. Box 25352
Oklahoma City, Oklahoma 73125
405/521-3801

Department of Human Resources
318 Public Service Building
Salem, Oregon 97310
503/378-3034

Adult and Family Services Division
Department of Human Resources
417 Public Service Building
Salem, Oregon 97310
503/378-3680

Stae Department of Public Welfare
Health and Welfare Building
Harrisburg, Pennsylvania 17120
717/787-2600/3600

Bureau of Medical Assistance
State Department of Public Welfare
7th and Forester Streets
Harrisburg, Pennsylvania 17120
717/787-1170/1174

Department of Health
P.O. Box 9342
Santurce, Puerto Rico 00908
809/723-2050

Health Economy Office
Department of Health
P.O. Box 10037
Caparra Heights Station
Rio Piedras, Puerto Rico 00922
809/765-9941

Department of Social and Rehabilitative Services
Aime J. Forand Building
600 New London Avenue
Cranston, Rhode Island 02920
401/464-2121

Division of Medicaid Services
Department of Social and Rehabilitative Services
Aime J. Forand Building
600 New London Avenue
Cranston, Rhode Island 02920
401/464-2174

State Department of Social Services
P.O. Box 1520
Columbia, South Carolina 29202
803/758-3244

Division of Medical Assistance
State Department of Social Services
P.O. Box 1520
Columbia, South Carolina 29202
803/758-2320

Division of Social Welfare
Department of Social Services
State Office Building III
Illinois Street
Pierre, South Dakota 57501
605/224-3491

Office of Medical Services
Department of Social Services
State Office Building III
Pierre, South Dakota 57501
605/224-3495

Department of Public Health
344 Cordell Hull Building
Nashville, Tennessee 37219
615/741-3111

Bureau of Medicaid
Adminstration and Coordination
Department of Public Health
344 Cordell Hull Building
Nashville, Tennessee 37219
615/741-7894

Department of Human Resources
John H. Reagan Building
Austin, Texas 78701
512/475-5777

Department of Human Resources
John H. Reagan Building
Austin, Texas 78701
512/475-2541

Department of Social Services
150 West North Temple
Salt Lake City, Utah 84110
801/533-5331

Office of Medical Services
Department of Social Services
150 West North Temple
Salt Lake City, Utah 84110
801/533-5038

Department of Social Welfare
State Office Building
Four East State Street
Montpelier, Vermont 05602
802/828-3421

Division of Medical Care
Department of Social Welfare
State Office Building
Four East State Street
Montpelier, Vermont 05602
802/828-3441

Department of Health
Charlotte Amalie
St. Thomas, Virgin Islands 00801
809/774-1321

Bureau of Health Insurance and Medical Assistance
Department of Health
Franklin Building
Charlotte Amalie
St. Thomas, Virgin Islands 00801
809/774-4624

State Department of Health
109 Governor Street
Richmond, Virginia 23219
804/786-3561

Medical Assistance Program
State Department of Health
109 Governor Street
Richmond, Virginia 23219
804/786-7933

Department of Social and Health Services
Mail Stop OB-44
Olympia, Washington 98504
206/753-3395

Office of Medical Assistance
Department of Social and Health Services
Mail Stop LK-11
Olympia, Washington 98504
206/753-5839

West Virginia Department of Welfare
1900 Washington Street, East
Charleston, West Virginia 25305
304/348-2400

Division of Medical Care
Department of Welfare
1900 Washington Street, East
Charleston, West Virginia 25305
304/348-8990

Department of Health and Social Services
One West Wilson Street
Madison, Wisconsin 53702
608/266-3681

Bureau of Health Financing Control
Division of Health
Department of Health and Social Service
One West Wilson Street
Madison, Wisconsin 53702
608/266-2522

Department of Health and Social Services
Hathaway Building
Cheyenee, Wyoming 82002
307/328-9657

Medical Assistance Services
Division of Health and Social Services
Department of Health and Social Services
State Office Building
Cheyenne, Wyoming 82002
307/777-9533

D. STATE MENTAL HEALTH OFFICES

State Department of Mental Health
Mr. Glenn Ireland, II
Commissioner
135 Union Street
Montgomery, Alabama 36130

Tel. (205) 834-4350

Same as Authority

Alaska Dept. of Health and Social Services
Helen A. Beirne, Ph.D.
Commissioner
Pouch H-01
Juneau, Alaska 99811

Tel. (907) 465-3030

Verner Stillner, M.D., M.P.H.
Director
Division of Mental Health and Developmental Disabilities
Alaska Dept. of Health and Social Services
Pouch H-04
Juneau, Alaska 99811

Tel. (907) 465-3370

Arizona Dept. of Health Services
Suzanne Dandoy, M.D., M.P.H.
Director
1740 West Adams Street
Phoenix, Arizona 85007

Tel. (602) 255-1024

Mr. Jack Beveridge, Acting Chief
Bureau of Community Services
Div. of Behavioral Health Services
Arizona Dept. of Health Services
2500 East Van Buren
Phoenix, Arizona 85008

Tel. (602) 255-1231/2

Arkansas State Hospital
Div. of Mental Health Services
Mr. Patrick Hamilton
Acting Commissioner Mental Health Services
4313 West Markham Street
Little Rock, Arkansas 72201

Tel. (501) 664-4500 X401

Larry R. Faulkner, M.D.
Deputy Commissioner for Community Mental Health Services and Affiliated Programs
Div. of Mental Health Services
Dept. of Human Services
4313 West Markam Street
Little Rock, Arkansas 72201

Tel. (501) 664-4500 X381

California Dept. of Mental Health
Dale H. Farabee, M.D.
Director
2260 Park Towne Circle
Sacramento, California 95826

Same as Authority

Colorado Dept. of Institutions Raymond Leidig, M.D. Executive Director 3550 West Oxford Avenue Denver, Colorado 80236 Tel. (303) 761-0220 X225	Sutherland Miller, Ph.D. Director Division of Mental Health Colorado Dept. of Institutions 3520 West Oxford Avenue Denver, Colorado Tel. (303) 761-0220 X201
Connecticut Dept. of Mental Health Eric A. Plaut, M.D. Commissioner 90 Washington Street Hartford, Connecticut 06115 Tel. (203) 566-3650	Same as Authority
Dept. of Health & Social Services Mrs. Patricia C. Schramm Secretary Adminstration Bldg., 3rd Floor Delaware State Hospital New Castle, Delaware 19720 Tel. (302) 421-6705	Mr. Sheldon Schweidel Director Division of Mental Health Delaware State Hospital C.T. Building New Castle, Delaware 19720 Tel. (302) 421-6101
Department of Human Resources Mr. Albert P. Russo Director District Building 1350 E Street, N.W. Washington, D.C. 20004 Tel. (202) 727-0310	Evelyn Ireland, Ph.D. Acting Adminstrator Mental Health Administration Department of Human Resources 1875 Connecticut Avenue, N.W. Washington, D.C. 20009 Tel. (202) 673-6720
Florida Dept. of Health and Rehabilitative Services Mr. Abe Lavine Assistant Secretary for Program Planning and Development 1323 Winewood Boulevard Tallahassee, Florida 32301 Tel. (904) 487-1111	Robert R. Furlough, Ph.D. Acting Mental Health Program Staff Director Mental Health Program Office 1323 Winewood Boulevard Tallahassee, Florida 32301 Tel. (904) 488-8304

Department of Human Resources W. Douglas Skelton, M.D. Commissioner 47 Trinity Avenue, S.W. State Office Building, Room 620 Atlanta, Georgia 30334 Tel. (404) 656-5680	Mr. R. Derril Gay, Director Div. of Mental Health and Mental Retardation Department of Human Resources 47 Trinity Avenue, S.W. Health Building, Room 315-H Atlanta, Georgia 30334 Tel. (404) 656-4908
State Department of Health Mr. George A.L. Yuen, Director Post Office Box 3378 Honolulu, Hawaii 96801 Tel. (808) 548-6505	Denis Mee-Lee, M.D., Chief Mental Health Division State Department of Health Post Office Box 3378 Honolulu, Hawaii 96801 Tel. (808) 548-6335
Dept. of Health and Welfare Mr. Milton Klein, Director 700 W. State STATEHOUSE Mail Boise, Idaho 83720 Tel. (208) 334-2336	Dr. Robert W. Glover Administrator Div. of Community Rehabilitation Dept. of Health and Welfare 700 W. State STATEHOUSE Mail Boise, Idaho 83720 Tel. (208) 334-4000
Illinois Dept. of Mental Health and Developmental Disabilities Robert A. deVito, M.D., Director 160 N. LaSalle Street, Room 1500 Chicago, Illinois 60601 Tel. (312) 793-2730	Same as Authority
Indiana Dept. of Mental Health Dr. William E. Murray, Commissioner 5 Indiana Square Indianapolis, Indiana 46204 Tel. (317) 232-7844	Same as Authority
Iowa Mental Health Authority Dr. Herbert L. Nelson, Director Oakdale Campus Oakdale, Iowa 52319 Tel. (319) 353-3901 RE: 314(d) State Mental Health Plan, Community Mental Health Authority	Same as Authority

Department of Social Services
Div. of Mental Health Resources
Mr. Charles M. Palmer, Director
Hoover State Office Building
Des Moines, Iowa 50319

Tel. (515) 281-6003

RE: State Hospial Authority

Same as Authority

State Dept. of Social and
Rehabilitation Services
Dr. Robert C. Harder, Secretary
State Office Building
Topeka, Kansas 66612

Tel. (913) 296-3271

Mr. Ken Keller, Acting Director
Div. of Mental Health and
Retardationn Services
State Dept. of Social and
Rehabilitation Services
State Office Building
Topeka, Kansas 66612

Tel. (913) 296-3774

Department for Human Resources
Mr. J.E. DeShazer, Secretary
275 East Main Street
Frankfort, Kentucky 40621

Tel. (503) 564-7130

Mrs. Verna Fairchild, R.N.
Acting Director
Bureau for Health Services
Department for Human Resources
275 East Main Street
Frankfort, Kentucky 40621

Tel. (502) 564-4360

Department of Health and
Human Resources
William A. Cherry, M.D.
Secretary
Post Office Box 3776
Baton Rouge, Louisiana 70821

Tel. (504) 342-6711

Carolyn T. Kitchin, M.D.
Assistant Secretary
Office of Mental Health and
Substance Abuse
Department of Health and
Human Resources
Post Office Box 106
Baton Rouge, Louisiana 70821

Tel. (504) 342-2544

Maine Dept. of Mental Health
and Corrections
Mr. Ronald R. Martel
Acting Commissioner
411 State Office Building
Augusta, Maine 04330

Tel. (207) 289-3161

Mrs. Chase Whittenberger
Director
Bureau of Mental Health
Maine Department of Mental
Health and Corrections
411 State Office Building
Augusta, Maine 04330

Tel. (207) 289-2711

Maryland Department of Health and Mental Hygiene Stanley R. Platman, M.D. Assistant Secretary for Mental Health and Addictions Herbert R. O'Connor State Office Building 201 W. Preston St., 5th floor Baltimore, Maryland, 21201 Tel. (301) 383-2686	Dr. Gary W. Nyman, Director Mental Hygiene Administration Maryland Department of Health and Mental Hygiene Herbert R. O'Connor State Office Building 201 W. Preston St., 4th floor Baltimore, Maryland 21201 Tel. (301) 383-2695
Massachusetts Dept. of Mental Health Robert L. Okin, M.D., Commissioner 160 North Washington Street Boston, Massachusetts 02114 Tel. (617) 727-5600	Same as Authority
Michigan Dept. of Mental Health Frank M. Ochberg, M.D., Director Lewis Case Building Lansing, Michigan 48926 Tel. (517) 373-3500	Same as Authority
Department of Public Welfare Mental Health Bureau Mr. Harvey Caldwell Assistant Commissioner Centennial Office Building St. Paul, Minnesota 55155 Tel. (612) 296-2791	Mr. James (Terry) Sarazin Director Mental Illness Program Division Department of Public Welfare Centennial Office Buiding St. Paul, Minnesota 55155 Tel. (612) 296-2710
State Dept. of Mental Health William L. Jaquith, M.D Executive Director 607 Robert E. Lee Office Bldg. Jackson, Mississippi 39201 Tel. (601) 354-6132	A.G. Anderson, M.D., Director Division of Mental Health State Dept. of Mental Health 607 Robert E. Lee Office Bldg. Jackson, Mississippi 39201 Tel. (601) 354-7041
Department of Mental Health Paul R. Ahr, Ph.D., M.P.A., Director 2002 Missouri Boulevard Jefferson City, Missouri 65101 Tel. (314) 751-3070	Nancy Barron, Ph.D. Program Evaluation and Planning Coordinator Department of Mental Health 2002 Missouri Boulevard Jefferson City, Missouri 65101 Tel. (314) 751-4933

Montana State Dept. of Institutions
Mr. Lawrence M. Zanto, Director
1539 11th Avenue
Helena, Montana 59601

Tel. (406) 449-3930

Dr. Peter S. Blouke
Administrator
Mental Health and Residential
Services Division
Montana State Department of
Institutions
1539 11th Avenue
Helena, Montana 59601

Tel. (406) 449-3964

State Department of Public
Institutions
W. Ralph Michener, J.D., Director
Post Office Box 94728
Lincoln, Nebraska 68509

Tel. (402) 471-2851

Charles W. Landgraf, Jr., M.D.
Acting Director
Division of Medical Services
State Department of Public
Institutions
Post Office Box 94728
Lincoln, Nebraska 68509

Tel. (402) 471-2851

Department of Human Resources
Ralph R. DiSibio, Ed.D., Director
Kinkead Building, Room 600
505 E. King Street
State Capitol Complex
Carson City, Nevada 89710

Tel. (702) 885-4730

Mr. Jerome Grienpentrog
Administrator
Division of Mental Hygiene/
Mental Retardation
1937 North Carson St., Suite 244
Carson City, Nevada 89701

Tel. (702) 885-5943

Department of Health and Welfare
Mr. Edgar J. Helms, Commissioner
Hazen Drive
Concord, New Hampshire 03301

Tel. (603) 271-4331

Gary E. Miller, M.D., Director
Division of Mental Health
Hazen Drive
Concord, New Hampshire 03301

Tel. (603) 271-4680

New Jersey State Department of
Human Services
Ann Klein, Commissioner
Post Office Box 1237
Trenton, New Jersey 08625

Tel. (609) 292-3717

Michail Rotov, M.D., Director
Division of Mental Health and
Hospitals
Capital Place One
222 South Warren Street
Trenton, New Jersey 08625

Tel. (609) 292-4242

New Mexico Department of Health
and Environment
George S. Goldstein, Ph.D., Secretary
Post Office Box 968
Santa Fe, New Mexico 87503

Tel. (505) 827-5671, x200

Marshall Fitz, M.D., Chief,
Mental Health Bureau
Division of Behavioral Health
Services
New Mexico Department of Health
and Environment
Post Office Box 968
Santa Fe, New Mexico 87503

Tel. (505) 827-5271

Office of Mental Health James A. Prevost, M.D. Commissioner 44 Holland Avenue Albany, New York 12229 Tel. (518) 474-4403	Donald G. Miles, Ed.D. Deputy Commissioner Division of Program Operations Office of Mental Health 44 Holland Avenue Albany, New York 12229 Tel. (518) 474-6567
North Carolina Department of Human Resources Sarah T. Morrow, M.D., M.P.H. Secretary 325 N. Salisbury Street Raleigh, North Carolina 27611 Tel. (919) 733-4534	Mr. Ben W. Aiken, Director Division of Mental Health and Mental Retardation Services North Carolina Department of Human Resources 325 N. Salisbury Street Raleigh, North Carolina 27611 Tel. (919) 733-7011
State Department of Health North Dakota Division of Mental Health and Retardation Mr. Samih A. Ismir, Acting Director Post Office Box 476 Jamestown, North Dakota 58401 Tel. (701) 253-2964	Mr. Samih A. Ismir Assistant Director Mental Health and Retardation Services North Dakota Division of Mental Health and Retardation State Department of Health 909 Basin Avenue Bismarck, North Dakota 58505 Tel. (701) 224-2766
Ohio Department of Mental Health and Mental Retardation Timothy B. Moritz, M.D., Director 30 E. Broad Street, Room 1182 Columbus, Ohio 43215 Tel. (614) 466-2337	Same as Authority
State Department of Mental Health J. Franklin James, M.D., Director Post Office Box 53277 Capitol Station Oklahoma City, Oklahoma 73152 Tel. (405) 521-2811	Mr. John H. Holt, Deputy Director for Hospital Services State Department of Mental Health Post Office Box 53277 Capitol Station Oklahoma City, Oklahoma 73152
Mental Health Division J.H. Treleaven, M.D., Assistant Director, Human Resources and Administration of Mental Health 2575 Bittern Street, N.E. Salem, Oregon 97310 Tel. (503) 378-2671	Same as Authority

State Department of Public Welfare
Mrs. Helen O'Bannon
Secretary of Welfare
Health and Welfare Bldg., Rm, 333
Harrisburg, Pennsylvania 17120

Tel. (717) 787-3600 or 2600

Mr. Robert P. Haigh, Acting
Deputy Secretary for
Mental Health
State Dept. of Public Welfare
Health and Welfare Bldg.
Room 308
Harrisburg, Pennsylvania 17120

Tel. (717) 787-6443

Rhode Island Dept. of Mental Health
Retardation and Hospitals
Joseph J. Bevilacqua, Ph.D., Director
The Aime J. Forand Building
600 New London Avenue
Cranston, Rhode Island 02920

Tel. (401) 464-3201

Mr. Neil Meisler, Adminstrator
Mental Health
Office of Community Mental
Health Service
Rhode Island Dept. of Mental
Health, Retardation, and
Hospitals
Rhode Island Medical Center
Cottage # 403
Cranston, Rhode Island 02920

Tel. (401) 464-3291

State Department of Mental Health
Dr. William S. Hall, Commissioner
Post Office Box 485
Columbia, South Carolina 29202

Tel. (803) 758-7701

Same as Authority

State Dept. of Social Services
Office of Mental Health
Mr. Mike Adamski, Acting Program
Adminstrator
State Office Bldg., 3rd floor
Illinois Street
Pierre, South Dakota 57501

Tel. (605) 773-3115

Same as Authority

Tennessee Dept. of Mental Health
and Mental Retardation
James S. Brown, M.D., Commissioner
501 Union Building, 4th floor
Nashville, Tennessee 37219

Tel. (615) 741-3107

Robert Fink, M.D., Acting
Assistant Commissioner
Division of Mental Health
Services
Tennessee Dept. of Mental
Health and Mental Retardation
501 Union Bldg., lower level
Nashville, Tennessee 37219

Tel. (615) 741-3348

Texas Dept. of Mental Health and Mental Retardation
John J. Kavanagh, M.D., Commissioner
Capitol Station
Post Office Box 12668
Austin, Texas 78711

Tel. (512) 454-3761

Jon D. Hannum, Ph.D.
Deputy Commissioner
Community Services
Texas Dept. of Mental Health and Mental Retardation
Capitol Station
Post Office Box 12668
Austin, Texas 78711

Tel. (512) 454-3761

State Dept. of Social Services
Anthony W. Mitchell, Ph.D.
Executive Director
Post Office Box 2500
Salt Lake City, Utah 84110

Tel. (801) 533-5331

Wilfred H. Higaski, Ph.D.
Director
Division of Mental Health
Utah Dept. of Social Services
Post Office Box 2500
Salt Lake City, Utah 84110

Tel. (801) 533-5783

Vermont Dept. of Mental Health
Richard C. Surles, Ph.D.
Commissioner
State Office Building
Montpelier, Vermont 05602

Tel. (802) 241-2610

Same as Authority

State Dept. of Mental Health and Mental Retardation
Leo E. Kirven, Jr., M.D., Commissioner
Post Office Box 1797
Richmond, Virginia 23214

Tel. (804) 786-3921

Miss Margaret L. Cavey, R.N.
Acting Assistant Commissioner
Division of Mental Health
State Dept. of Mental Health and Mental Retardation
Post Office Box 1797
Richmond, Virginia 23214

Tel. (804) 786-3902

Mental Health Divison
Delbert M. Kole, M.D., Director
Mail Stop OB-42F
Olympia, Washington 98504

Tel. (206) 753-5414

Same as Authority

Office of Community Health Services
Mel Henry, Ph.D., Director
State Capitol Complex
1800 Washington Street, East
Charleston, West Virginia 25305

Tel. (304) 348-0025

Mr. Randy Myers, Acting Director
Division of Behavioral Health Services
Office of Community Health Services
1800 Washington Street, East
Charleston, West Virginia 25305

Tel. (304) 348-2411

Wisconsin Department of Health and Social Services
Mr. Donald E. Percy, Secretary
State Office Bldg., Room 663
1 West Wilson Street
Madison, Wisconsin 53702

Tel. (608) 266-3681

Mr. Burton A. Wagner
Adminstrator
Division of Community Services
Wisconsin Department of Health and Social Services
State Office Bldg., Room 534
1 West Wilson Street
Madison, Wisconsin 53702

Tel. (608) 266-2701

Division of Community Programs
Mr. Guy Noe, Administrator
The Hathaway Building
2300 Capitol Avenue
Cheyenne, Wyoming 82002

Tel. (307) 777-7121

Same as Authority

Government of American Samoa
Department of Medical Services
Julia Grach, M.D., Director
LBJ Tropical Medical Center
Pago Pago, Tutuila
American Samoa 96799

Tel. Overseas Operator and 633-5732

Guy Spinello, M.D., Director
Mental Health Clinic
LBJ Tropical Medical Center
Pago Pago, Tutuila
American Samoa 96799

Tel Overseas Operator and 633-5139

Government of Guam
Mental Health and Substance Abuse Agency
Mr. Peter S. San Nicolas, Administrator
Post Office Box 20999, Main Facility
Guam 96921

Tel. Overseas Operator and 477-9704/5

Same as Authority

Commonwealth of the Northern Mariana Islands
Division of Mental Health
Dr. Frances Schwaninger-Morse
Dr. Torres Hospital
Saipan, Mariana Islands 96950

Tel. Overseas Operator and 6110 or 9314

Same as Authority

Department of Health
Dr. Jaime Rivera Dueno, Secretary
Box 9342
Santurce, Puerto Rico 00908

Tel. (809) 765-7453

Dr. Aida Guzman
Assistant Secretary for Mental Health
G.P.O. Box 61
San Juan, Puerto Rico 00936

Tel. (809) 781-5660

Office of the High Commissioner
Masao Kumangai
Medical Officer, M.P.H.
Director of Health Services
Trust Territory of the Pacific Islands
Saipan, Mariana Islands 96950

Tel. Overseas Operator and 9422 or 9355

Government of the Virgin Islands
Virgin Islands Department of Health
Roy L. Schneider, M.D.
Commissioner of Health
St. Thomas, Virgin Islands 00801

Tel. (809) 774-0117

Paul W. Dale, M.D., Chief
Mental Health Branch
Bureau of Health Services
Office of the High Commissioner
Trust Territory of the Pacific Islands
Saipan, Mariana Islands 96950

Tel Overseas Operator and 9422 or 9355

Chester D. Copemann, Ph.D.
Director
Division of Mental Health Services
Department of Health
Post Office Box 7309
St. Thomas, Virgin Islands 00801

Tel. (809) 773-1992

E. NATIONAL ORGANIZATIONS

Action for Independent Maturity
1909 K Street, N.W.
Washington, DC 20049
202/728-4466

Al-Anon Family Group Headquarters
One Park Avenue
New York, NY 10016
212/683-1771

Alcohol and Drug Problems Association of North America
1101 15th Street, N.W.
Washington, DC 20005
202/452-0990

Alzheimer's Disease and Related Disorders Association
360 N. Michigan Avenue, Suite 601
Chicago, Illinois 60601
312/853-3060

American Aging Association
c/o Denham Harman, M.D.
College of Medicine
University of Nebraska
Omaha, Nebraska 68105
402/559-4416

American Association of Homes for the Aging
1050 17th Street, N.W., Suite 770
Washington, DC 20036
202/296-5960

American Association of Retired Persons
1909 K Street, N.W.
Washington DC 20049
202/872-4700

American Cancer Society
777 Third Avenue
New York, New York 10017
212/371-2900

American College of Nutrition
New York University Medical Center
Goldwater Memorial Hospital
Roosevelt Island, New York 10044
212/308-3633

American Council of the Blind
1211 Connecticut Avenue, N.W.
Suite 506
Washington, DC 20036
202/833-1251

American Council of the Blind
1211 Connecticut Avenue, N.W.
Suite 506
Washington, DC 20036
202/833-1251

American Council on Alcoholism
Medical Center Suite 16-B
300 E. Joppa Road
Baltimore, Maryland 21204
301/296-5545

American Diabetes Association
Two Park Avenue
New York, New York 10016
212/683-7444

American Dietetic Association
430 N. Michigan Avenue
Chicago, Illinois 60611
312/280-5000

American Foundation for the Blind
15 W. 16th Street
New York, New York 10011
212/620-2000

American Geriatrics Society
Ten Columbus Circle
New York, New York 10019
212/582-1333

American Health Care Association
1200 15th Street, N.W.
Washington, DC 20005
202/833-2050

American Heart Association
7320 Greenville Avenue
Dallas, Texas 75231
214/750-5300

American Institute of Nutrition
9650 Rockville Pike
Bethesda, Maryland 20814
301/530-7050

American Lung Association
1740 Broadway
New York, New York 10019
212/245-8000

American Mental Health Counselors Association
UPO 1321
Morehead State University
Morehead, Kentucky 40351
800/354-2008

American Mental Health Foundation
Two E. 86th Street
New York, New York 10028
212/737-9027

American Occupational Therapy Association
1383 Piccard Drive, Suite 301
Rockville, Maryland 20850
301/948-9626

American Parkinson Disease Association
116 John Street, Suite 417
New York, New York 10038
212/732-9550

American Physical Therapy Associaton
1156 15th Street, N.W.
Washington, DC 20005
202/466-2070

American Psychological Association
Division of Adult Development and Aging
1200 17th Street, N.W.
Washington, DC 20036
202/833-7600

American Rheumatism Associaton
Arthritis Foundation
3400 Peachtree Road, N.E.
Atlanta, Georgia 30326
404/226-0795

American Society for Mature Catholics
740 N. Plankington Avenue
Milwaukee, Wisconsin 53203
414/271-8926

Arthritis Foundation
1314 Spring Street, N.W.
Atlanta, Georgia 30309
404/872-7100

Arthritis Information Clearinghouse
P.O. Box 9782
Arlington, Virginia 22209
703/558-8250

Assembly of Skilled Nursing and Related Long Term Care Services
American Hospital Association
840 N. Lake Shore Drive
Chicago, Illinois 60611
312/280-6382

Association of Community Cancer Centers
11600 Nebel Street, Suite 201
Rockville, Maryland 20852
301/984-9496

Association of Mental Health Clergy
c/o George E. Doebler
Lakeshore Mental Health Institute
5908 Lyons View Drive
Knoxville, Tennessee 37919
615/584-0521

Association of Rehabilitation Nurses
2506 Gross Point Road
Evanston, Illinois 60201
312/475-7530

Cancer Guidance Institute
5501 Fair Oaks Street
Pittsburgh, Pennsylvania 15217
412/521-2290

Catholic Golden Age
400 Lackawanna Avenue
Scranton, Pennsylvania 18503
717/342-3294

Center for the Study of Aging
706 Madison Avenue
Albany, New York 12208
518/465-6927

Concerned Relatives of Nursing Home Patients
P.O. Box 11820
Cleveland, Ohio 44118
216/321-0403

Consumer Protection Center
2000 L Street, N.W., Suite 307
Washington, DC 20052
202/676-7585

Daughters of the Elderly Bridging the Unknown Together
c/o Jane Norris
S. Central Community Mental Health Center
645 S. Rogers
Bloomington, Indiana 47401
812/339-1691

Ebenezer Society
2722 Park Avenue
Minneapolis, Minnesota 55407
612/871-7112

Elder Craftsmen
135 E. 65th Street
New York, New York 10021
212/861-5260

Family Mediation Association
5530 Wisconsin Avenue, Suite 1250
Chevy Chase, Maryland 20815
301/654-7708

Gerontological Society of America
1835 K Street, N.W., Suite 305
Washington, DC 20006
202/466-6750

Gray Panthers
3635 Chestnut Street
Philadelphia, Pennsylvania 19104
215/382-3300

Heartline/National Association of Older Americans
129 N. Cherry
Eaton, Ohio 45320

Help the Aged
1010 Vermont Avenue, N.W., #712
Washington, DC 20005
202/638-5915

Independent Citizens Research Foundation for the Study of Degenerative Diseases
P.O. Box 97
Ardsley, New York 10502
914/478-1862

Institute for Research of Rheumatic Diseases
Box 955, Ansonia Station
New York, New York 10023
212/595-1368

Institute for Retired Professionals
New School for Social Research
66 W. 12th Street
New York, New York 10011
212/741-5682

Jewish Association for Services
for the Aged
40 W. 68th Street
New York, New York 10023
212/724-3200

Leadership Council of Aging
Organizations
c/o National Council of Senior
Citizens
925 15th Street, N.W.
Washington, DC 20005
202/347-8800

Legal Counsel for the Elderly
1909 K Street, N.W.
Washington, DC 20049
202/331-4215

Legal Services for the Elderly
132 W. 43rd Street, 3rd Floor
New York, New York 10036
212/595-1340

National Alliance of Senior
Citizens
101 Park Washington Court
Falls Church, Virginia 22046
703/241-1533

National Association for Hearing
and Speech Action
10801 Rockville Pike
Rockville, Maryland 20852
301/897-8682

National Association for Human
Development
1620 Eye Street, N.W.
Washington, DC 20006
202/393-1881

National Association for
Visually Handicapped
305 E. 24th Street
New York, New York 10010
212/889-3141

National Association of Area
Agencies on Aging
600 Maryland Avenue, S.W.
West Wing, Suite 208
Washington, DC 20024
202/484-7520

National Association of Black
Social Workers
271 W. 125th Street
New York, New York 10027
212/749-0470

National Association of
Hispanic Nurses
1024 Hanshaw Road
Ithaca, New York 14850

National Association of
Mature People
Box 26792
Oklahoma City, OK 73126
405/848-1832

National Association of
of Social Workers
7981 Eastern Avenue
Silver Spring, Maryland 20910
301/565-0333

National Association of
Rehabilitation Facilities
P.O. Box 17675
Washington, DC 20015
703/556-8848

National Association for Rural
Mental Health
c/o Mental Health, UWEX
414 Lowell Hall
610 Langdon
Madison, Wisconsin 53706
608/263-2088

National Association of State
Mental Health Program Directors
1001 Third Street, S.W., Suite 114
Washington, DC 20024
202/554-7807

National Association of State
Units on Aging
600 Maryland Avenue, S.W.,
Suite 208
Washington, DC 20024
202/466-8529

National Association of the Deaf
814 Thayer Avenue
Silver Spring, Maryland 20910
301/587-1788

National Black Nurses Association
P.O. Box 18358
Boston, MA 02118
617/266-9703

National Cancer Foundation
One Park Avenue
New York, New York 10016
212/679-5700

National Caucus and Center on Black Aged
1424 K Street, N.W., Suite 500
Washington, DC 20005
202/637-8400

National Center on Arts and the Aging
600 Maryland Avenue, S.W., West Wing 100
Washington, DC 20024
202/479-1200

National Committee on Art Education for the Elderly
Culver Stockton College
Canton, Montana 63435
314/288-5221

National Council for Senior Citizens
925 15th Street, S.W.
Washington, DC 20005
202/347-8800

National Council of Community Mental Health Centers
6101 Montrose Road, Suite 360
Rockville, Maryland 20852
301/984-6200

National Council of Health Centers
2600 Virginia Avenue, N.W., Suite 1100
Washington, DC 20037
202/298-7393

National Council on Black Aging
Box 8813
Durham, NC 27707
919/684-3175

National Council on the Aging
600 Maryland Avenue, S.W.
West Wing 100, Suite 208
Washington, DC 20024
202/479-1200

National Federation of Licensed Practical Nurses
P.O. Box 11038
214 S. Driver Street
Durham, North Carolina 27703
919/596-9609

National Federation of Societies for Clinical Social Work
c/o Marsha Winebrugh
315 E. 68th Street
New York, New York 10021
202/223-6134

National Geriatrics Society
212 W. Wisconsin Avenue, 3rd Floor
Milwaukee, Wisconsin 53203
414/272-4130

National Homecaring Council
235 Park Avenue, S.
New York, New York 10003
212/674-4990

National Indian Council on Aging
P.O. Box 2088
Albuquerque, New Mexico 87103
505/766-2276

National Institute on Adult Daycare
600 Maryland Avenue, S.W., West Wing 100
Washington, DC 20024
202/479-1200

National Institute on Aging, Work and Retirement
c/o National Council on the Aging
600 Maryland Avenue, S.W.
West Wing 100
Washington, DC 20024
202/479-1200

National Institute of Arthritis, Diabetes, and Digestive and Kidney Diseases
c/o Dr. George Brooks
Westwood Bldg., Rm. 637
Bethesda, Maryland 20205
301/496-7277

National Interfaith Coalition on
Aging
P.O. Box 1924
298 S. Hull Street
Athens, Georgia 30603
404/353-1331

National League for Nursing
Ten Columbus Circle
New York, New York 10019
212/582-1022

National Mental Health Association
1800 N. Kent Street
Rosslyn, Virginia 22209
703/528-6405

National Pacific/Asian
Resource Center on Aging
811 First Avenue, Suite 210
Seattle, Washington 98104
206/622-5124

National Rehabilitation
Information Center
4407 Eighth Street, N.E.
Washington, DC 20017
202/635-5826

National Senior Citizens Law Center
1424 16th Street, N.W., Suite 300
Washington, DC 20036
202/232-6570

North American Association of
Jewish Homes and Housing for
the Aging
2525 Centerville Road
Dallas, Texas 75228
214/327-4503

One/Fourth, The Alliance for Cancer
Patients and Their Families
36 S. Wabash, Suite 700
Chicago, Illinois 60603
312/346-1414

The Church of the Brethren Homes
and Hospitals Association
1451 Dundee Avenue
Elgin, Illinois 60120
312/742-5100

Urban Elderly Coalition
600 Maryland Avenue, S.W.,
Suite 204
Washington, DC 20024
202/554-2040

APPENDIX: MODEL ADULT PROTECTIVE SERVICES ACT

The goal of this Act prepared by the Senate Select Committee on Aging was to provide guidelines for the states to use in the development and implementation of elder neglect and abuse legislation. There is no data available as yet which indicates which states have utilized the model and to what degree. Nevertheless, this Act is significant in that it addresses the key issues in elder neglect and abuse so comprehensively. When we review state-level legislation since 1977, a clear pattern of progress emerges. Before 1980, 19 states had passed some type of elder abuse legislation. Since 1980, 18 more have done so. In addition, there are 9 states with legislation pending, and only 4 states not considering legislation at the present time.

At the federal-level, elder neglect and abuse legislation is also taking place. Since 1979, Representatives Mary Oakar and Claude Pepper have submitted legislation which would establish a national center on elder abuse, and provide financial assistance for programs which would address the issues of prevention, identification and treatment of elder neglect, abuse and exploitation. This year, 1984, the bill failed once again. However, another bill was introduced, H.R. 1904, which called for the establishment of a family violence center which would include elder abuse. This bill did pass and has become Public Law 98-457.

Introductory Comments

As with any model statute, the general purpose of the Model Protective Services Act is to provide prototype legislation which the States may uti-

---

*Source: Protective services for the elderly, a working paper. Prepared for the Special Committee on Aging, U.S. Senate, July, 1977.

lize in drafting their own protective services statutes. This act also has three particular objectives: (1) To provide the authority for a Stat to develop, organize, and supervise a State program of protective services; (2) to outline guidelines and criteria for the design and operatio of a protective services system; (3) to authorize the courts to issue orders for involuntary protective services and protective placement after making specific findings and following designated procedures.

The last objective should be seen in a wider context. All States currently permit certain types of involuntary intervention in the lives o their citizens, including the elderly. The kinds of intervention relevan to the elderly are typically authorized through civil commitment proceedings involving admission to a State mental hospital or guardianship proceedings transferring authority over the ward or his property to a court-appointed fiduciary. This act does not modify or replace such legislation, but rather is intended to provide legal authority to intervene involuntarily in situations requiring less drastic interference with a person's civil rights.

Two specific situations receive particular attention. The first concerns the person whose health or living conditions pose serious danger to himself or others and consequently short-term emergency action is necessary. The court order for this problem is called an "emergency orde for protective services." Intervention for a longer period must follow the existing guardianship laws.

The other situation for which legally authorized intervention is necessary is the involuntary transfer of an elderly person's residence to an institution other than a mental hospital, such as a nursing home. Thi intervention is referred to as "protective placement."

In both instances, current State law concerning civil commitment or guardianship is either wide of the mark, which is to fill a particular need of a person, or offers too drastic a solution by declaring the perso incompetent and stripping him of all or most of his rights. The Model Protective Services Act attempts to fill the gaps in existing law and at the same time to authorize only the least restrictive and appropriate for of intervention.

This explanation of the act's methods for authorizing involuntary intervention through legal channels should not, however, divert attention from the act's other objectives. The protective services system contemplated by this act will function on a voluntary basis in the vast majority of cases. Indeed, a system which requires frequent involuntary intervention may well be suspect. It is expected that the wide range of services provided in this system to assist the elderly in maintaining independent lifestyles will prove attractive to them and invite their cooperation. The potential for involuntary intervention, and hopefully, its infrequent but necessary occurrence under the provisions of this act, will distinguish the protective services system created by this act from existing programs of home or community-centered services.

Accompanying the Model Protective Services Act is other suggested legislation. One important adjunct is the Model Public Guardian Act designed to provide guardianship services for the financially needy. Suggested revisions of the State guardianship, conservatorship, and power of attorneys laws based largely on the Uniform Probate Code are also proposed. The final proposal contains a short but significant change in State civil commitment to require courts to consider whether less drastic alternative programs than commitment are available and adequate.

The net results of the enactment of all this proposed legislation will be a program of services to the elderly to assist them to avoid institutionalization and a spectrum of alternative forms of legally authorized intervention in the elderly person's life calibrated to provide only the specific services necessary to meet immediate needs and avoid more drastic interference.

Suggested Legislation

(Title, enacting, clause, etc.)

SECTION 1. (Short title). This act may be cited as the Adult Protective Services Act.

SECTION 2. (Declaration of Policy and Legislative Intent). The legislature of the State of [__________] recognizes that many elderly citizens of the State, because of the infirmities of aging, are unable to manage their own affairs or to protect themselves from exploitation, abuse, neglect, or physical danger. Often such persons cannot find others able or willing to render assistance. The legislature intends through this act to establish a system of protective services designed to fill this need and to assure their availability to all elderly citizens. It is also the intent of the legislature to authorize only the least possible restriction on the exercise of personal and civil rights consistent with the person's need for services, and to require that due process be followed in imposing such restrictions.

Comments on Section 2.
The protective services system established by this act is designed to benefit only the elderly because, as an identifiable segment of society, their need for such services is imperative. Moreover, many States have already developed for their elderly citizens systems of supportive and preventive services which can be readily integrated into the proposed protective services system. The additional costs of the proposed program for the elderly will therefore be small, as compared with the costs of creating an entirely new services program for all residents of the State.

SECTION 3. Definitions -- As used in this act:
(1) "Conservator" means a person who is appointed by a court to manage estate of a protected person.
(2) "Court" means the court or branch having jurisdiction in matters relating to the affairs of decedents, this court in this State is known as [ ].
(3) "Department" means the [State agency responsible for community-based services to the elderly].
(4) "Elderly" means a person 60 years of age or older, who is a resident of the State.

(5) "Emergency" means that an elderly person is living in conditions which present a substantial risk of death or immediate and serious physical harm to himself or others.

(6) "Emergency services" are protective services furnished to an elderly person in an emergency pursuant to the provisions of section 10 of this act.

(7) "Geriatric evaluation service" is a team of medical, psychological, psychiatric, and social work professionals established by the [State agency responsible for community-based services to the elderly] for the purpose of conducting a comprehensive physical, mental, and social evaluation of an elderly person for whom a petition has been filed in a court for commitment to a mental hospital, appointment of a conservator or guardian, an emergency order for protective services, or an order for protective placement.

(8) "Guardian" means a person who has qualified as a guardian of an incapacitated person pursuant to testamentary or court appointment, but excludes one who is merely a guardian ad litem.

(9) "Hazardous living conditions" means a mode of life which contains a substantial risk of or actual exploitation, abuse, neglect, or physical danger.

(10) "Incapacitated person" means [alternative A: any person who is impaired by reason of mental illness, mental deficiency, physical illness or disability, advanced age, chronic use of drugs, chronic intoxication, or other causes (except minority) to the extent that he lacks sufficient understanding or capacity to make or communicate responsible decisions concerning his person]. [alternative B: any person for whom a guardian has been appointed by court.]

(11) "Independent living arrangements" means a mode of life maintained on a continuing basis outside of a hospital, Veterans' Administration hospital, nursing home, or other facility licensed by or under the jurisdiction of any State agency.

(12) "Infirm person" means a person who, because of physical or mental disability, is substantially impaired in his ability to provide adequately for his own care or custody.

(13) "Interested person" means any adult relative or friend of an elderly person, or any official or representative of a protective services agency or of any public or nonprofit agency, corporation, board or organization eligible for designation as a protective services agency.

(14) A "protected person" is a person for whom a conservator has been appointed or other protective order has been made.

(15) "Protective placement" means the transfer of an elderly person from independent living arrangements to a hospital, nursing home, or domiciliary or residential care facility, or from one such institution to another, for a period anticipated to last longer than 6 days.

(16) "Protective services" means the services furnished by a protective services agency or its delegate, as described in section 6 of this act.

(17) "Protective services agency" means a public or nonprofit private agency, corporation, board or organization authorized by the Department pursuant to section 4(f) of this act to furnish protective services to elderly infirm, protected or incapacitated persons and/or to serve as conservators or guardians of the person for elderly protected or incapacitated persons upon appointment by a court.

(18) "Public guardian" means the office of the public guardian.

(19) A "ward" is a person for whom a guardian has been appointed.

Comments on Section 3.

The terminology of the Uniform Probate Code has been adopted here to describe the persons principally involved in guardianship and conservatorship proceedings. "Incapacitated persons" are those for whom guardians (of the person) are appointed, while "protected persons" are those for whom conservators have been appointed or other protective orders issued by a court.

The term "infirm persons" refers to the elderly whose degree of impairment is substantial, but is not so serious as to justify appointment of a guardian or conservator.

SECTION 4. Establishment of protective services system.

(a) Planning and development of system. -- The Department shall develop a coordinated system of protective services for elderly infirm and incapactitated persons. In planning this system, the Department shall obtain the advice of agencies, corporations, boards, and associations currently involved in the provision of social, health, legal, nutritional, and other services to the elderly, as well as of organizations of the elderly themselves.

(b) Advisory board. -- In order to provide continuing advice to the Department concerning the protective services system, an advisory board composed of [nine] members appointed by the Governor is established.

(c) Provision of services by Department. -- The Department may provide direct protective services.

(d) Contracts for services. -- The Department may contract with any protective service agency for the provision of protective services.

(e) Utilization of resources. -- The Department shall utilize to the extent appropriate and available existing resources and services of public and nonprofit private agencies in providing protective services.

(f) Designation of protective services agencies. -- The Department may designate any public or nonprofit private agency, corporation, board or organization as a protective services agency. The Department shall issue regulations establishing criteria and procedures for the designation of protective services agencies. Preference shall be given to agencies with consumer or other citizen representation.

(g) Limitation. -- No public or private agency, corporation, board or organization may furnish protective services to an elderly person under court order or serve as guardian of the person unless the Department has designated such a body as a protective services agency pursuant to subsection (f) above.

(h) Emergencies. -- The Department shall designate at least one protective services agency in each [city and county] which shall be responsible for rendering protective services in an emergency.

(i) Coordination and supervision of system.--Upon establishment of the protective services system, the Department shall be responsible for continuing coordination and supervision of the system. In carrying out these duties, the Department shall:

(1) Adopt rules and regulation for the system;
(2) Continuously monitor the effectiveness of the system and perform evaluative research about it; and
(3) Utilize to the extent available grants from Federal, State, and other public and private sources to support the system.

Comments on Section 4.

This section sets forth the powers and duties of the State agency responsible for organizing a protective services system. The structure and detailed organization of this system, however, are left to the agency and are not included in the legislation.

The chief duties of the agency are: (1) to develop a protective services system; (2) to obtain wide ranging professional and consumer advice in planning and operating the system; (3) as part of the system, to designate local protective services agencies for emergency situations; and (4) to coordinate and supervise the system on an ongoing basis.

The State agency is given a variety of powers in providing protective services, but States may wish to select those it believes most in accord with its system and resources and therefore delete other powers. Thus the agency itself may provide protective services; it may contract for these services at State expense; it may simply designate existing organizations as providers protective services; or it may choose a combination of these approaches. Subsection (e) states a preference for the use of existing community resources, while subsection (h) indicates a further preference for organizations with broad citizen representation.

Where protective services are to be furnished by an organization, subsection (g) requires this organization to be approved for this purpose by the State agency. The requirement for approval as well as its power will enable the State agency to limit the provision of services to responsible organizations which meet agency criteria.

SECTION 5. Protective services agencies.

(a) Powers. -- A protective services agency is authorized:

(1) to furnish protective services to an elderly person with his consent;

(2) to petition the court for appointment of a conservator or guardian, for issuance of an emergency order for protective services, or for an order for protective placement;

(3) to furnish protective services to an elderly infirm person without his consent on an emergency basis pursuant to section 10 of this act;

(4) to furnish protective services to an elderly incapacitated or protected person with the consent of such person's guardian or conservator;

(5) to serve as conservator, guardian, or temporary guardian of an elderly protected or incapacitated person;

(6) to enter into protective arrangements and to conduct single transactions authorized by a court pursuant to [section 5-409 of the Uniform Probate Code].

(b) Reports. -- A protective services agency shall make such reports as the Department or a court may require.

Comments on section 5.

Once having been designated a "protective services agency" by the State agency, the protective services agency is required to obtain permission before it may provide services. This permission may come from the elderly person himself (subsection (a) (1)), that person's conservator or guardian (subsection (a) (4)), or a court. Court authorization will be given by issuance of an emergency order (subsection (a) (3)), by appointment of the protective services agency as conservator or guardian (subsection (a)(5)), or by granting power to conduct particular transactions for the elderly person (subsection (a)(6)).

The protective services agency is also empowered under subsection (a)(2) to petition the court for appointment of a conservator or guardian and for issuance of orders for protective services on an emergency basis or for protective placement.

SECTION 6. Nature of Protective Services.

(a) Definition. -- Protective services are services furnished by a protective services agency or its delegate to an elderly infirm, incapacitated, or protected person with the person's consent or appropriate legal authority, in order to assist the person in performing the activities of daily living, and thereby maintain independent living arrangements and avoid hazardous living conditions.

(b) Services. -- The services furnished in a protective services system may include but are not limited to: social case work; psychiatric and health evaluation; home care; day care; legal assistance; social services; health care; and other services consistent with the purpose of this act. Such services do not include protective placement.

(c) Service-related activities. -- In order to provide the services listed in subsection (a) above, a protective services system may include but is not limited to the following service-related activities: outreach; identifying persons in need of services; counselling; referring persons for services; evaluating individuals; arranging for services; tracking and following up cases; referring persons to the public guardian; petitioning the courts for the appointment of a conservator or guardian of the person; and other activities consistent with the purposes of this act.

(d) Costs of services. -- The costs of providing protective services shall be borne by the provider of such services, unless the elderly person agrees to pay for them or a court authorizes the provider to receive reasonable reimbursement from the person's assets after a finding that the person is financially able to make such payment.

Comments on Section 6.

The definition of protective services in subsection (a) indicates that such services are intended to be only a specific portion of a broader program whose purpose is to prevent or delay institutionalization of the elderly. The characteristics that distinguish protective services from these larger programs are: (1) their target population is the infirm, incapacitated, or protected elderly; (2) the services are provided by a designated protective services agency or its delegate; and (3) unless the elderly client consents to accept the services, the protective services agency may intervene only with court authorization.

Subsections (b) and (c) provide examples of the services that may be included in a protective services program. Protective placement, defined in section 3(15) above, is excluded from these services. Section 11 establishes special proceedings to obtain court authorization for involuntary transfers of residence.

Subsection (d) establishes the presumption that the protective services will be paid for by the provider agency, which may in turn be reimbursed from Federal or State sources if such funding is available. The provider agency may obtain reimbursement from the elderly person only if the client consents or a court authorizes such payment. The criterion to be applied by the court is deliberately framed in general terms, viz, the "financial ability" of the elderly person to afford the services. See also section 9(c). "Financial ability" is a variable dependent on the nature, extent, and liquidity of the person's assets; his disposable net income; the type, duration and complexity of the services required and rendered; and any other foreseeable expenses.

A rigid means test should be avoided. On the other hand, elderly persons who desire to receive protective services and can afford to pay for them are not precluded from receiving them under this section.

In the event that the elderly client will pay for protective services, the criterion for reimbursement is the reasonable cost of the services.
See also section 9(c).

SECTION 7. Geriatric evaluation service --
(a) Establishment. -- The Department shall establish a geriatric evaluation service for the purpose of conducting a comprehensive physical, mental, and social evaluation of an elderly person for whom a petition has been filed in a court of commitment to a mental hospital, appointment of a conservator or guardian, an emergency order for protective services, or an order for protective placement.
(b) Evaluation. -- The evaluation of an elderly person conducted by the geriatric evaluation service should include at least the following:
(1) The name and address of the place where the person is residing and of the person or agency, if any, who is providing services at present;
(2) A description of the treatment and services, if any, presently being provided to the person;
(3) An evaluation of the person's present physical, mental, and social conditions; and
(4) A recommendation concerning the least restrictive course of services, care or treatment consistent with the person's needs.
(c) Costs. -- The cost of this evaluation should be borne by the Department.

Comments on Section 7.
The geriatric evaluation service (GES) is a team of medical, psychological, psychiatric, and social work professionals. Its function is to provide the courts with impartial professional advice to assist them in making determinations which by their very nature involve the assessment of an elderly person's capacity to continue independent living and decision-making. The direct responsibility of the GES is to the court, not the petitioner or the elderly person, and therefore its recommendations will hopefully be free of partisanship. For the same reason, the costs of this evaluation are borne by the State under subsection (c) instead of by the parties to the proceedings. At the same time, however, the evaluation conducted by the GES is not exclusive, and therefore the parties to the proceedings may also offer similar evaluations in evidence. See section 12(a) (4).
One important feature of the evaluation described in subsection (b)(4) is the GES' recommendation concerning the least restrictive course of services, care or treatment consistent with the elderly person's needs. The theme that intervention should be as minimal as necessary to achieve valid goals for the person appears elsewhere in the act. See sections 9(b), 11(a)(6), 11(g)(3), and 11(l). Section 14 also authorizes the elderly person to appeal the court's findings on this issue required in section 11(a)(6).

SECTION 8. Voluntary protective services.
(a) Consent required. -- Any elderly person may receive protective services, provided the person requests or affirmatively consents to receive these services. If the person withdraws or refuses consent, the services shall not be provided.
(b) Interference with services. -- No person shall interfere with the provision of protective services to an elderly person who requests or con-

sents to receive such services. In the event that interference occurs on a continuing basis, the Department, a protective services agency, or the public guardian may petition the court to enjoin such interference.

(c) Publicity for services. -- The Department shall publicize throughout the State the availability of protective services on a voluntary basis for elderly persons.

Comments on section 8

It is experienced that protective services will ordinarily be provided to the elderly who desire such assistance. In such case, proceedings to establish guardianship or conservatorships, if necessary, will be nonadversarial.

Subsections (b) and (c) are consistent with the principle of voluntary acceptance of services by prohibiting interference with these services by others and by requiring the State agency to make the elderly aware of the availability of this assistance.

SECTION 9. Involuntary protective services.

(a) Lack of consent. -- If an elderly person lacks the capacity to consent to receive protective services, these services may be ordered by a court on an involuntary basis, (1) through an emergency order pursuant to section 10 of this act, or (2) through appointment of a conservator or guardian pursuant to [the provision of the Model Guardianship and Conservatorship Act].

(b) Least restrictive alternative. -- In ordering involuntary protective services, the court shall authorize only that intervention which it finds to be least restrictive of the elderly person's liberty and rights, while consistent with his welfare and safety. The basis for such finding shall be stated in the record by the court.

(c) Payment for services. -- The elderly infirm, incapacitated, or protected person shall not be required to pay for involuntary protective services unless such payment is authorized by the court upon a showing that the person is financially able to pay. In this event the court shall provide for reimbursement of the reasonable costs of the services.

Comments on Section 9.

Protective services may be provided to elderly persons without their consent only with court authorization. Such authorization may take two forms: (1) the issuance of an emergency order under section 10 or (2) the appointment of a conservator or guardian. If this authorization has not been obtained or has been denied and the elderly person refuses to accept the services voluntarily, no organization or individual may intervene on its own authority.

The underlying principle here is that the elderly person alone should decide whether or not to accept these services, regardless of the opinion of others about the possible detrimental effects on the person who refuses to accept assistance. Involuntary intervention authorized by the courts, therefore, requires findings that: (1) The elderly person lacks capacity to consent to services, for example, to make intelligent decisions about his person or property; and (2) that conditions exist justifying an emergency order under section 10 or appointment of a conservator or guardian. It is not enough that the older person refuses services or other persons disagree with his decisions.

Discussions of subsection (b) appear in the comments on section 7 and of subsection (c) in the comments on section 6.

SECTION 10. Emergency order for protective services.

(a) Petition and findings. -- Upon petition by the Department, the public guardian, a protective services agency, or an interested person, a court may issue an order authorizing the provision of protective services on an emergency basis to an elderly person after finding on their record, based on clear and convincing evidence, that:

(1) the elderly person is infirm or incapacitated, as defined in Section 3 of this act;
(2) an emergency exists, as defined in section 3(5) of this act;
(3) the elderly person lacks the capacity to consent to receive protective services;
(4) no person authorized by law or court order to give consent for the elderly person is available to consent to emergency services; and
(5) the proposed order is substantially supported by the findings of the geriatric evaluation services, or if not so supported, there are compelling reasons for ordering services.

(b) Limitations on emergency order. In issuing an emergency order, the court shall adhere to the following limitations:

(1) Only such protective services as are necessary to remove the conditions creating the emergency shall be ordered; and the court shall specifically designate the approved services in its order.
(2) Protective services authorized by an emergency order shall not include hospitalization or a change of residence unless the court specifically finds such action is necessary and gives specific approval for such action in its order.
(3) Protective services may be provided through an emergency order only 72 hours. The original order may be renewed once for a 72 hour period upon a showing to the court that continuation of the original order is necessary to remove the emergency.
(4) In its order the court shall appoint the petitioner, another interested person, or the public guardian as temporary guardian of the elderly person with responsibility for the person's welfare and authority to give consent for the person for the approved protective services until the expiration of the order.
(5) The issuance of an emergency order and the appointment of a temporary guardian shall not deprive the elderly person of any rights except to the extent validly provided for in the order or appointment.
(6) To implement an emergency order, the court may authorize forcible entry of premises of the elderly person for the purpose of rendering protective services or transporting the person to another location for the provision of such services only after a showing to the court that attempts to gain voluntary access to the premises have failed and forcible entry is necessary. Persons making authorized forcible entry shall be accompanied by a peace officer.

(c) Contents of petition. -- The petition for an emergency order shall set forth the name, address, and interest of the petitioner; the name, age, and address of the elderly person in need of protective services; the nature of the emergency; the nature of the person's disability, if determinable; the proposed protective services; the petitioner's reasonable belief, together with facts supportive thereof, as to the existence of the facts stated in subsection (a)(1) through (4) above; and facts showing petitioner's attempts to obtain the elderly person's consent to the services and the outcomes of such attempts.

(d) Notice of petition. -- Notice of the filing of such petition, and other relevant information, including the factual basis of the belief that emergency services are needed and a description of the exact services to be rendered, the rights of the person in the court proceeding, and the consequences of a court order, shall be given to the person, to his spouse, or if none, to his adult children or next of kin, to his guardian, if any, to the public guardian, and to the geriatric evaluation service. Such notice shall be given in language reasonably understandable by its intended recipients at least 24 hours prior to the hearing for emergency intervention. The court may waive the 24-hour delay, and (2) reasonable attempts have been made to notify the elderly person, his spouse, or if none, his adult children or next of kin, his guardian, if any, and the public guardian. Notice of the court's final order shall also be given to the above named parties.

(e) Hearing on petition. -- Upon receipt of a petition for an emergency order for protective services, the court shall hold a hearing pursuant to the provisions of section 12 of this act. This hearing shall be held no earlier than 24 hours after the notice required in subsection (d) above has been given, unless such notice has been waived by the court.

(f) Review of court order. -- The elderly person, the temporary guardian, or any interested person, may petition the court to have the emergency order set aside or modified at any time, notwithstanding any prior findings by the court that the elderly person is infirm.

(g) Report. -- Where protective services are rendered on the basis of an emergency order, the temporary guardian shall submit a report describing the circumstances including the name, place, date, and nature of the services, and the use of forcible entry, if any, to the court and the public guardian. This report shall become part of the court record.

(h) Continued need for services. -- If the person continues to need protective services after the renewal order provided in subsection (b)(3) above has expired, the temporary guardian or the public guardian shall immediately petition the court to appoint a conservator or guardian and/or to order protective placement pursuant to section 11 of this act.

(i) Immunity of petitioner. -- The petitioner shall not be liable for filing the petition if he acted in good faith.

(j) Emergency placement. -- When from personal observation of a peace officer, it appears probable that an elderly person will suffer immediate and irreparable physical injury or death if not immediately placed in a health care facility, that the elderly person is incapable of giving consent, and that it is not possible to follow the procedures of this section, the peace officer making such observation may transport the elderly person to an appropriate medical facility. The Department and the persons entitled to notice under subsection (d) above shall be notified of such detention within 4 hours. The Department shall file a petition pursuant to subsection (a) above within 24 hours after the transfer of the elderly person has taken place. The court shall hold a hearing on this petition and render its decision within 48 hours after the transfer has occurred.

Comments on section 10.

This section provides the legal authority to deal with a situation where an elderly person is living in highly dangerous conditions or is himself in a state of severe physical deterioration, and therefore swift action is necessary to provide a remedy. Despite the emergency character of the situation, court authorization on an expedited basis is still required for involuntary intervention. The only exception to the need for a court order is the provision for emergency placement in subsection (j).

Subsection (a) lists the findings which the court must make to support issuance of an order for protective services to be furnished in an emergency. These findings must be supported by "clear and convincing evidence" and not merely a preponderance of the evidence to emphasize the caution with which involuntary intervention must be authorized. The basis for these findings should appear in the court record and are appealable under section 14.

Even though a court finds issuance of an order to be justified, the scope and duration of the order are subject to the limitations of subsection (b). In conformity with the "least restrictive action" principle enunciated earlier, the court may authorize only those services needed to remove the emergency, not an extended care program of rehabilitation or treatment designed to restore the elderly person to his full potential. These services must be specified in the court order, and may not include hospitilization or a change of residence except as provided in subsection (b)(2). Two 72-hour programs of services are permissible under subsection (b)(3). If emergency protective services are needed beyond this 6-day period, proceedings for appointment of a guardian or conservator or full protective placement must be initiated, as provided in subsection (h). Forcible entry of the elderly person's premises to implement the court order is also controlled in subsection (b)(16).

To avoid having the elderly person exclusively in the care of the provider of services for the duration of the court order, subsection (b)(4) requires the court to appoint a temporary guardian for this period whose duties are to be responsible for the elderly person's welfare, and to petition further court actions under subsection (h) if services continue to be necessary. The provider of services may be appointed as temporary guardian if the court so chooses, but it is preferable that some other party serve as guardian to prevent the elderly person from becoming completely dependent on the provider even for the limited duration of the emergency order.

This section is intended to replace for elderly persons section 5-310 of the Uniform Probate Code, which authorizes the appointment of a temporary guardian in two situations. The UPC provides that, when an incapacitated person has no guardian and an emergency exists, the court may exercise the power of a guardian pending notice and hearing. This provision appears to be unnecessary in the light of section 10 of the Adult Protective Services Act. Under the UPC a temporary guardian may also be appointed, with or without notice, when an appointed guardian is not effectively performing his duties and the court finds that the welfare of the incapacitated person requires immediate action. Again, the combination of a short-term guardianship under section 10 of this act and further proceedings for a new appointment of a permanent guardian seems better suited to protect the interests of the elderly person because of their strict criteria and procedural requirements.

Subsections (c), (d) and (e) describe the procedure to be followed by the petitioner and the court for issuance of an emergency order for protective services. A philosphy of full disclosure has been adopted, both as the contents of the petition and as to the persons entitled to be notified of the filing of the petition. Such disclosure will afford interested parties the opportunity to intervene or participate in the proceedings, to assist the court, and to protect the interests of the elderly person.

The provision for emergency placement in subsection (j) attempts to deal with the situation which there is not sufficient time to obtain an emergency court order. Peace officers are authorized to make on-the-spot determination based on personal observation that certain specified conditions probably exist. This determination is analogous to decisions based on probable cause, with which police are familiar in the areas of warrantless arrests and searches in criminal contexts. Once the transfer to a health care facility has occurred, however, appropriate parties must be notified of this action and regular proceedings under section 10 must be started. The court is required to reach a decision within a specified time limit because transfer of the elderly person has already occurred and should be validated or not as quickly as possible.

SECTION 11. Protective placement.

(a) Findings.--If the elderly person refuses to consent, protective placement shall not take place unless ordered by a court after a finding on the record based on clear and convincing evidence that:

(1) The elderly person is incapacitated, as defined in section 3(10) of this act [or as defined in sections ______ or ______ of the State code], and a petition to appoint a guardian accompanies this petition for protective placement;
(2) The elderly person is so totally incapable of providing for his own care or custody that his condition creates a substantial risk of serious physical harm to himself or others. Serious harm may be occasioned by overt acts or acts of omission;
(3) The elderly person has a disability which is permanent or likely to be permanent;
(4) The elderly person needs full-time residential care or treatment;
(5) The proposed order is substantially supported by the recommendation of the geriatric evaluation service, as provided for in subsection (g) below, or if not so supported, there are compelling reasons for ordering such placement; and
(6) No less restrictive alternative course of care or treatment is available which is consistent with the incapacitated person's welfare and safety.

(b) Who may petition. -- The Department, a protective services agency, a conservator, a guardian, the public guardian, or a person applying for a conservatorship or guardianship pursuant to [the provisions of the uniform probate code] may petition the court for protective placement.

(c) Contents of petition. -- The petition shall state with particularity the factual basis for the allegations specified in subsection (a) above and shall be based on the petitioner's personal knowledge of the elderly person alleged to need protective placement.

(d) Order for consideration. -- A petition for appointment of a conservator or guardian accompanying a petition for protective placement shall be heard and decided prior to the petition for protective placement.

(e) Notice of petition. -- Notice of a petition for protective placement shall be served upon the elderly person sought to be placed by personal service at least 10 days prior to the time set for a hearing. Notice shall be given in language reasonably understandable by the elderly person, and he shall be informed orally of its complete contents. The notice shall include the names of all petitioners, the factual basis of the belief that protective placement is needed, the rights of the elderly person in the court proceedings, the name and address of the proposed placement, and the consequences of an order for protective placement. The person serving the notice shall certify to the court that the petition has been delivered and notice given. Notice shall also be given to the person's guardian ad litem; legal counsel persons having physical custody of the elderly person whose names and addresses are known to the petitioner or can with reasonable diligence be ascertained; any governmental or private body or group from whom the elderly person is known to be receiving aid; the geriatric evaluation service; the public guardian; and such other persons or entities as the court may require.

(f) Hearing on petition. -- Upon receipt of a petition for protective placement, the court shall hold a hearing pursuant to the provisions of section 12 of this act.

(g) Evaluation of person. -- In order to make the finding required in subsections (a)(2), (3), (4), and (6) above, the court shall direct that a comprehensive evaluation of the elderly person alleged to be in need of placement be conducted by the geriatric evaluation service. The evaluation shall include at least the following information:

(1) The address of the place where the person is residing and the person or agency, if any, which is providing care treatment or services at present;
(2) A resume of the professional treatment and service provided to the person by the Department or agency, if any, in connection with the problem creating the need for placement;
(3) A medical, psychological, a psychiatric, and social evaluation and review, where necessary, and any recommendations for or against maintenance or partial legal rights as provided in ____________ of this code. Such evaluation and review shall include recommendations for placement consistent with the least restrictive environment required.

(h) Choice of facilities. -- In ordering protective placement, the court shall give consideration to the choice of residence of the elderly person. The court may order placement in such facilities as hospitals, nursing homes, domiciliary or personal care facilities, sheltered care residences, foster care homes, or other appropriate facilities. It may not order placement in facilities for the acutely mentally ill; placement in such facilities is governed by [the civil commitment provisions] of this code.

(i) Duration of order. -- The court may authorize protective placement of an elderly person for a period not to exceed 6 months.

(j) Renewal of order. -- At the time of expiration of an order for protective placement, the guardian, the original petitioner, or any interested person may petition the court to extend its order for protective placement for an additional period not to exceed 6 months. The contents of the petition shall conform to the provisions of subsections (a) and (c) above. Notice of the petition for the extension of placement shall be made in conformity with subsection (e) above. The court shall hold a hearing to determine whether to renew the order. Any person entitled to a notice under subsection (e) above may appear at the hearing and challenge the petition; in this event, the court shall conduct the hearing pursuant to the provisions in section 12 of this act.

(k) Transfer. -- The residence of an elderly person which has been established pursuant to an order for protective placement shall not be changed unless the court authorizes the transfer of residence after finding compelling reasons to justify the transfer.

(l) Temporary placement. -- When an elderly person lives with his guardian, the guardian may petition the court order an alternative temporary placement of the elderly person for good cause, such as to allow the guardian to take a vacation or to release the guardian temporarily for a family emergency. Such placement may be made for not more than 18 days, but the court may grant upon application an additional period not to exceed 30 days. The petition shall include such information as the court deems necessary and adequate. In ordering the alternative placement, the court shall provide for the least restrictive placement consistent with the needs of the elderly person and comparable to his previous residence. Petitions for alternative temporary placement shall not be granted more than once a year except in an emergency.

(m) Discharge from placement. -- Prior to discharge from protective placement, the Geriatric Evaluation Service shall review the need for continued protective services after discharge, including the necessity for a conservator or guardian. Such recommendation and report shall be made to the Department, the public guardian, the elderly person's conservator or guardian, all persons notified of the original petition for protective placement, and the court where appropriate.

(n) Duties of the guardian. -- A guardian of an elderly person placed under this section shall have the duty to take reasonable steps to assure that the elderly person is well treated, properly cared for, and provided with the opportunity to exercise his legal rights.

(o) Confidentiality of records. -- Any records of the Department of other agency pertaining to an elderly person who is protected under this act or for whom an application has ever been made for such protection are not open to public inspection. Information contained in such records may not be disclosed publicly in such a manner as to identify individuals, but the record shall be available upon application for cause to persons approved by court.

(p) Voluntary request for placement. -- Any elderly person may request protective placement under this act. No legal rights are relinquished or modified as a result of such placement.

(q) Costs of placement. -- The costs of providing protective placement shall be borne by the elderly person, unless he is placed in a public facility or is eligible for assistance under Federal or State programs, or the facility is willing to provide placement without charge.

Comments on Section 11.

An involuntary change of residence of an elderly person to an institutional setting, or from one institution to another, often produces major effects in the person's physical and mental health as well as in his civil rights, and therefore special proceedings to authorize such actions are necessary. The degree of incapacity required to justify protective placement as compared with protective services is greater, in that for the former the person must be found to be incapacitated to the extent that appointment of a guardian is justified. The definition of an "incapacitated person" in subsection (a)(1) is presented in the alternative to permit a jurisdiction with a different definition in its guardianship laws to utilize that definition in lieu of the one offered in section 3(10) of this act. The other findings required in subsection (a), particularly as to the gravity of the person's disability and its consequent risk of harm to others or himself, again emphasize that orders for protective placement should be given only when a solid justification for such action has been established in court.

The procedural provisions of subsections (c), (e), and (j) generally follow those discussed earlier under section 10 for emergency orders for protective services. Because the order for protective placement requires a finding that the person is incapacitated, subsection (d) requires that the accompanying petition for appointment of a guardian be heard and decided first, in that such appointment includes a finding of incapacity.

The role of the geriatric evaluation service has already been discussed under section 7.

Subsection (h) requires the court to consider the preference of the elderly person himself for placement, even though by definition he has refused consent to such action. This section may not be used as a vehicle to avoid the State's civil commitment law, and therefore the court may not authorize placement in a mental hospital.

Orders for protective placement are only temporary; that is, 6 months in duration, under subsection (i). The burden to obtain renewal of the order is placed by subsection (j) on a party other than the elderly person. If no such party seeks renewal, the elderly person is free to leave the residence established by the last court order. To obtain renewal of the order, the petitioner must file a petition similiar in form to that previously filed and notify the persons previously entitled to notice. The court's hearing on the petition for renewal, however, may be of an ex-parte nature unless the elderly person himself or any other party entitled to notice desires to contest the petition. In this event, a hearing pursuant to section 12 must be held.

Subsection (k) places an additional burden of justification on a petitioner who wishes to transfer again the residence of a person who has already experienced displacement as a result of an order for protective placement. This provision is designed to prevent transfers of "convenience" intended to benefit the provider or the petitioner rather than the elderly person.

Subsection (m) requires the geriatric evaluation service to evaluate the person's need for assistance if discharge from protective placement occurs. The GES' recommendations are intended to assist the guardian or conservator in caring for the person or his property. If the guardianship or conservatorship is also terminated upon discharge, then the elderly person is free to accept or not the GES' recommendations.

Subsection (n) emphasizes that a guardian of an institutionalized person has a special responsibility to monitor the care and treatment of this person. If this care and treatment prove deficient, the guardian should exercise the remedies provided by Federal or State law.

Unlike section 6(d) which placed initial responsibility for the costs of protective services on the provider subsection (g) makes the elderly person himself primarily responsible for the costs of protective placement. This principle is consistent with current Federal and State law concerning institutional care of the elderly. The alternative of making the institution responsible without providing for reimbursement would create insurmountable difficulties and nullify protective placement except for those eligible for governmental assistance.

SECTION 12. Hearing on petiton.

(a) Hearing procedure. -- The hearing on a petition for an emergency order for protective services or for an order for protective placement shall be held under the following conditions:

(1) The elderly person shall be present unless he has knowingly and voluntarily waived the right to be present or cannot be present because of physical or mental incapacity. Waiver

or incapacity may not be presumed from nonappearance but shall be determined on the basis of factual information supplied to the court by counsel or a visitor appointed by the court.

(2) The elderly person has the right to counsel whether or not he is present at the hearing, unless he intelligently and voluntarily waives the right. If the person is indigent or lacks the capacity to waive the counsel, the court shall appoint counsel. Where the person is indigent, the State shall pay reasonable attorney's fees; that is, such compensation as is customarily charged by attorneys in this State for comparable services.

(3) The elderly person shall have the right to trial by jury upon request by the person or his counsel.

(4) The elderly person has the right at his own expense, or if indigent at the expense of the State, to secure an independent medical and/or psychological or psychiatric examination relevant to the issue involved in any hearing under this section, and to present a report of this independent evaluation or the evaluator's personal testimony as evidence at the hearing.

(5) The elderly person may present evidence and cross-examine witnesses.

(b) Duties of counsel. -- The duties of counsel representing an elderly person for whom a petition for an emergency order for protective services of for an order of protective placement has been filed shall include: personally interviewing the elderly person; counselling the person with respect to this act, his rights, and any available alternative resources or causes of action; arranging for an independent medical and/or psychological or psychiatric examination of the person relevant to the issue involved in the hearing; and providing competent representation at all proceedings.

(c) Statement of findings. -- The court shall issue for the record a statement of its findings in support of any order for emergency protective services or protective placement.

Comments on Section 12.

Subsection (a) sets forth the basic procedural rights of the elderly person at hearings on petitions for an emergency order for protective services or an order for protective placement. In some details these provisions are more protective of the person than many State laws concerning guardianship and conservatorship, or even the Uniform Probate Code itself. This added protection appears warranted by the substantial deprivation of personal liberty which may be the outcome of these hearings.

If anything, those State should consider strengthening the procedural rights of parties who are the subject of guardianship and conservatorship proceedings to emphasize the fact that such proceedings are at root adversarial in nature, and rightly so, and therefore the paternalistic undercurrents of many older laws should be abandoned. The rights and interests of all parties to these proceedings are best preserved when proceedings are truly adversarial.

The right to counsel provided in subsection (a)(2) is of special importance in these proceedings. Waiver of the right is permitted, but the court should exercise caution in concluding that the person is waiving this right, because the petitions in these cases may be based on allegations of mental incapacity of the person to make responsible decisions.

If these allegations are taken at face value, then a waiver of the right to counsel may be subject to the same incapacity.

This subsection and subsection (a)(4) require the State to afford the indigent elderly counsel and professional evaluations at public expense. Counsel might be provided through legal aid or legal services offices or by the Public Defender. In appointing counsel the courts should be sensitive to their responsibility to appoint as counsel, where possible, attorneys with special competence or expertise in mental health proceedings.

Subsection (b), by listing in detail some of the duties of counsel, is intended to avoid permitting attorneys to provide only pro forma representation similar to that given by the guardian ad litem in many jurisdictions.

SECTION 13. Duty to report.

(a) Nature of duty. -- Any person having reasonable cause to believe that an elderly person is infirm, incapacitated, or in need of protection shall report such information to the Department or the public guardian.

(b) Procedure for reporting. -- The report shall be made orally or in writing. It shall include the name, age, and address of the elderly person; the name and address of any other person responsible for the elderly person's care; the nature and extent of the elderly person's condition; the basis of the reporter's knowledge; and other relevant information.

(c) Immunity. -- Any person making a report pursuant to subsection (a)above, testifying in any judicial proceeding arising from the report, or participating in a required evaluation, shall be immune from civil or criminal liability on account of such report, testimony, or participation, unless person acted in bad faith or with a malicious purpose.

(d) Action on report. -- Upon receipt of a report, the Department shall make a prompt and thorough evaluation to determine whether the elderly person is in need of protective services and what services are needed, unless the Department determines that the report is frivolous or is patently without a factual basis. The evaluation shall include a visit to the person and consultation with others having knowledge of the facts of the particular case. After completing the evaluation, the director shall make a written report of his findings to the elderly person, his spouse or next of kin, and the person making the report.

If the director determines that the elderly person needs protective services according to the criteria set forth in section 10(a) of this act, the director, the elderly person, his spouse or any interested person may petition the court for an emergency order for protective services pursuant to section 10 of this act.

Comments on Section 13.

Subsection (a) imposes a duty on all citizens to inform the State agency or the public guardian of the status of persons who are believed to be infirm, incapacitated, or in need of protection. No penalty, however, is imposed on one who fails to make such a report. Subsection (c) authorizes immunity from civil or criminal liability for persons making a report, except where the reporter acted in bad faith or with a malicious purpose, such as intent to harass the elderly person or to force the person to undertake a transaction against his will. The State agency is expected to investigate all such reports unless it finds that the report is frivolous or clearly without a basis in fact.

SECTION 14. Right to appeal.

An elderly person, his conservator or guardian may appeal any findings of a court under sections 10(a), 11(a), 11(j), or 11(k) of this act. Such appeal shall be handled on an expedited basis by the appellate court.

Comments on Section 14.

The provision for an explicit right to appeal particular findings of a court is consistent with the act's philosphy that the proceedings authorized under it be truly adversarial and that the findings of courts be specific and based on clear evidence.

SECTION 15. Severability. (Insert serverability clause).
SECTION 16. Repeal. (Insert repealer clause).
SECTION 17. Effective date. (Insert effective date.)

AUTHOR INDEX

In the list below, the numbers after each name refer to item numbers in the Bibliography.

About the Compilers

TANYA F. JOHNSON, Ph.D., is a Family Sociologist and Fellow at the Center for the Study of Aging and Human Development, Duke University Medical Center, Durham, North Carolina. Her earlier works include publications in *Acta Paeedologica, Parenting Studies, The Roeper Review*, and a chapter in *Studies in the Anthropology of Play.*

JAMES G. O'BRIEN, M.D., is Associate Chairman and Professor of Family Practice at Michigan State University. His earlier works include *Family Medicine Curriculum and Care of the Elderly*, and he has contributed to *Textbook of Family Practice, Family Systems Medicine*, and *Post Graduate Medicine.*

MARGARET F. HUDSON, R.N., G.N.P., is Associate Professor of Nursing at the University of North Carolina, Chapel Hill. She has published articles in *Nursing, Journal of Nursing Education, Public Health Nursing*, and a chapter in *Recent Advances in Nursing: Care of the Aging.*